Jack,

You're always a cut above!

Christ's blessings,

Steve

Faith Food

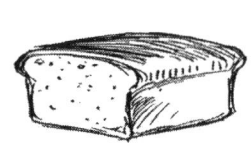

A Spiritual Smorgasbord
of Daily Devotions

Steve Stranghoener

Copyright © 2018 Steve Stranghoener.

All rights reserved. No part of this book may be used or reproduced by any means, graphic, electronic or mechanical, including photocopying, recording, taping or by any information storage retrieval system without the written permission of the author except in the case of brief quotations embodied in critical articles and reviews.

For all those servants of the Incarnate Word; broken tools called and empowered by God, who feed our hungry souls.

"He saith unto him the third time, Simon, son of Jonas, lovest thou me? Peter was grieved because he said unto him the third time, Lovest thou me? And he said unto him, Lord, thou knowest all things; thou knowest that I love thee. Jesus saith unto him, **Feed my sheep**."

(Jesus Christ, John 21:17)

FOREWORD

What is the secret to success? Is it measured by the amount of wealth we can amass during our lifetime? Can it be gauged by the fame we've attained or the legacy we've left to mankind? Our most priceless treasures offer absolutely no bargaining power when death approaches and, sadly, our greatest accomplishments are mere fleeting blips on time's finite continuum. This life is brief and all of time is but a blink of an eye when compared to eternity.

The extent of one's true success can be determined with one simple question: "Where will I spend eternity?" We can try to dispute the undeniable truth but to no avail for we will all spend eternity in the glories of heaven with God or forever separated from Him in hell. There's only one way to heaven and that is through God-given faith in Jesus Christ who has secured our success by conquering death. For us, success is simple and easy. We only need to repent and believe.

Why then should we bother with the Bible if our salvation is a done deal? Simply put, faith can grow weak and even be lost without proper nourishment. God through His inspired Apostle explained it this way as recorded in John 20:31,

"But these are written, that ye might believe that Jesus is the Christ, the Son of God; and that believing ye might have life through his name." Jesus offered these perfect guidelines to His disciples and all of us in John 8:31-32, "Then said Jesus to those Jews which believed on him, If ye **continue in my word**, then are ye my disciples indeed; And ye shall know the truth, and the truth shall make you free."

Faith Food is designed to feed us daily with spiritual nourishment and strengthen and keep us in the one true Christian faith unto life everlasting. There is no substitute for God's word in the Holy Bible and this book is no exception. But I hope and pray that *Faith Food* will serve as a useful tool to help draw many into God's word in a way that can help us relate our common, everyday experiences to the extraordinary wisdom and power of Holy Scripture. God's dinner bell is ringing; come and get it!

Table of Contents

Times and Seasons (P. 2)

- Advent
    - Advent-ure
- Christmas
    - Three Precious Stocking Stuffers
    - The Heart of Christmas
    - Christmas … Virgin Territory
    - That Twinkle in Your Eye
    - Joy to the World
    - Re-Gifting
    - White Christmas
- New Year
    - Resolute in the New Year
    - Ringing in the New
- Epiphany
    - Flipping the Switch
- Lent
    - Bitter Pill (St. Patrick's Day)
    - Helpful Reminder
    - Staying Focused
    - What's My Line?
- Easter
    - The Mystery of Easter
    - Jericho to Jerusalem
- Summer Vacation
    - On the Road Again
- Independence Day
    - God and Country
- Reformation

- Halloween Costumes
- The Tweet Heard Round the World
- The Test of Time
- Reformation, Easter & Judgment Day
- Thanksgiving
  - Promises, Promises

The Word (P. 75)

- Back to the Past
- Consistency
- Spiritual Smorgasbord
- Fact or Fable?
- Flame On!
- Forget-Me-Not
- A Heavenly Diet
- Indoctrination
- Mission Impossible
- Super Power!
- The Book
- Uncommon Sense
- The Bambino, Beatles & Methuselah

Comfort, Peace, Promise and Prayer (P. 113)

- Are You a Name Dropper?
- Consolation Prize
- Cool as a Cucumber
- It's Just Not Fair!
- Quantity and Quality
- Godly Economics 101

- Sticks and Stones
- The Ultimate Body Guard
- Sweet & Sour
- Super Glue
- Time Flies
- Words of Comfort and Promise

Stewardship and Service (P. 142)

- Two Natures of Members
- Time, Talent & Treasure

Kingdoms of the Left and Right Hand: God, Government and Society (P. 150)

- Devouring Their Young
- All Men Evolved Equally?
- Faint Not!
- Whoppers
- Government: From Bloated to Blessed
- Failure of Leadership
- Marriage: Back to Basics
- The Last Child
- The Tax Man Cometh
- Mother Hen
- Unconventional Wisdom

Seeing the World through Spiritual Lenses (P. 184)

- Generating Profit
- Invisible Things

- Life's Love/Hate Relationship
- Money Isn't Everything

Evangelism (P. 195)

- The Greatest Speech Ever (Part 1)
- The Greatest Speech Ever (Part 2)
- Calling All …
- Bad Company
- Be Careful What You Ask For
- Fear Factor
- In the Spotlight
- Literally Wrong
- Opportunity Knocks

Love (P. 221)

- Why Am I Here?
- Friend or Foe?
- Can't Buy Me Love
- Endless Love
- Summer of Love
- Are You a Hater?
- Prized Possessions
- To Know Him is to Love Him
- Puppy Love

Grace (P. 246)

- Oil and Water
- Righteous Work
- The Right or Requirement to Work?

- Sacrifice Makes Perfect
- Pro-Choice

Faith, Justification & Redemption (P. 260)

- Show-Me Skeptics
- God's Palette
- Spoiler Alert!
- Born to be Wild
- The Great Exchange
- Silver Lining
- The Great Emancipator
- Have You No Shame?
- Knock, knock … Who's There?
- Signposts to Salvation

Law & Gospel (P. 286)

- Buried Treasure
- The Law & Gospel in a Nutshell

Sanctification (P. 293)

- Goldilocks and the Three Beers
- Courage from Above
- Tongue-Tied

Humility (P. 302)

- Full-Service or Self-Service?
- The Gospel for Dummies
- Humble Pie

- I Am the Greatest!
- Young at Heart

The Nature of God (P. 315)

- Rolling in the Dough
- Rotten Apples
- Relativity
- Proof Positive
- Endless Summer
- Mountain Man
- Clover and Ice
- The Great Unifier

Eternal Life and End Times (P. 337)

- Our Inheritance
- Quality of Life
- Noah, Lot and John
- Fountain of Youth
- Perfect Imperfections
- Here Today, Gone Tomorrow
- Old Age Isn't for Sissies
- Home Sweet Home

Faith Food Steve Stranghoener

So that thou incline thine ear unto wisdom, and apply thine heart to understanding. (Proverbs 2:2)

Faith Food — Steve Stranghoener

Times and Seasons

Advent

ADVENT-URE

Are you a fan of adventure films? Do you marvel while watching a swashbuckler like *Indiana Jones* brave untold perils in searching for ancient treasures like the lost Ark of the Covenant containing the stone tablets inscribed by God with the Ten Commandments? As a child, I was captivated by reruns of *The Seventh Voyage of Sinbad*, a 1958 Hollywood release that featured the genius of Ray Harryhausen and brought fantastic creatures to life through stop-motion animation. Long before today's wonders of computer-generated images, the original master concocted special effects that included Sinbad the Sailor battling a monstrous cyclops and fire-breathing dragon. His treacherous journey and death-defying feats were prompted by his love for the beautiful Princess Parisa whom he rescued from the clutches of Sokurah, the evil magician who shrunk her to the size of a mouse.

My favorite was another Harryhausen classic, *Jason and the Argonauts*. Jason set sail as the captain of the Argo with a crew comprised of such legendary figures as Hercules to retrieve the Golden Fleece. In order to capture this most prized treasure, the hero and his comrades faced daunting mythological creatures like the harpies, sirens, a seven-headed hydra and an army of diabolical skeleton warriors. Most imposing was their encounter with Talos, the gargantuan bronze statue that came to life to terrorize the Argonauts. In an interesting twist, Jason used the mystical powers of the fleece to bring his love interest, Medea, back to life after she was felled by an arrow intended for him.

To keep the adventurous spirit of my youth alive, I've shared DVDs of these old classics with my grandkids. Not surprisingly, one of their favorite games is playing Talos with Pop-o posing as the bronze menace. If you're not into old B movies, we have another, even more fantastic adventure at our disposal. I like to picture our annual December pilgrimage to figurative Bethlehem as an advent-ure. Nothing could be more thrilling or meaningful. God's cosmic plot far exceeds all the best Greek tragedies combined.

Some forty centuries passed while the multitudes anxiously awaited the coming of a hero for the ages. The most vile and cunning supervillain the world has ever known plotted against the Promised Savior and His people with a host of evil minions at his command. Against all odds, humanly speaking, the Christ arrived in the fullness of time through a miraculous virgin birth as a tiny baby in the humblest surroundings possible. From there, our Champion embarked on the greatest adventure of all while confronted with the direst of consequences. The fate of all mankind hung in the balance for all eternity.

Christ Jesus faced the most formidable phalanx of foes ever assembled: sin, the devil and death itself. His motivation was similar to Sinbad's and Jason's except that His love was perfect, unconditional and undeserved. He conquered all and vanquished our worst enemies through the most unexpected means that could only be conceived by Almighty God. He sacrificed Himself, suffered our punishment in hell and died in our place so that we might live eternally with Him in heaven. He didn't need the aid of a golden fleece. Jesus Christ broke forth from the empty tomb to live again that we might never die. That's what I'd call an advent-ure!

Christmas

Three Precious Stocking Stuffers

How did the Christmas carol *We Three Kings of Orient Are* become so embedded in our culture, even in Christian circles? There seems to be so much misinformation not supported by Scripture. Nowhere does the Bible tell us that just three kings or wise men followed God's guiding star to Bethlehem. Perhaps many more made the journey. It also does not chronicle their arrival on the day of Christ's birth as is so often depicted in our nativity scenes. Perhaps it's natural to assume three travelers since we're told Jesus' visitors offered three gifts of gold, frankincense and myrrh. However, a careful reading shows that we can't say definitively that only these three gifts were offered by just three wise men.

Still I like the notion of three gifts; not gifts presented **to** God but instead bounties offered **from** God to us. If we meticulously un-wrap Matthew 2 and look deep within its treasure trove, I think there are three precious stocking stuffers that are worth much more to us than anything this world has to offer. The first precious gift is God's grace. Think about it. How did these wise men come to know about the Savior?

Although we can't say so definitively, these Magi were likely astronomers from Persia. Certainly, they were not part of God's chosen people, the Jews. Yet, God reached out to them in miraculous ways to bring the good news to them. It's quite possible that Daniel's witness to the Babylonians had been handed down to them across a 600-year span. Or perhaps they were exposed to God's Old Testament prophesy of the guiding star in Numbers 24:17 by some other means. In any case, God clearly shared the gospel with nations besides ancient Israel. God has continued to shower His amazing grace upon us Gentiles unto today.

Matthew's inspired account also destroyed any doubt about God's promises. The Lord not only foretold of the coming Savior but went to incredible lengths to fulfill every aspect of His prophesy down to the minutest detail. He equipped these ancient astronomers to be able to read the signs in the heavens and then produced a one-of-a-kind star to guide them on their journey when the fullness of time had come. He didn't stop there but also protected them from Herod's evil intentions and even warned them in a dream to take a different route home to avoid the scheming king. As if equipped with an iPhone navigation app, the Magi were led not only to Bethlehem but precisely to Jesus, Joseph and Mary. Then He instructed Joseph to flee Bethlehem for Egypt before the murderous Herod could dispatch his bloodthirsty minions to commit infanticide. As such, God has provided every reason for us to put our hope and trust in the Lord.

To top things off, Matthew's account shared the jubilation that the Wise Men experienced when the guiding star's illumination rested over the long-promised Babe of Bethlehem. Their people had patiently waited 600 years for this moment and they had endured an arduous journey to reach this land of promise. Their exultation has echoed unto us today. True and lasting joy was God's gift to them and has remained ours too.

Amidst all of our other celebrations, let's take time to un-wrap the greatest gift of all. Gather by the Christmas tree and take time to read Luke's account of Jesus' birth and then turn to Matthew 2 and revel in God's promises fulfilled. In reading about the Magi's thoughtful display of immense gratitude in offering gold, frankincense and myrrh to the Newborn King, Jesus Christ, let us rejoice all the more of the hidden treasures revealed therein: God's grace, our sure hope and the unbridled joy of God's everlasting gospel gift given to us on that first Christmas.

The Heart of Christmas

I really look forward to watching my favorite Christmas specials at this time of year. In reviewing the list, I noticed a common thread. Maybe you can pick it out from these capsules. In *Christmas Vacation*, Clark Griswold's holiday is ruined when his penny-pinching boss eliminates his sizable bonus in favor of a Jelly-of-the-Month membership. After well-intentioned but hair-brained Cousin Eddy kidnaps the skinflint, Mr. Shirley reconsiders and reinstates Clark's windfall in a show of Christmas generosity.

In contrast, George Bailey's nemesis, Mr. Potter, never veers from his evil ways in *It's a Wonderful Life*. George is so beaten down by the ogre's nefarious deeds that he spirals into a depression that makes him wish he were never born. After George is given a chance to see the difference he has made in the lives of others as a type of Christ, he learns to cherish his own life even more.

As outcasts, Rudolf and Herbie the Elf feel just as dejected as George Bailey until they are thrust into the unfamiliar role of Christmas heroes in *Rudolph the Red-Nosed Reindeer*. Amazingly, they and their intrepid friend Yukon Cornelius enlist the unlikeliest of allies when the beastly abominable is turned into a humble bumble.

In *A Christmas Carol*, miserly Ebenezer Scrooge is completely devoid of the tiniest morsel of Christmas joy until he's given the chance to recount his life and peer into his frightening future. His classic metamorphosis is best reflected in Tiny Tim's face as it glows with unbridled thankfulness.

In *How the Grinch Stole Christmas*, the morbidly morose Mr. Grinch can only find sadistic happiness in ruining Christmas for the others in Whoville until his tiny, frozen ticker is warmed by wide-eyed waif, Cindy Lou Who. The Grinch's amazing transformation delights everyone including his reluctant, downtrodden pooch, Max.

The best of all, in my opinion, is *A Charlie Brown Christmas*. This turnabout tale is my favorite because the inspiration is provided by Linus quoting Scripture to reveal the true meaning of Christmas. Everyone is moved by the Holy Spirit working through the word except for clueless, happy-go-lucky Snoopy.

Did you make the connection? Yes, every story involved a change of heart. Isn't that what Christmas is all about Charlie Brown? We were reconciled to God by our Savior Jesus Christ as revealed in 2 Corinthians 5:18, "And all things are of God, who hath reconciled us to himself by Jesus Christ, and hath given to us the ministry of reconciliation." God accomplished this impossible feat through the virgin birth of the perfect, sinless Babe of Bethlehem. God's loving heart was revealed to us in His gospel plan of salvation as it unfolded in the fullness of time on that first Christmas.

It's summed up perfectly in John 3:16-17, "For God so loved the world that he gave his only begotten Son, that whosoever believeth in him should not perish, but have everlasting life. For God sent not his Son into the world to condemn the world; but that the world through him might be saved." And so, as Tiny Tim said, "A Merry Christmas to us all; God bless us, every one!"

Christmas ... Virgin Territory

One day, I was listening to a local radio talk show and the host, Dave, followed his habit of delving into theology, an area where, unfortunately, he appeared clueless. During past such forays, his guests represented a myriad of theological views which were often woefully inaccurate. Sometimes, a faithful

Christian called in and made a good point on the basis of Scripture. Dave often dismissed them using the rationale that the Bible could be interpreted in a wide variety of ways. He considered anyone's point equally valid if they simply referred to the Bible no matter how they misused or even contradicted it. Seemingly, Dave didn't have enough command of the Holy Bible to mount a challenge.

This day's discussion offered a perfect example. Dave, an openly avowed non-believer, was discussing the virgin birth of Christ and recounted how he once asked a group of Rabbis why they didn't believe that Jesus was the Messiah. Dave said that one outspoken Rabbi claimed the virgin birth was a myth created by New Testament Christians. The Rabbi claimed that there was no mention of it in the Old Testament Torah.

My first question for the Rabbi would have been, "Are you discounting all of the other books of the Old Testament besides the Books of Moses? Anyway, according to Dave, the Rabbi went on to claim that the notion of the Messiah being God incarnate or the Son of God was just a New Testament phenomenon. According to the Torah, the Messiah would be just a man; a special man but a man nonetheless.

I was aghast. I wanted to call the station and set the record straight but couldn't get through. I would have said the Old Testament, including the Torah, was full of messianic prophesies that described the Savior in ever increasingly specific terms that pointed to no one other than Jesus. These prophesies included His earthly ancestry, place of birth and, most telling, His virgin birth by the power of the Holy Spirit.

I would have pointed the Rabbi to the first prophesy in the first Book of Moses, Genesis 3:15, "And I will put enmity between thee and the woman, and between thy seed and her seed; it shall bruise thy head, and thou shalt bruise his heel." I would have asked if he noticed that it mentioned the woman's seed. I would have asked why it didn't refer to the Savior as the seed of an earthly mother and father. Now, a skeptic like the Rabbi might have said this was a stretch and how could I get the virgin birth out of this passage?

Rather than argue the point on human logic or reason, I would have gone straight to Isaiah 7:14, "Therefore the Lord himself shall give you a sign; Behold, a virgin shall conceive, and bear a son, and shall call his name Immanuel." This not only foretold that the Messiah would be born of a virgin but it spelled it out in no uncertain terms that the Messiah would be the Son of God. That's what Immanuel meant … God with us. If that wasn't enough, I would have referred to Isaiah 9:6 where the Son is called "the mighty God." Wouldn't this have settled the argument once and for all? But I could hear the wily Rabbi's retort. *Wait just a minute sir. Modern translations of Isaiah 7:14 say that a **young woman** will conceive. There's nothing in there about a virgin.*

This, of course, would have been ignorance or sophistry. I would have guessed the latter since the Rabbi was no dummy. He surely knew that the Hebrew word used in the original text was almah. This term in either its feminine form (almah) or masculine form (elem) was used nine times in the Old Testament (Gen. 24:43; Ex. 2:8; 1 Sam. 17:56, 20:22; Psa. 68:25; Prov. 30:19; S. of Sol. 1:3, 6:8; Isa. 7:14). The feminine form referred to someone who was unmarried but of marriageable age which, in that culture and time, was around fourteen or so. The connotation was that the young maiden was chaste. Thus, the word almah was synonymous with virgin as used in the passages noted above.

Such verbal battles can be annoying and frustrating. But remember this. Don't give up. Keep fighting the good fight of faith with the one weapon at our disposal: the sword of the spirit which is the word of God. And don't allow the naysayers to ruin Christmas. We celebrate the truth of God's word and the absolute surety of His promises. God became flesh in the person of Jesus Christ, the Babe of Bethlehem, through the miracle of the virgin birth by the power of the Holy Spirit. This is essential to our faith and joy just as are the Easter cross and empty tomb. Let's celebrate once again the promises fulfilled and look forward with great anticipation to those that remain to be accomplished when Christ returns. Come Lord Jesus, come. And a very merry Christmas to all!

That Twinkle in Your Eye

God's ways are not our ways and our puny intellects are not capable of comprehending the mind of God. Thus, at some point, every Christian faces a choice. That is, whether to concede the authority of God's word over human reason or vice versa. So many people try to have it both ways but the outcome is always foolish. For example, theistic evolution tries to reason that God must have used evolution to create us but this only serves to undermine the Christian faith by presupposing that Almighty God is not powerful enough to have created the universe and everything in it within six days as revealed in Genesis. If we can't trust the creation account, then the whole foundation crumbles including the truth of Jesus' life, death and resurrection.

In another example, the Roman Catholics teach that Mary must have been sinless in order for Jesus to have been born sinless. This opens up a real can of worms because it requires that Mary's mother, Anne by some traditions, and all of her predecessors had to be sinless. How could that be if they were descended from our first parents, Adam and Eve, who transgressed in the Garden and passed along the curse of original sin to all their descendants? Mary even confessed her faith in her Savior in Luke 1:47. She knew she was a sinner like the rest of us.

This is where reason has tried to kick in. Despite being a virgin, Mary was a sinner. So how could she have borne a sinless child? It had to be one of God's

Faith Food   Steve Stranghoener

great miracles. The Holy Spirit took a speck of her flesh containing her genetic material and purified it from the corruption of sin that clings to all human flesh. Our human reason shouted, *Not so! If Mary's flesh was corrupted by sin, this would be impossible!* But with God, all things are possible (Matthew 19:26).

Now think about it. Does this require more faith than to believe that Jesus Christ was raised from the dead and is alive today unto eternity? Of course, there is no difference. So again, I say; if we try to remove any of the building blocks of our faith, the whole thing crumbles. The authority and veracity of God's word is essential, beyond feeble human reason.

Our resurrection hope is totally dependent upon our faith in Christ's resurrection. Similarly, our eternal salvation rests upon the truth of the Christmas miracle. Yes, God did take corrupt human flesh from Mary and transform it in giving His only Begotten Son a perfect, sinless body. We must believe this if we are to have any hope of shedding our own corrupt flesh.

Not to worry, it's a sure thing. God is going to perform this same miracle for each of us come Judgment Day. He tells us so in 1 Corinthians 15:52, "In a moment, in the twinkling of an eye, at the last trump: for the trumpet shall sound, and the dead shall be raised incorruptible, and we shall be changed." Throughout the year and especially during Christmastime, when I see a faithful Christian with a joyful twinkle in their eye, I like to think it's a reflection of that miraculous, twinkling star that God used to point to His sinless Son, our Lord and Savior, the God-man, Jesus Christ.

Joy to the World

I've often referenced *A Charlie Brown Christmas* in my seasonal devotions. It's been over fifty years since Charles Schulz penned his Christmas classic and yet it has remained amazingly relevant whenever Charlie Brown has asked the timeless question "Isn't there anyone who knows what Christmas is all about?" Has it warmed your heart too when faithful Linus turned to Luke 2 to point to the fulfillment of God's plan of salvation in baby Jesus? It's become a tradition for me but this year I'd like to turn to the Old Testament to kindle the kind of joy accompanied by the familiar heralding of the Savior's birth in the New Testament. The true meaning of Christmas was a source of joy for King David thousands of years before Jesus' birth as recorded in Psalm 103.

What kind of Savior was embodied in the Babe of Bethlehem, the Word Made Flesh; God Incarnate, Jesus Christ? King David, that repentant and forgiven sinner, the adulterer and murderer, knew the answer long before Christ ever appeared in the flesh. He knew all about the Messiah based on God's promised plan of salvation and was able to joyfully and thankfully put his trust in the Promised One by God-given faith. King David described Him to a T in Psalm 103.

"Who forgives all your iniquities, who heals all your diseases (Most importantly He heals the soul-destroying sickness of sin.), who redeems your life from destruction. (He rescues us from everlasting separation from God in hell.) Who crowns you with loving kindness and tender mercies, who satisfies your mouth with good things, so that your youth is renewed like the eagle's. (He showers us with blessings in mind, body and spirit.) The LORD executes righteousness and justice for all who are oppressed. (If not in this life then He surely will do so in the next. True justice will be served on Judgment Day.) The LORD is merciful and gracious; slow to anger, and abounding in mercy. (He lavishes us with undeserved, unconditional love rather than the punishment we deserve.) He will not always strive with us, nor will he keep his anger forever. (He has poured out His wrath against our sins on the Sinless One. Jesus suffered our hellfire on the cross. He stood in our place.) He has not dealt with us according to our sins, nor punished us according to our iniquities. (Christ imputed His righteousness to us while taking all of our sins upon Himself.) For as the heavens are high above the earth, so great is his mercy toward those who fear him. (Even our fear; love, respect & reverence, is a God-given gift. He provides for all or our needs, both temporal and spiritual.) As far as the east is from the west, so far has he removed our transgressions from us." (We have been reconciled to God in Christ and have been adopted into His forever family.)

That's the true meaning of Christmas. That's the reason for the season. In the fullness of time, God fulfilled all of His gracious promises of salvation in a stable in Bethlehem. Joy to the world, the Lord is come!

Re-Gifting

One of my favorite television shows was *Everybody Loves Raymond*. It had a special knack for revealing the sometimes-dysfunctional nature of our families in a hysterical way. A recurring theme in several episodes was the law of unintended consequences in giving and receiving gifts. Once, Ray tried to outshine his brother, Robert, by buying an expensive aquarium filled with exotic fish for their father, Frank. This underhanded deed backfired when one of the fishes died making Ray believe he'd reminded his dad of his own mortality. Actually, Frank resented the exorbitant cost.

Another time, Ray presented his parents with a Fruit-of-the-Month membership to which his mother, Marie, exclaimed in abject horror, "You mean this is going to happen every month? Who can eat so much fruit?" Perhaps the funniest disaster occurred when Frank and Marie returned the toaster Ray had given them in exchange for a coffee maker. They didn't realize that Ray had paid to have the toaster engraved with the names of their children and grandchildren.

I can remember times when such foibles weren't so funny. Have you ever sacrificed a lot of thought and hard-earned money in offering what you felt was the perfect gift only to have it fall flat? This has led to depression, hurt feelings or even anger. How dare the recipient not be thrilled with the precious treasure I deliberated over so thoughtfully for so long! Have you ever received such a gift and uncomfortably feigned gratitude and joy over something you actually loathed? Have you ever had your heart strings broken after an eager child put their heart and soul into personally crafting a gift only to be crushed by the poorly disguised disappointment of the recipient?

Can you imagine how Christ felt? After living the perfect life that we couldn't lead, He suffered scorn, ridicule, torture and crucifixion. Outside of time, on that bloody cross for three of our hours, He endured the torments of hell that all of us deserved for all eternity. He did this to justify everyone who has ever lived or will live, so that none would have to experience eternal separation from God. Furthermore, He redeemed us while we were still filthy sinners and enemies of God and all as a free gift!

This amazing truth was summed up beautifully in Romans 5:18, "Therefore as by the offence of one judgment came upon all men to condemnation; even so by the righteousness of one the free gift came upon all men unto justification of life." Jesus' atoning sacrifice was and remains the most precious, costly, thoughtful and loving gift imaginable. Yet, so many thoughtless thousands have spurned it. Even at His crucifixion this cruel paradox played out in front of our Lord when one criminal was brought to faith while the other one railed against Jesus.

If we were in the same position, by our very nature we would lash out at all the ungrateful scorners and banish them to hell forever. We certainly would never make the ultimate sacrifice for loathsome creatures who we knew beforehand would reject us. But God is love and showed as much when Jesus said this about His executioners, "Father, forgive them; for they know not what they do," (Luke 23:34). Jesus didn't begrudge His all-availing sacrifice from those who He knew would throw His priceless gift back in His face but instead showed true compassion toward them, "O Jerusalem, Jerusalem, thou that kills the prophets, and stones them which are sent unto thee, how often would I have gathered thy children together, even as a hen gathers her chickens under her wings, and ye would not!" (Matthew 23:37).

We can't do anything to make up for the injustice and cruel treatment our Lord received but we can nevertheless do something Christ-like. At Christmastime, re-gifting is usually frowned upon but in this case, nothing could be more fitting. Let's take the precious gift of God's grace, mercy and forgiveness and share it with as many other undeserving people like us as possible unto life everlasting.

White Christmas

Who wants a white Christmas? I say bah humbug! Yeah, I know this sounds detestable, especially at this time of the year. I'm sorry but that's the way I feel. Sure, if I was a kid again I'd be wishing for snow;

Faith Food   Steve Stranghoener

piles and piles and deep drifts of the glistening white stuff. For children, snow means racing down the slopes on a Flexible Flyer, rambunctious snow ball fights, holly, jolly snow men and, best of all, the prospect of an unplanned hiatus from school.

However, I'm no spring chicken. I'm an old geezer and, thus, snow only means snarled traffic, perilous roadways, sooty slush on the cars and garage floor, filthy footprints in the foyer and, worst of all, shoveling the driveway in bone-chilling weather. Nah, you can keep your jingling sleigh bells, marshmallow world and idyllic winter wonderland where snowflakes stay on your nose and eyelashes. As for this old Grinch, I'll settle for a good, old-fashioned, Indian summer any day.

I realize that I'm in the minority on this one. Most people can overlook the ominous snow plows that rumble along like Sherman tanks, harsh salt that corrodes like acid and scraping shovels that grate the ears like fingernails being dragged across a chalk board. To most, this is a small price to pay in exchange for the marvel of gazing at an endless, silvery-white, fluffy blanket covering everything as far as the eye can see, especially when it reflects the warm glow of every hue and shade imaginable that are cheerfully and softly emitted from twinkling Christmas lights and decorations.

Now, don't get me wrong. I like chestnuts roasting over an open fire and halls decked with boughs of holly as much as the next guy. And I admit that I'm a sucker for Irving Berlin's classic version of *White Christmas* as sung by the inimitable Bing Crosby. There's a reason why this song topped the charts in 1942 and has been selling ever since. Today it still stands as the best-selling single of all time at over fifty million copies or more than one hundred million records if you include all the other versions released over the years.

Ah, nothing can warm the heart and fill a room with holiday cheer quite like Bing's bass-baritone floating along with the lyrical, lilting melody of *White Christmas*. Hey, wait a minute! What am I saying? I hate the white stuff, Bing or no Bing. Yeah, I like Bing but I'd much rather be sitting on my lanai in Honolulu hearing the consummate crooner oozing, "Mele Kalikimaka is the thing to say on a bright Hawaiian Christmas day." That's the ticket all right, eighty degrees and palm trees swaying.

Come to think of it though, for some reason, it seems like it would be hard to focus on the real meaning of Christmas with all the distractions of an island paradise. That is, God solved our biggest problem, our impossible sin problem in the most miraculous, marvelous way. He came to earth Himself, in the person of Jesus Christ. This He did in the most unique, mind-boggling way imaginable. God was born into the flesh as a little baby through virgin birth, without any taint of sin. Only the Holy Spirit could perform such a feat.

That little baby, true God and true man, went on to lead the perfect, holy, sinless life that none of us could ever do. He earned a mantle of righteousness, one that is gleaming white and spotless. Then, in a cosmic exchange that transcended anything that our feeble, human brains could comprehend without the aid of the Holy Spirit, He took our filthy, hell-deserving sins upon Himself and covered us with His perfect, white robe of righteousness. This was recorded for us in 2 Corinthians 5:21, "For he hath made him to be sin for us, who knew no sin; that we might be made the righteousness of God in him."

Isn't that something? We've been reconciled to God, us undeserving sinners, by the Babe of Bethlehem. Eternal salvation is ours because of the greatest Christmas gift of all, a perfect, white, spotless covering of divine righteousness purchased at an infinite, unimaginable price that none of us could ever afford. Yeah, the more I think about it, I am dreaming of a white Christmas, snow or no snow.

Faith Food   Steve Stranghoener

New Year

Faith Food   Steve Stranghoener

Resolute in the New Year

Have you made your New Year's resolutions? What, you've already broken them? I'm just kidding because I'm sure we all mean well. What's in your plan for this year: losing weight, getting in shape, advancing your career? Maybe you've resolved to break a bad habit or just be a nicer person.

Wouldn't it be nice to stop sinning so much this year? Good luck in tackling that project on your own! I'm not trying to make light of New Year's resolutions. Even though most don't last for long, it's still admirable and worthy to try to improve ourselves and the world around us. It's next to impossible to achieve anything without having a firm goal in mind. Nothing ventured, nothing gained.

As Christians, we face a peculiar dilemma. Like everyone else, we want to strive for success but we realize that our lives are not our own. We can wander way off course and end up in a terrible mess if we try to go it alone, apart from God. But how can we know what God has in store for us? Should we idle away the time waiting for a clear sign from God? Is prayer the solution?

Prayer is of course a good thing but is not our only guide. The surest way to seek God's direction is through His verbally inspired, inerrant word in the Holy Bible. In wrestling with this question of how to move forward without losing sight of God, I came across some very helpful guidance from the Lord. In

Proverbs 16, God tells us our endeavors should be a joint venture with Him. Two passages really stand out. In verse 3 we're told, "Commit thy works unto the Lord, and thy thoughts shall be established." Verse 9 adds that, "A man's heart devises his way: but the Lord directs his steps." This means that, if our hearts are committed to serving the Lord, everything that follows will work out. God tells us that we must act but He will light the way for us.

Like the Psalmist (Psalm 119:70) and the Apostle Paul (Romans 7:22), if we delight in the law and earnestly seek to conform to God's word and will, everything else will take care of itself. This is easier said than done though since we often get impatient and want immediate results. God has advice for us here too in Psalm 27:4, "Wait on the Lord: be of good courage, and he shall strengthen thine heart: wait, I say, on the Lord." Sometimes God encourages us to act decisively but at other times requires patience.

Therefore, we can approach the New Year eagerly with energy and much determination but also prudence and patience. Most importantly, we can also strive to live in cooperation with God with His word and will leading the way.

Ringing in the New Year

As we ring in the New Year, let's take a moment to compare old and new. Perhaps the best way to do this is to compare and contrast the two worlds in which we live: the temporal and spiritual or Satan's domain and God's kingdom of grace.

Here's how God describes the condition of our present, fallen world in Ecclesiastes 1:9, "The thing that hath been, it is that which shall be; and that which is done is that which shall be done: and there is no new thing under the sun." We should keep this in mind as we make our resolutions. Exchanging last year's calendar with a new one will not change anything in this world. In a temporal sense, the New Year will bring the same sin, corruption, injustice and discord as every other year since the fall of Adam and Eve into sin.

There will be no satisfaction but only frustration and disappointment for those who pursue a social gospel in an attempt to create a better world; a utopia on this earth. Here's how God puts this in Ecclesiastes 1:14, "I have seen all the works that are done under the sun; and, behold, all is vanity and vexation of spirit." Let's face it. No matter how hard we try, the labor of our hands will not change the nature of our present world.

It is doomed by sin and corruption and its fate is sealed. It will be destroyed by God on the last day as is made abundantly clear in 2 Peter 3:10, "But the day of the Lord will come as a thief in the night; in the which the heavens shall pass away with a great noise, and the elements shall melt with fervent heat, the earth also and the works that are therein shall be burned up." The War on Poverty, the battle against global warming and all of our misguided attempts to salvage this lost and fallen world will come to naught.

However, there is no need to dismay. Most thankfully, Christ reminds us in John 18:36 and elsewhere that His kingdom is not of this world. Christ's kingdom is a spiritual one, an everlasting one. We're living and reigning with Him even today as citizens of His new kingdom. But this is not meant to be in spirit alone. We are not relegated to live as disembodied spirits in an ethereal, spiritual realm forever.

First of all, as noted in 1 Corinthians 15:52, Jesus promises that we will be resurrected and given new, perfect, glorified bodies, "In a moment, in the twinkling of an eye, at the last trump: for the trumpet shall sound, and the dead shall be raised incorruptible, and we shall be changed." And just as importantly, we will have a new place to live forever in the presence of God. In 2 Peter 3:13, God proclaims, "Nevertheless we, according to his promise, look for new heavens and a new earth, wherein dwells righteousness." Furthermore, He also promises through his prophet in Isaiah 65:17, "For, behold, I create new heavens and a new earth: and the former shall not be remembered, nor come into mind." Isn't that marvelous to know that we won't have any memory of this lost and fallen world?

So, you may be wondering what to do next. Should we forget about turning over a new leaf with the New Year? Should we avoid the futility of trying to change this sinful, old world and sit back patiently and quietly while awaiting Christ's return? No, that is certainly not God's calling for us. In Ecclesiastes 9:7 He tells us to go on with our lives joyfully, "Go thy way, eat thy bread with joy, and drink thy wine with a merry heart; for God now accepts thy works."

Yes, God is pleased with the things we do in accordance with His word out of love for Christ. God gives us more specific direction in Ecclesiastes 11:11, "Cast thy bread upon the waters: for thou shalt find it after many days." What kind of investment is God encouraging us to make. Yes, spiritual ones, everlasting ones. That's why He's given us His Great Commission to make disciples of all nations. Okay, so we have a lot of work in store for us; joyful, rewarding, everlasting work. Thus, it is a good time to remember to ring in the new, in spirit, by recalling God's promise in 2 Corinthians 5:17. "Therefore if any man be in Christ, he is a new creature: old things are passed away; behold, all things are become new."

Epiphany

Flipping the Switch

Have you ever come home after nightfall to a dark house and been touched with a fear of the unknown as you slid your outstretched hand back and forth along the wall searching frantically for that elusive light switch? Or do you remember as a kid being in your parents' basement, turning off the light switch and then bounding up the stairs like a cannon shot in an attempt to out-pace the imaginary goblins lurking in the darkness?

I think most of us, no matter how old or brave, get a little nervous when we're in pitch black surroundings, even for just a few moments. Is it a natural instinct or the product of silly superstitions? There are good practical reasons to be afraid of the dark. Have you ever stubbed your toe on a chair or banged your shin against a coffee table in the dark? But there's a lot more to this practical fear than self-preservation against bumps, bruises and turned ankles.

Throughout Scripture, God uses light and darkness as symbols to impart important spiritual messages. God makes it abundantly clear that light represents good while darkness stands for evil. For example, He cautions in 2 Corinthians 6:14, "Be ye not unequally yoked together with unbelievers: for what fellowship hath righteousness with unrighteousness? And what communion hath light with darkness?" The two are exact opposites and so diametrically opposed that they cannot coexist. 1 John 1:5 drives this point home further by revealing the source of all light and goodness, "This then is the message which we have heard of him, and declare unto you, that God is light, and in him is no darkness at all."

Matthew 4:16 describes how God flipped the switch for all mankind with the birth of Christ the Savior, "The people which sat in darkness saw great light; and to them which sat in the region and shadow of death light is sprung up." Yes, darkness represents sin and its consequence; death. Jesus used this same symbolism to deliver His precious gospel message to us in John 8:12, "Then spake Jesus again unto them, saying, I am the light of the world: he that followeth me shall not walk in darkness, but shall have the light of life."

In everyday life we have small epiphanies all the time. We say the light bulb went on when we finally grasp something that has escaped our understanding for a long while. But an Epiphany with a capital E can only come from God. The wise men had heard prophesies of the coming Savior but it took the original light source, God, to throw the switch and guide their path to Him with the help of the miraculous star.

Likewise, we are unable to grasp the good news by ourselves in our former, fallen state. Apart from God, we are by nature dead in our trespasses and sins and cannot flip the switch. But God comes to us daily and continually through His means of grace, His precious word and sacraments connected to the word.

This truth is revealed clearly in 1 Corinthians 12:3, "Wherefore I give you to understand, that no man speaking by the Spirit of God calls Jesus accursed: and that no man can say that Jesus is the Lord, but by the Holy Ghost."

Most of us can recall being afraid of the dark but how about the opposite? Have you ever read a passage of Scripture for the umpteenth time when, all of a sudden, you've gained a new insight that has never crossed your mind before? Sure, we've all had this happen many times. So that's the key. When we want an Epiphany with a capital E; when we want to flip our spiritual light switches on, it's easy. All we have to do is open the book, the Holy Bible and, voila, instant light of the best kind! Christ, the Incarnate, Living Word, is the Light of the World, and the world to come (Revelation 21:23) where there will be no need of the sun.

Lent

Bitter Pill

Do you believe in leprechauns? Is there a pot of gold at the end of the rainbow? The answer of course is no since it would be foolish to put one's faith and trust in folklore and myths. Some in Christ's day thought that faith in the resurrection of believers was just such a fool's errand. Most notably, the Sadducees taught that there was no resurrection of the dead.

These Jewish religious leaders were supposedly experts on the Scriptures, the Books of Moses. They hated Jesus because they felt He undermined their authority. As recorded in Mark chapter 27, they conspired to expose Him as a fraud and even would have laid hands on Him were it not for their fear of the people following Jesus.

How did Christ turn the tables on them? First Jesus applied the law to the Jewish authorities as a loving, brotherly admonition, by sharing the parable of the owner of the vineyard and the wicked husbandmen who killed his son. He made it abundantly clear that they were the object of the lesson when He talked about how the builders rejected the stone that is the head of the corner.

The Pharisees and Herodians had the next crack at Jesus when they asked Him about paying Tribute to Caesar. He easily swatted away their childish riddle by advising them to give unto Caesar what is Caesar's and unto God what is God's.

Next the Sadducees, in their hubris, intended to set Jesus straight. They posed a hypothetical situation on the basis of two presuppositions, neither of which were valid. First, they presumed that, if there was a resurrection, believers would remain male and female in marriage. Second, and more importantly to them, they posited that God did not have the power to resurrect the dead. In structuring their argument this way, they showed that they were Scriptural shams rather than the scholars they claimed to be.

They asked if a woman was widowed and remarried multiple times, who would be her husband after the resurrection. Jesus corrected them bluntly by telling them there would no longer be marriage in heaven. Then He hit them with the knockout punch. Jesus drew them back to the Books of Moses which they claimed to know so well and reminded them how God told Moses from the burning bush, "I am the God of Abraham, the God of Isaac and the God of Jacob." They understood His point because Abraham, Isaac and Jacob were dead in body by that time. Yet their spirits lived on. Then came the glorious truth in Mark 12:27 when Jesus proclaimed, "He is not the God of the dead, but the God of the living: ye therefore do greatly err."

Now, did Jesus do this to embarrass and belittle them? No, this was a hard truth and a bitter pill for them to swallow but He did it out of love. It was the truth they needed to hear. Even though they conspired against Him and rejected Him, Jesus kept applying the law so that they might be receptive to the gospel.

And let's not forget that not all their hearts were hardened to the point of despair. We know that some Jewish leaders like Nicodemus, Joseph of Arimathea and Saul of Tarsus were brought to faith by the gospel. So, what they felt was a myth was in fact the truth, the veracity for which God would provide indisputable evidence through the cross and empty tomb.

It's ironic yet fitting that St. Patrick's Day and Easter are so close together. One is frivolous and the other is glorious. No there are no leprechauns. But there is a treasure available to you and me that is infinitely more valuable than any pot of gold. It's not at the end of the rainbow. It's only found at the foot of the cross and the empty tomb. Rather than chasing rainbows we should turn to the word of God in the Holy Bible and His promise of forgiveness, redemption and salvation.

Helpful Reminder

A not so funny thing happened to me at the beginning of Lent. While many of my Roman Catholic friends practiced their annual rite of giving up alcohol, soda, sugary foods or other vices and flocked to Friday night fish fries, I pondered anew the solemnity of the season. I tried to avoid feelings of haughty superiority while comparing Lutheran Lenten practices to their oftentimes self-serving sacrifices. Then an insidious thought knocked me off my pedestal. Did I really have my heart and mind focused on our Lord's Passion or had Lent become a familiar routine where I dutifully went through the motions? I didn't want to believe it but had to admit the tendency of my sinful human nature toward complacency.

While I didn't realize it at the time, God already had a solution to my problem in mind. The day before the first Sunday in Lent, an odd feeling overcame me. By early afternoon, I could tell a nasty virus of some sort had invaded my body. It was only a matter of time. That night, my insides painfully rebelled until I retched over and over to expel the vile poison from my system. You know the feeling: helplessness and despair. I tossed and turned late into the night until the ordeal ended. Thankfully, I never felt sorry for myself but simply asked the Lord to help see me through it. After a few hours of sleep, I awoke feeling well enough to drag myself into church for a much-needed spiritual refresher. After that, I felt like I was out of the woods.

My optimism held through most of the day on Monday but then it became apparent that God still needed to plow this field. Apparently, the enemy still maintained a stronghold and my system fought to expel the foe in a fierce battle. My first trip to the restroom occurred around 7:00 p. m. and the interminable suffering continued in roughly fifteen-minute intervals until about 8:00 a. m. on Tuesday. Eventually, the discomfort, lack of sleep and, worst of all, perception of there being no end in sight laid me low in deep despair. I had no choice but to put myself in the Lord's hands. Again, thankfully, I didn't feel the urge to cry, "Why me God?" Of course, I begged for relief but found, by God's grace, the patience to bow to His will alone.

As I recovered enough to attend our Lenten service on Wednesday night, the blessing of my chastisement became apparent. I couldn't have been more focused on Christ's passion as our pastor preached about Jesus' suffering in the Garden of Gethsemane. The rich meaning of Christ's words in Mark 14:36 hit home, "And he said, Abba, Father, all things are possible unto thee; take away this cup from me: nevertheless not what I will, but what thou wilt." My suffering suddenly seemed infinitesimally small compared to the cosmic grief that caused the Lord to literally sweat blood. He knew the pain and suffering His cup withheld; the cross that loomed and, most importantly, God's wrath over our sins that would be poured out on Him in our place.

Most assuredly I would have escaped my own puny chastisement if I had possessed the power to end my sickness and suffering. Amazement gripped me as I realized that Jesus could have easily turned away from His horrendous cup of sorrows. But that would have derailed God's plan of salvation for us. Jesus willingly forged ahead and suffered all for us. He paid an incredible price that none of us could have afforded. This Lenten reminder, however unpleasant, proved to be a great blessing. It focused my attention on Christ's suffering like a laser and helped me to marvel at Jesus' great love toward us. Oh, thank the Lord for He is good and His mercy endures forever.

Staying Focused

Lent is a solemn season with an all-encompassing, singularly critical purpose. That is, we are to keep our focus on Christ alone and His passion in accomplishing our redemption from sin, death and the devil. Here is how Paul put it in the third chapter of his God-inspired letter to the church at Galatia.

First, he grabbed their attention in his sternest, no-nonsense fashion in verse 1. "O foolish Galatians, who hath bewitched you, that ye should not obey the truth, before whose eyes Jesus Christ hath been evidently set forth, crucified among you?" The Galatians had wandered from the true gospel. Heterodox teachings and heresies had infiltrated the congregation. They had retreated to the harsh yoke of the law.

Paul didn't beat around the bush. He turned their focus back to Christ and His crucifixion in verse 13. "Christ hath redeemed us from the curse of the law, being made a curse for us: for it is written, Cursed is every one that hangs on a tree." He couldn't say it any plainer. Christ became sin and took all our sins upon Himself and paid the price, the infinite price we couldn't afford: death on a cross and the hellfire of God's just wrath that we deserved.

Paul proclaimed the truth that they couldn't go back and claim the blessings of their Jewish heritage by returning to the Old Covenant law. He pointed to the New Covenant fulfilled through the Promised One of Israel in verse 14. "That the blessing of Abraham might come on the Gentiles through Jesus Christ; that we might receive the promise of the Spirit through faith." Paul wanted them to know that both Jew and Gentile were spiritual children of Abraham, saved by the same faith that saved Abraham.

He said in verse 22 that the law could not save anyone, including Jews, because they were all sinners. "But the scripture hath concluded all under sin; that the promise by faith of Jesus Christ might be given to them that believe." He pointed them to Jesus, the Promise Fulfilled, through the God-given gift of faith.

Paul pointed the Galatians to their heavenly heritage as God's adopted children in verses 26-28, "For ye are all the children of God by faith in Christ Jesus. For as many of you as have been baptized into Christ have put on Christ. There is neither Jew nor Greek, there is neither bond nor free, there is neither male nor female: for ye are all one in Christ Jesus." Paul proclaimed them and us to be all one in the same, spiritual Israel. He showed us all to be branches connected to the True Vine, Jesus Christ.

Thus we, like the Galatians, are privileged to live thankfully in God's grace and walk by faith and not by sight, justified not by the deeds of the law but rather the perfect righteousness of Jesus Christ, our

Savior. If we remember these words, we will not be led astray. We will stay focused on Christ and His all-availing death and glorious resurrection.

What's My Line?

What's My Line was a popular game show in the 1950s and 1960s. It was hosted by a guy named John Charles Daly and featured a panel of now forgotten stars that included, from time to time, Arlene Francis, Bennett Cerf, Steve Allen, Fred Allen and Soupy Sales among others. The premise was pretty simple. The panel asked questions to try to determine the occupation of the guest. If they didn't figure it out within the time allowed, the contestant was awarded a cash prize. Oftentimes, the guest had a strange vocation like counting worms in a bait shop. The best part of the show was the mystery guest. The panelists were blindfolded and a celebrity guest came out and disguised their voice to try to stump the questioners.

I was thinking about this the other day and my mind began to wander. I couldn't help but ponder what it would have been like if Jesus Christ was the mystery guest. Do you think the panel would have identified the Lord correctly? Do most people today, even Christians, really know who Jesus was? Unfortunately, many have been rendered clueless.

Some say He was a great prophet. Others claim He was a wise teacher. Many have gone so far as to say He was the Son of God but no more. I think that Bible-believing Christians have even had trouble wrapping our minds around His true identity at times. We've tended to make Him too small.

I think Lent is the perfect season for a refresher as we head toward Easter. So, this would be a good time to revisit Christmas, right? If you're having a tough time making this connection, please bear with me. Don't we often go from the manger to the cross during Advent to fully grasp the meaning of Christmas? I think we can derive a similar benefit by doing the reverse.

We're all familiar with the Christmas message of John 1:1-14 in seeking the true identity of Christ. Let's look at another familiar Christmas passage and see if it can help us better understand just who it was that went to the cross for us on that first Easter. Isaiah 9:6 reads, "For unto us a child is born, unto us a son is given: and the government shall be upon his shoulder: and his name shall be called Wonderful, Counsellor, the Mighty God, the Everlasting Father, the Prince of Peace."

The passage we just read is really quite profound; astonishing actually. A closer look reveals Jesus' true identity. He is not just the Son of God. Jesus is also one with God the Father, in majesty co-equal just as we confess in the Athanasian Creed. Jesus is one with God the Holy Ghost. Yeah that's what is meant by Counsellor. In John 14:16, Jesus refers to the Holy Ghost in saying, "And I will pray the Father, and he shall give you another Comforter that he may abide with you forever." The word Comforter here is translated from the Greek parakletos which means intercessor, counsellor, comforter and advocate.

Can you imagine how the game show panel would have handled this mystery guest? Jesus Christ is a distinct person, the Son of God; God incarnate in human flesh. But He is also God; the one true and Triune God. The panel might have accused him of having a split personality. How else could they have explained someone claiming to be three persons: Father, Son and Holy Spirit while simultaneously proclaiming His oneness as the only God?

Surely, they would have been completely baffled by this unfathomable conundrum. But could we blame them? No, I don't think so because we'd be in the same boat if not enlightened by the Holy Spirit. We're told in 1 Corinthians 12:3, "Wherefore I give you to understand, that no man speaking by the Spirit of God calls Jesus accursed: and that no man can say that Jesus is the Lord, but by the Holy Ghost." Thank the Lord that He has chosen to reveal this marvelous, miraculous, incredible truth to us. Let's keep this in mind as we follow Him to the cross during Lent.

Easter

The Mystery of Easter

Paul sounds like a mystery writer in 1 Corinthians 2:1-10 but, as inspired by God, he was not an author of fiction. "And I, brethren, when I came to you, came not with excellency of speech or of wisdom, declaring unto you the testimony of God. For I determined not to know anything among you, save Jesus Christ, and him crucified. And I was with you in weakness, and in fear, and in much trembling. And my speech and my preaching was not with enticing words of man's wisdom, but in demonstration of the Spirit and of power: That your faith should not stand in the wisdom of men, but in the power of God. Howbeit we speak wisdom among them that are perfect: yet not the wisdom of this world, nor of the princes of this world, that come to naught: but we speak the wisdom of God in a mystery, even the hidden wisdom, which God ordained before the world unto our glory: which none of the princes of this world knew: for had they known it, they would not have crucified the Lord of glory. But as it is written, eye hath not seen, nor ear heard, neither have entered into the heart of man, the things which God hath prepared for them that love him. But God hath revealed them unto us by his Spirit: for the Spirit searches all things, yea, the deep things of God."

I like to write Christian murder mysteries. Sometimes it may be a whodunit. Other times the killer is known right off the bat and the question is more one of why or how did they do it. Easter falls into the latter category. We know exactly what happened and have heard the story over and over. The question is how and why?

Paul's lead-in to the Easter story was rather puzzling. Here was Paul, the great apostle, one of the most brilliant, intelligent and learned men of all time. Paul was also one of the greatest orators and most gifted writers in all of history who was inspired by Almighty God. He was incredibly courageous and suffered interminably for the sake of the gospel. And yet, he introduced the greatest mystery of all not with sophisticated pomp and flowery prose but in the simplest language possible. He admitted to being weak and timid and that he knew nothing out of the ordinary except for Jesus Christ and His crucifixion.

He declared his sole purpose as pointing to the cross of Christ alone and nothing else. Paul admitted that he had no enchanting words with which to persuade. Furthermore, he declared that no man had the wisdom to unravel God's great mystery. Then he exposed the utter folly of worldly wisdom by laying bare the blame for the worst tragedy that has ever or will ever occur. Man's spiritual blindness and total lack of Godly wisdom led to the crucifixion of Jesus Christ. Paul added another layer to the mystery's labyrinth by calling us "perfect." How could this be?

Then he shared the secret and solved the mystery for us. We sinners could only be perfected by God through the cover of Christ's righteousness which is outside us. He explained that we could only solve the mystery by turning aside from our own feeble reason and seeking the hidden wisdom of God as revealed in His word of truth, the Holy Bible.

The mysterious plot thickened as Paul pointed us to the unfathomable "deep things of God." Then therein he revealed that we must walk by faith and not by sight. The crucifixion, this seemingly terrible, senseless tragedy, was ordained by God before the foundation of the world unto our glory. God came into this world, incarnate in the person of our Savior, His Son, Jesus Christ, to pay the price for our sins. It was the only way. God was the only one that could accomplish our salvation. He paid the price, an infinite price that we could never afford upon a bloody torture tree, the cross.

Fittingly, Paul concluded with the motive, the final piece of the puzzle. The greatest mystery of all was no longer how God redeemed us but why? The answer was found in one simple word: love.

Jericho to Jerusalem

Join me on a trip from Jericho to Jerusalem. No, we won't need to go to Google Maps for directions. This will be a mind trip of eternal proportions, spiritually speaking, without us taking a single step. Let's use the Book of Joshua as our travel guide for the first leg.

After God had miraculously used His servant Moses to free His people from bondage in Egypt, He led them on a long, difficult journey that resulted in death in the wilderness for many. The children of Israel were sustained by God's solemn promise that they would dwell in the land of Canaan. When they finally stood on the threshold of fulfillment, they encountered a major obstacle; a fierce enemy within the heavily fortified, walled city of Jericho. Against all odds, God assured Joshua and the Israelites that they would conquer the city in a fantastic, miraculous way. They demonstrated their God-given faith and followed His mysterious instructions by marching around the city for seven days and then blowing their horns. The walls tumbled down and God claimed the victory for His people.

Another promise sustained God's people after Jericho. It was the same promise that had been given to Adam and Eve and all of their descendants thereafter. The Messiah, the Christ, would be God in the flesh, a perfect sacrificial lamb and suffering servant. Jesus fulfilled this promise in Jerusalem in a way uncannily reminiscent of the Jericho miracle. Here's what happened when Jesus announced His victory on the cross that first Good Friday as recorded in Matthew 27:51, "And, behold, the veil of the temple was rent in twain from the top to the bottom; and the earth did quake, and the rocks rent."

Similar to the walls that separated the children of Israel from the Promised Land, the Temple curtain represented an even more imposing partition between Holy God and man: sin. Only the High Priest could enter the Holy of Holies where God's presence dwelled to offer the sacrifice on behalf of the people on the Day of Atonement. This partition was made incredibly strong by sewing together multiple cloths to form a veil several inches thick and impenetrable in a spiritual sense. In a gracious, merciful display of divine symbolism, God split the partition in two to show that the sacrifice of Jesus' death had atoned for the sins of all mankind and reconciled us sinners to God once and for always.

Good Friday and Easter remind us that we're all following the same map as Adam and Eve in the Garden to Joshua at Jericho and the witnesses at Christ's death and resurrection: God's plan of salvation in Jesus Christ. Paul offered this poignant reminder to the Ephesians and us in verse 2:14 of his epistle, "For he is our peace, who hath made both one, and hath broken down the middle wall of partition between us." We've been reconciled to God through our Lord and Savior, Jesus Christ, who destroyed the iron curtain of sin that separated us from Him.

Faith Food   Steve Stranghoener

Summer Vacation

On the Road Again

It never fails. I always get so excited when summer vacation time approaches. Actually, if the truth be known, my eager anticipation builds for months, through Lent's reverent solemnity and Easter's unabashed joy. I think I enjoy the planning and preparation almost as much as the actual event.

Summer means a lot of things. Radios blast an aging rocker's timeless anthem of summer announcing to kids that *School's Out*. The cold weather flees, pools are opened and tantalizing aromas waft from sizzling barbeque grills. And most thrilling of all, the masses prepare to embark on that time-honored tradition of the great American family vacation.

Vacation is, in some respects, all about getting away. It's escaping from the job and all that pressure and stress for a while. It means getting out from under a boss's or teacher's thumb. Even for the self-employed, it means freedom from normal obligations for a while. Vacation is a welcome break from our tired routines and the same old scenery. Sure, we have to come back to the grind but getting away for a while helps us to appreciate what we have since absence makes the heart grow fonder.

Vacations are much more than a get-away though. The best thing about a family vacation is togetherness. It gives us a chance to share quality time with the ones we love the most, away from all the normal duties and distractions that can keep us apart.

Vacation holds a rare blessing for my family now that our kids have jobs and families of their own. For one special week, we come together as a clan on what amounts to almost a coordinated military maneuver: fifteen people, three or four vehicles, umpteen pieces of luggage, GPS maps, budgets and itineraries of fun-filled activities. If it sounds a little too rigid and well-planned, it's not really. All the prep work just satisfies my buttoned-downed tendencies. Actually, once we're on the road, my laissez-faire side takes over and we all relax and enjoy playing things by ear.

We love the beach so Gulf Shores is one of our favorite destinations. Ah, is there anything better than sitting on a balcony, watching the emerald green and aqua blue waters roll into the shore on foamy, white-tipped waves while being fanned by the cool ocean breezes? How about frolicking in those same breakers, being buried in the sand by giggling grandkids and building a majestic sandcastle replete with a saltwater moat and shell-capped towers?

We love to walk on the beach or out on the pier to watch the anglers haul in a big one. I don't know what's better, Gulf food or Southern hospitality. We can't wait to walk barefoot in the sand to the Sea 'n Suds, right at the water's edge, for hot, juicy cheeseburgers and frosty, cold beer or soft drinks. As Mizzou fans, we love the friendly fraternization with other SEC football fans sporting their Bama, LSU and Gator colors.

The best part of our special time together is that there will be a sixteenth guest joining us, our Lord and Savior Jesus Christ. Yes, Jesus promises us in Matthew 28:20, "I am with you always, even unto the end of the world." Wherever we go, Jesus will be our constant companion. Isn't that great?

Before we depart, we will pray to our Heavenly Father in Jesus' name for our safekeeping. Every time we gather for our meals, we will pray and ask Jesus' blessings upon us and all the gifts He offers; not only the food but every temporal and spiritual blessing He provides in mind, body and spirit. When we gather for family devotions around God's word, we know with certainty that the Incarnate Word will be there with us, the Holy Spirit will bless us and our loving, Heavenly Father will be watching over us and dispatching His holy angels to guard and protect us.

Like our family, we hope you and yours will be incredibly blessed during the special time you share with each other and God on your vacations this summer; that He will help you to grow in your love toward one another and our Lord and Savior, Jesus Christ.

Faith Food   Steve Stranghoener

Independence Day

God and Country

In the year of our Lord 2018, we celebrated the 242nd anniversary of our nation's Declaration of Independence from England when we extricated ourselves out from under King George III's rule. I couldn't help being overcome by a keen sense of nostalgia and, regrettably, some deep misgivings. No, I had no regrets about our independence but admittedly felt some remorse over what we'd become. Amidst the frequent hullaballoo about the United States being the greatest nation on earth, I couldn't help but see through the charade by comparing the present to what once was.

It made my chest expand and heart soar when I heard the old patriotic standard, *The Battle Hymn of the Republic*, until the words sank into my psyche. The title alone gave me pause as I thought *this cherished anthem could not be penned in America today*. Three key words: battle, hymn, and republic were no longer politically correct in the USA.

When this song was written, it was considered good, worthy and righteous to take up arms in a just cause. Americans have never been anxious for warfare but we've never backed down from a fight if it was necessary for the cause of freedom.

I found it noteworthy that this tune was referred to as a hymn rather than just a song. God and country were inextricably linked. There was no foolish notion of separating our nation from God and His church. By and large we lived by the truth of Psalm 33:12 that, "Blessed is the nation whose God is the Lord."

I marveled at the term used to describe our Constitutional government. It wasn't deemed a democracy but rather a republic: a representative government of, by and for the people with unalienable rights bestowed not from Washington, D. C. but rather by Almighty God.

The Battle Hymn of the Republic originated when, like today, our nation faced a great divide that resulted in Civil War. It was penned by Julia Ward Howe in 1861 and first published in the Atlantic Monthly in February 1862. Julia and her husband, Samuel Gridley Howe, were politically active anti-slavery advocates. She used the familiar melody from *John Brown's Body*, a song that had recently come to popularity among Union troops. I don't have enough time here to publish the entire lyrics but I encourage you to review them for yourself. What struck me about the lyrics was the unabashed use of Scripture and clear references to the gospel.

A major theme of the song is to equate the temporal battle of the Civil War in ending slavery to the coming wrath of God in the final judgment. There is also significance to *John Brown's Body* serving as the foundation for the *Battle Hymn of the Republic*. Like *Onward Christian Soldiers*, the *Battle Hymn* is a reminder that temporal battles are superseded by a spiritual one. While John Brown's body lay decomposing in his grave, his soul lived on. Many on the side of emancipation saw the Civil War as much more than a fight over economic systems and political autonomy. It was a battle for goodness and truth, a spiritual mission encompassing the soul of the nation.

Please allow me to share two verses of the *Battle Hymn of the Republic* that will leave no doubt regarding the Christian underpinnings.

"I have read a fiery gospel, writ in burnished rows of steel; 'As ye deal with my contemners, so with you my grace shall deal; Let the hero, born of woman, crush the serpent with his heel, Since God is marching on.'"

"In the beauty of the lilies Christ was born across the sea; with a glory in his bosom that transfigures you and me; as he died to make men holy let us die to make men free; While God is marching on."

I pray that God will bless America with not only a president but many other leaders who aren't afraid to publicly express the truth that we should worship God and not government. I can't think of a more fitting way to close than with the chorus from the *Battle Hymn of the Republic* "Glory, glory hallelujah!"

Reformation

Halloween Costumes

Halloween has been commercialized to the point where it rivals Christmas in the secular sense. It has become a multi-billion-dollar industry that, oddly enough, caters as much if not more to adults than children. Every year, Hollywood has produced a spate of new horror flicks just in time for Halloween and businesses have flooded us with new products ranging from decorations to candy to elaborate spook-house experiences to everything we might conceivably need to throw the biggest monster mash of a party. The question, "What are you going to be for Halloween?" has become more a topic of conversation for adults than the kids.

What will be your choice if you're invited to a costume party? Will you be a princess or a pirate? In this year of 2018, there will surely to be a lot of Donald Trumps out there and maybe even a few Nancy Pelosi and Chuck Schumer masks. In keeping with the secular reason for the season, many people will opt for the maximum fright value by heading to the nearest store for more gore. Why must people dwell on the macabre? What's the purpose of dressing up as zombies, ghosts, goblins and witches? It seems as foolish as trying to conjure up evil spirits with a Ouija board.

I've found it unnecessary to spend a lot of money on scary things since I've had my spine chilled for free by reading the Bible. The most frightening costumes ever donned were used by evil angels, demons in Satan's service, back in the days when Christ walked the earth. These ghouls clothed themselves in the most realistic costumes ever devised. They possessed or occupied human beings.

Talk about a fright-fest! The truth is stranger than fiction. Stephen King and Edgar Allen Poe have nothing on these dudes. There are many accounts of demon possession in the Scriptures. Here's one from several select verses in Luke chapter 8. "And they arrived at the country of the Gadarenes, which is over against Galilee. And when he (Jesus) went forth to land, there met him out of the city a certain man, which had devils long time, and ware no clothes, neither abode in any house, but in the tombs. And Jesus asked him, saying, what is thy name? And he said, Legion: because many devils were entered into him. Then went the devils out of the man, and entered into the swine: and the herd ran violently down a steep place into the lake, and were choked."

I submit that these true accounts are much more harrowing than anything you'll see or hear in our Halloween myths, legends and folklore. Yet, there's no need to be worried. Please take note that even though no one could control the naked, immensely strong, rampaging lunatic of the Gadarenes who skulked among the tombstones, he was no match for Jesus Christ. The legion of demons that possessed the man was powerless when confronted by the King of Kings and Lord of Lords.

This was always the case when Christ confronted the evil angels, including the chief among them, Satan. So, if you see any goblins wandering about on Halloween, don't be alarmed. Use it as an opportunity to witness on behalf of the one whose voice they must obey, the Son of God, Jesus Christ.

I have another suggestion. If you must get dressed up for Halloween, how about this idea? Since it is, more importantly, Reformation Day, how about a Martin Luther costume? Go ahead and give it a try. Just don a rough-hewn tunic tied at the waist, pad on a few extra pounds and give yourself a funny haircut. Oh, and most importantly, carry a Bible with you at all times. To make things really authentic, in deference to Reformation Day, keep the Bible open to Romans 1:17. Trick or treat!

The Tweet Heard Round the World

Outsider Donald Trump changed the political landscape in America in 2016 with his unorthodox approach to communicating on the campaign trail. He flummoxed the largely hostile, mainstream media by bypassing them and taking his message directly to the voters. Candidate Trump eschewed conventional wisdom by relying on free media coverage of raucous campaign rallies where his incendiary rhetoric made constant headlines and often controlled the 24/7 news cycle.

Once in the Oval Office, he continued this habit against incessant, fierce opposition from a politically motivated, media-led resistance movement. Early morning Twitter rants remained one of his favorite tools. Although scorned and roundly denounced by his detractors, the President's tweets often proved immensely effective in getting around what he labeled as fake news to reach out to the common folks.

This reminded me of something even more earth shattering that occurred in 16th century Europe. How could I draw comparisons to a time so technologically different from ours? The means of communication in the 16th century were light years behind today. The power contained in our handheld smart phones alone has rendered the two ages worlds apart, separated by a seemingly impassable gap. There were no phones or even telegraphs and Gutenberg's primitive printing press had only been in existence for less than a century. Travel occurred on foot or horseback since automobiles, planes and even trains remained far off in the future. The dissemination of information occurred mostly by word of mouth.

That was the world of an obscure German monk named Martin Luther. Yet, he fired off the equivalent of a Twitter rant that not only spread across Europe and throughout the world but has continued to resonate today with the force of a thousand Trumpian tweets. When Martin Luther nailed his *95 Theses* to the church door in Wittenberg, Germany, he publicly challenged the most powerful forces in the world: The Roman Catholic Church under Pope Leo X and Holy Roman Emperor Charles V. Called by God and guided and protected by the Holy Spirit, Luther dared to proclaim the truth and ignited the Protestant Reformation on October 31, 1517.

Despite the passage of over 500 years and the incredible transformation the world has undergone, I think Luther's *95 Theses* and President Trump's campaign tweets were comparable in a way. Both Luther and Donald Trump were incredibly bold and courageous and each appeared to have been called and equipped by God to serve His good purposes even though posterity hasn't weighed in on the latter yet.

However, there were also some important distinctions. For example, Luther faced the very real threat of torture and death for taking a stand. Most importantly, Luther clearly operated primarily as a servant of the word rather than a politician.

President Trump's legacy remains to be seen but history has already spoken for Luther. God used Martin Luther as His empowered servant to rescue, restore and spread the gospel that was nearly lost. God has blessed us with the same glorious opportunity more than 500 years after the Reformation began. With that in mind, Christ has offered this timeless guidance for us as recorded in John 8:31-32, "Then said Jesus to those Jews which believed on him, If ye continue in my word, then are ye my disciples indeed; And ye shall know the truth, and the truth shall make you free."

The Test of Time

Have you seen those novelty shop booklets that cite noteworthy events from your birth year? In 1955 when I was born, the Brooklyn Dodgers won the World Series, Lee Merriweather was Miss America, teen idol James Dean died in a car crash, Bill Haley & His Comets scored a number one hit with *Rock Around the Clock* and *Abbott and Costello Meet the Mummy* was a blockbuster at the box office. Reading these factoids really made me feel old and offered a sobering lesson about the irrelevance of much of history, especially pop culture.

To reinforce this point, I recently turned the dial back to the 16th century and wondered if anything happened then that really mattered today. I put time to the test with this sampling of historical facts from the 1500s. Leonardo da Vinci painted the Mona Lisa and Michelangelo sculpted David and painted the ceiling of the Sistine Chapel. Nicolas Copernicus suggested that the earth moved around the sun. Henry VIII appointed himself head of the Anglican Church after being excommunicated by the Pope. Ivan the Terrible was crowned Czar of Russia. The pencil was invented in England. Kabuki Theater began in Japan. Shakespeare began writing and the Globe Theater was built in London near the River Thames.

While some great accomplishments occurred, these 16th century celebrities and their then astounding works have now just become footnotes in history. Time and astonishing technological advancements have eclipsed them all. Mona Lisa and David have been imprisoned in museums, light years removed from the mainstream of modern pop culture. Even the great bard, William Shakespeare, has only lived on in stories that have morphed into unrecognizable forgeries aimed at the itching ears of our nearly-illiterate masses.

However, one priceless treasure from our distant past has lost none of its value, even in our coarse, materialistic culture. Our church's namesake, Martin Luther, nailed his *95 Theses* to that church door in Wittenberg, Germany. On October 31, 2017, we had a special celebration of this momentous act which triggered the Reformation of the Christian Church 500 years before. We recognized Luther but gave the credit to Almighty God because only He could have saved what was nearly lost: the true gospel of Jesus Christ as handed down in God's Holy Bible.

God mightily used His servant Luther to overcome Satan and his minions: an empire and the apostate church. God's Reformation of His Church, started so inauspiciously by Luther in Wittenberg, caused a spark that ignited the entire world in spiritual flames that have burned brightly ever since. While much from that day has been lost to history, the 16th century gave us blessings that have remained indispensable unto the present. During the Reformation, Luther translated the Bible into the language of the people and later Tyndale gave us the first English translation of the New Testament. The

Geneva Bible gave us our current chapter and verse enumerations.

Two Bible passages come to mind that perhaps have best summed up the enduring, earth shattering significance of the Reformation. "Heaven and earth shall pass away, but my words shall not pass away," (Matthew 24:35). The Reformation had to happen in some shape, way or form because God said so and He always keeps His promises. "Then said Jesus to those Jews which believed on him, If ye continue in my word, then are ye my disciples indeed; And ye shall know the truth, and the truth shall make you free," (John 8:31-32). By God's grace, Luther knew, preserved and spread the truth that God's word possesses the power to create faith and sustain us, especially in spirit unto life everlasting. Thank God for using an obscure German monk to save the Church. Thank the Lord for restoring us and all believers to health and life everlasting in the Incarnate Word; our Lord and Savior, Jesus Christ.

Reformation, Easter & Judgment Day

What God accomplished through His servant Martin Luther in reforming His church during medieval times was arguably as miraculous as the six days of creation, Christmas and Easter. This may sound like a bold and, some might say, ludicrous claim considering the following. In the beginning, God created the earth, universe and everything therein by calling them into existence over six literal, twenty-four-hour days. He exercised His omnipotent power simply by speaking the word. At the first Christmas some 4,000 years later, God took on human flesh in the person of His perfect, sinless Son, Jesus Christ, through a virgin birth initiated and carried out by the power of His Holy Spirit. Thereafter, Christ's life, suffering, death and Easter resurrection fulfilled hundreds of Old Testament prophecies perfectly and offered God's proof-positive that Jesus had conquered sin, Satan and death itself.

How could I compare the act of a German monk nailing his *95 Theses* to the church door at Wittenberg to the most miraculous acts of Almighty God? I arrived at this conclusion by looking through spiritual lenses, beyond the flesh, sinew and feeble reason of a mere mortal. God and not Martin Luther saved the church. Of course, Luther served in a key role but God supplied the power. He used Martin Luther as He had miraculously used Abraham, Moses, the Apostles and all of His flawed but faithful servants including you and me. As I looked beyond mere men, these heroes of the Bible and Luther, I recognized the unmistakable similarities between their mighty acts since each miracle hinged, first and foremost, on the word of God.

In Luther's time, the gospel had been almost completely lost. God's grace had been perniciously replaced with a system of works righteousness that even included a monetary quotient for salvation. The Roman Catholic Church was selling indulgences that granted forgiveness in exchange for filthy lucre. One could supposedly even gain access into heaven's express lane if the price was right. People were by and large ignorant of God's true plan of salvation because they were denied access to the Holy Bible.

God changed all of this through His humble servant with the same divine power He used to call our world into being. God used Luther to restore and spread His word of truth. Although the Reformation lacked the conspicuous extravagance of creation, Christmas and Easter, it was no less miraculous. While some are apparent to the naked eye, other miracles, like when a helpless baby is brought to faith through baptism, are no less extraordinarily powerful even though they must be perceived through spiritual lenses.

Only God could save the church from the false teachers and He blessed Martin Luther to serve this divine purpose. He kept His promise of salvation by grace through faith the same way He kept all of His promises; through the power of His word. God is not finished. We await the final reformation when Christ will return, put an end to this sin-sick world and create the new heavens and earth through His all-powerful word.

Faith Food   Steve Stranghoener

Thanksgiving

Promises, Promises

November is special because, in our country, it's the month in which we celebrate our national day of thanksgiving. We're grateful for our freedom, liberty and all the wonderful blessings we enjoy. Unfortunately, sometimes we forget the source of our blessings.

In 2016 it was easy to be distracted because of the election. Did you catch all the campaign promises made by Hillary Clinton, Donald Trump and your congressional candidates? This was no small task considering the plethora of pledges made to us voters but was crucial in order to keep track of how many vows were actually kept. Sadly, many campaign promises have often gone unfulfilled. Hollow promises have too frequently been the norm in politics for such is the nature of man.

Despite the political realities of an election year and sinful man's inherent nature to renege on every form of commitment, we still had every reason to be eternally thankful and joyful in 2016 and beyond. That's because we had so many promises from Almighty God who has never gone back on His word. God's promises have always been absolutely sure and infinitely more valuable than anything this world could offer.

Christ assured us in Isaiah 40:8 and John 15:11, "The grass withers, the flower fades, but the word of our God stands forever ... These things have I spoken unto you; that my joy might remain in you, and that your joy might be full."

We have so much to be thankful for since the Bible is chock full of God's immutable promises. There isn't space here to plumb the depths of God's providence toward us but this small sample is enough to last an eternity.

- "Who gave himself for our sins, that he might deliver us from this present evil world, according to the will of God and our Father," (Galatians 1:4).
- "And if ye be Christ's, then are ye Abraham's seed, and heirs according to the promise," (Galatians 3:29).
- "According as he hath chosen us in him before the foundation of the world, that we should be holy and without blame before him in love: having predestinated us unto the adoption of children by Jesus Christ to himself, according to the good pleasure of his will," (Ephesians 1:4-5).
- "Giving thanks unto the Father, which hath made us meet to be partakers of the inheritance of the saints in light: who hath delivered us from the power of darkness, and hath translated us into the kingdom of his dear Son," (Colossians 1:12-13).
- "Verily, verily, I say unto you, He that hears my word, and believeth on him that sent me, hath everlasting life, and shall not come into

condemnation; but is passed from death unto life," (John 5:24).

As we gather together for worship and family feasts of celebration on Thanksgiving Day, may we remember the promises that really count and Almighty God, our loving, Heavenly Father who is the fount and source of all our blessings. I pray this gratitude will reside in our hearts and upon our lips all the days of our lives.

Faith Food   Steve Stranghoener

The Word

Back to the Past

Blessed with prophetic power, Isaiah could have related to producer Steven Spielberg's blockbuster *Back to the Future*. However, seeing through God's eyes, Isaiah didn't need a tricked-out DeLorean to gaze ahead with perfect, miraculous accuracy. Today, Hollywood has continued to spin out futuristic films for hungry fans but ironically our obsession with what lies beyond has caused us to lose sight of history. Perhaps movie makers should reverse course and take us back to the past.

They could find an unlimited supply of untapped material in the Holy Bible, the greatest "screenplay" ever written. For example, the story of Persian King Cyrus would be perfect for the silver screen. God laid out a marvelous plot through His prophet in Isaiah 45. Although a gentile, God anointed Cyrus to do His bidding in subduing many nations. This led to the fulfillment of God's promise that a remnant of Israel would be released from their Babylonian captivity after seventy years and allowed to return to Jerusalem to rebuild the Temple. It also revealed God's true identity to the gentile nations as declared in Isaiah 45:5-6, "I am the LORD, and there is none else, there is no God beside me: I girded thee (Cyrus), though thou hast not known me: That they may know from the rising of the sun, and from the west, that there is none beside me. I am the LORD, and there is none else."

Cyrus may not have been a Christian but he recognized God's truth as he confessed in 2 Chronicles 36:23, "Thus saith Cyrus king of Persia, All the kingdoms of the earth hath the LORD God of heaven given me; and he hath charged me to build him an house in Jerusalem, which is in Judah. Who is there among you of all his people? The LORD his God be with him, and let him go up." Cyrus didn't waste time but, as recorded in Ezra 6:3, got busy with the Lord's work in the first year of his reign. This fact of history was corroborated by secular historian Flavius Josephus.

We could take a lesson from Cyrus. Instead of turning away from God and looking to vain yearnings about the future, we should turn back to the Bible and reflect on the mighty acts of God. Therein is revealed our certain future: Christ's return and eternal salvation.

Consistency

I couldn't help but chuckle when I've heard people, especially Christians, downplay the importance of the Old Testament. That's over and done with they've implied. The Old Covenant was done away with by the New. We should focus on the New Testament Scriptures and not waste time with that old relic.

Couldn't they see the fallacy in this argument? Christ didn't set aside the Old Covenant but rather fulfilled it. Creating a gulf between the Old and New Testaments would be the same as denying our biological descent from Adam, Eve and Noah or our spiritual connection to Abraham, Isaac, Jacob and Moses.

We can't read the New Testament and Christ's words without being reminded of the Old Testament's relevance. Jesus frequently quoted the Old Testament to illuminate the teachings of the New Covenant. For example, in Matthew 4 we're told about Jesus' temptation by Satan after fasting in the wilderness for forty days and nights. The devil offered Him food, comfort, worldly riches and power and the means to avoid His pending passion and death. Take note of how Jesus countered Lucifer's hateful, prideful and foolish attempt to derail God's plan of salvation for mankind. He didn't use His omnipotent, divine power to physically crush the Evil One. Instead, He simply quoted the Holy Scriptures and referred to Deuteronomy to make His iron clad case.

Many times, I've delighted in comparing the Old and New Testament Scriptures because of their marvelous consistency. It's more than that though because the two are inseparable, interwoven with a scarlet thread dipped in the righteous, cleansing blood of the Savior. God's plan of salvation was revealed to Old Testament believers just like to us in New Testament times. It is the exact same plan, a future foretold to them and a commitment fulfilled to us. However, they were not left to wonder what would happen after the Messiah's incarnation. God also revealed the end times to them regarding Christ's return, Judgment Day and the new heavens and earth.

I read a passage recently that reminded me anew of the miraculous synchronicity of the Scriptures. Most of us have heard of God's dire warning in Revelation 22:18-20 against changing or reinterpreting the Bible. "For I testify unto every man that hears the words of the prophecy of this book, If any man shall add unto these things, God shall add unto him the plagues that are written in this book: And if any man shall take away from the words of the book of this prophecy, God shall take away his part out of the book of life, and out of the holy city, and from the things which are written in this book. He which testifies these things saith, Surely I come quickly. Amen. Even so, come, Lord Jesus." This caution was not meant to terrify us but rather served as a loving admonition to always give proper respect to the veracity of the Holy Bible because it is the word that sustains and strengthens us on the path to salvation.

God offered this same stern but loving advice to His chosen people who, like us, were so inclined to stray. In Deuteronomy 4:2 He instructed the Hebrews, "Ye shall not add unto the word which I command you, neither shall ye diminish ought from it, that ye may keep the commandments of the LORD your God which I command you." Then as now, the application of God's law in this way was not a punishment meted out to satisfy God's wrath but rather shined His light of grace on the road leading to heaven. God please bless us that we may ever remain in the word.

Spiritual Smorgasbord

Ding, dong, ding; did you hear it ring? Was that the church bell calling us to Sunday worship and Bible study?

Please allow me to indulge my imagination for a few moments. When I hear that clarion call, it reminds me of something else that evokes wonderful childhood memories. It sounds like the dinner bell announcing Mom's nightly feast at the family table.

Now, to be quite honest, I've glamorized things a bit. We didn't actually have a dinner bell. Mom just yelled "Supper's ready!" out the back door. Also, we weren't always able to gather together around the family dinner table because of our parents' work schedules. In fact, sometimes when Mom and Dad weren't around, we fended for ourselves by whipping up some fried baloney sandwiches in a cast iron skillet. Ah, those were the days!

There is more to my fanciful trip down memory lane than fond recollections. Maybe it would be good for all of us to hear a figurative dinner bell when we head to church. If you're like me, you might be spiritually famished by the time Sunday morning rolls around. That's because sometimes I shortchange myself by treating private Bible study and family devotions like a trip through the drive-thru lane at a fast food joint. What really puts the tiger in my tank is the veritable feast, the full-course meal that is always served up by my pastor.

When I go to church hungry and thirsty, I'm never served syrupy soda, greasy burgers, tacos, fries, onion rings or America's deadliest missile: the hot dog. At my church's banquet table, I get nothing but the best: a spiritual smorgasbord! There my spiritual diet isn't limited by political correctness, misguided tact and diplomacy or timidity. God's chef, my pastor, serves up nothing but the truth, the whole truth of God's law and gospel.

Sometimes I've mistakenly chaffed under the law thinking that my pastor was singling me out from the pulpit. We've probably all felt such paranoia at one time or another. Still we could appreciate the law because we knew we needed to be convicted of our sins and reminded of our need for the Savior. That's when we've best enjoyed a delicious dessert to top things off: the sweet, precious gospel. In word and sacrament, we're always reminded and reassured of God's forgiveness and the promise of salvation. We're always pointed to the one and only solution: Jesus Christ and His cross and empty tomb.

When we're privileged to worship at a church where the truth of God's word is faithfully preached and taught, we receive an endless supply of the most delectable spiritual sustenance. Here's how God puts it in Psalm 19:10, "More to be desired are they (God's teachings) than gold, yea, than much fine gold:

sweeter also than honey and the honeycomb." This bounty is hard to find today. The full truth of God's word is rare indeed in today's world, including in many churches.

If we're blessed to belong to a faithful, right-teaching Christian church, we should be eternally grateful and take care to avoid becoming lax. We should remember the words of thankfulness of the Psalmist in 119:14-17. "I have rejoiced in the way of thy testimonies, as much as in all riches. I will meditate in thy precepts, and have respect unto thy ways. I will delight myself in thy statutes: I will not forget thy word. Deal bountifully with thy servant, that I may live, and keep thy word."

It's quite a shame that many such banquet tables aren't full every Sunday. The Lord has so much to offer and yet countless thousands pass by starving for God's promises and thirsting for the living water. If we keep that dinner bell in mind perhaps each of us can ring it throughout the week calling starving souls to share in our bounty, the bounty of the Lord. Put aside that fast food brothers and sisters and come enjoy a feast. It's free for the taking!

Fact or Fable?

Today we are told by the secular world that the Holy Bible is a book of fables that fly in the face of "settled science." They claim that the teachings of the Bible are completely contradictory to certain "indisputable facts" of science. Those of us who disagree on any of these points are labeled by progressives as crazies who must be shunned, ridiculed and silenced.

It's certainly true that some of the teachings of Holy Scripture are at direct odds with today's conventional wisdom. But does this really mean that true science and the Christian faith are incompatible? To the contrary, as an objective search for the truth through unbiased experimentation and empirical evidence, science provides amazing reinforcement for the veracity of God's word.

If we want to avoid being forced to choose between "science" and the Christian faith, we need to recognize that it's not Christians but rather the so-called experts who are relying upon fables. Here's what God has revealed about today's secular humanists in 2 Timothy 4:3-4, "For the time will come when they will not endure sound doctrine; but after their own lusts shall they heap to themselves teachers, having itching ears; And they shall turn away their ears from the truth, and shall be turned unto fables."

God proclaims in 2 Peter 1:16 that Christian believers have observable, hard evidence on our side, "For we have not followed cunningly devised fables, when we made known unto you the power and coming of our Lord Jesus Christ, but were eyewitnesses of his majesty." Consequently, we need to get into God's word to understand where the fables of "science" are in conflict with the truth of the Bible.

In demonstrating the compatibility between Christianity and true science, we can eliminate a lot of the confusion by weeding out three lies that have been spread by secular humanists and widely accepted in our modern society. These viewpoints are diametrically opposed to God's word and cannot be reconciled. We must choose to believe one or the other.

Fable 1: There is no God. The universe came into being out of nothing via an inexplicable big bang resulting in infinitesimally sophisticated and intricate systems and then slowly, over millions of years, life magically appeared and evolved by sheer chance into incredibly complex beings. Yes, blobs of goo eventually produced ape-like creatures which somehow turned into men with no guiding hand whatsoever.

God says (Genesis 1:27), "So God created man in his own image, in the image of God created he him; male and female created he them." **God adds** (Isaiah 45:12), "I have made the earth, and created man upon it: I, even my hands, have stretched out the heavens, and all their host have I commanded."

Just look around and consider what you observe. Does nothing produce something? Do cats become dogs or apes turn into men? Or is there a clear and firm imprint of an amazingly intelligent designer, our Creator God, that is evident everywhere in the world around us and within our own bodies?

Fable 2: Since there is no Creator God and mankind evolved from the animals by chance, it's okay to kill unborn babies through abortion. It's not a human being with an immortal soul. It's just a blob of fetal matter.

God says (Psalm 51:5), "Behold, I was shapen in iniquity; and in sin did my mother conceive me." **God adds** (Psalm 139:16), "Thine eyes did see my substance, yet being imperfect; and in thy book all my members were written, which in continuance were fashioned, when as yet there was none of them."

Is there really any dispute here? Back in 1973 when Roe v. Wade legalized abortion in the United States, perhaps one could have argued out of ignorance that a fetus (baby) was not a person. Today, science and genetics have advanced and caught up with the Bible and clearly support the truth that a baby in the womb is a person. A tiny speck of DNA contains all of the information unique to that person. Now that the tide of science has turned, have the pro-abortion folks conceded? No, they continue to willingly turn to fables in spite of scientific fact.

Fable 3: If you accept Fables 1 and 2, then you must have a cause to follow; an object of your secular humanist faith. You must save the planet from mankind! The air we exhale (5% CO_2) is not a naturally occurring element essential to life but is a pollutant created by mankind and the capitalist system. It must be eradicated at all costs, even if it impoverishes billions and destroys life as we know it.

Or else, the world will come to an end at the hand of evil mankind.

God says (Genesis 8:22), "While the earth remains, seedtime and harvest, and cold and heat, and summer and winter, and day and night shall not cease." In regard to the apocalypse, **God says** in 2 Peter 3:12 that the world will end by His power alone, "Looking for and hasting unto the coming of the day of God, wherein the heavens being on fire shall be dissolved, and the elements shall melt with fervent heat."

This is another easy one, isn't it? You don't need a computer model to discern the truth. Anyone can see that, over time, climate trends shift back and forth but we are definitely not experiencing a straight-line, global warming or cooling trend. And man-made CO_2 has nary a thing to do with changes in the climate. The impact of CO_2 in the atmosphere on temperatures is miniscule when compared to other factors like the sun and ocean temperatures and currents. As for how the earth will end, who are you going to trust?

Just three little lies. That's all it takes to undermine faith. And there is no middle ground. Either one is true or vice versa. The answer to this dilemma is simple. Will we trust the word of man; the ever-changing winds of doctrine (Ephesians 4:14), or will we stand on the truth of God's word, the Holy Bible? Only the latter is perfectly trustworthy and completely reliable (John 17:17).

Here's my final tip to you my friends. Don't rely on conventional wisdom. We have great scientific resources at our disposal that can edify us and reinforce our Christian faith. Turn to Creation Research and Answers in Genesis, among others, regularly. And let's put our money where our mouths are and support these ministries with our generous gifts.

Flame On!

People are obsessed with temporal power. Many strive for earthly power through political, economic and military means and some gain great wealth and influence thereby. Most of the rest of us must settle for a more cerebral substitute: our imaginations.

If you need convincing, just look at the legion of comic book heroes that we live through vicariously. There's something for everyone: *Super Man, Batman, Iron Man, Spider Man, the Incredible Hulk, Thor, Captain America, The Flash, Wonder Woman, Super Girl, Bat Girl and Robin the Boy Wonder*. If you're a Baby Boomer like me, you can vividly remember these wonderful characters from childhood. Today they are more popular than ever being resurrected and immortalized for the current generation through television and blockbuster movies.

Wouldn't it be great to possess super powers like the *Fantastic Four*? What if we could stretch and reshape our bodies like *Mr. Fantastic*, the brainy scientist, *Reed Richards*? Who wouldn't want to be invisible from time-to-time like *Sue Storm* and put up an impenetrable force field against the many dangers our perilous world presents? How about the brute strength and near indestructability of *The Thing, Ben Grimm*? Maybe the topper would be Sue's younger, impetuous brother, *Johnny Storm*. Yeah, just like the *Human Torch*, we could shout, "Flame on!" and soar through the air like a flaming comet while unleashing fiery fusillades with the flick of a fingertip. Such is the power of imagination from 1960's Marvel creators Stan Lee and Jack Kirby.

I find this to be deliciously ironic because, as Christians, we have real power that dwarfs anything the richest, most influential people in this world possess. It even far exceeds the imaginary powers of *Johnny Storm*. Like the *Human Torch*, we have immense power at our very fingertips. It's right there in that Bible sitting next to you.

I can almost hear you scoffing, *oh come on, surely you can't be serious*. Wrong, I most certainly am and don't call me Shirley; nyuk, nyuk. The word of God will still be around long after everything in this world, including Marvel and DC comics, have completely faded away. Christ has promised this in Matthew 24:35, "Heaven and earth shall pass away, but my words shall not pass away." God's word has no Kryptonite.

The power at our disposal, gospel power, is likened unto dynamite. Romans 1:16 cites power using the Greek word dunamis which refers to dynamic, explosive power. "For I am not ashamed of the gospel of Christ: for it is the (irresistible, explosive, dynamite) power of God unto salvation to everyone that believeth; to the Jew first, and also to the Greek (Gentile)."

Nothing in this world, not even the deadliest Samurai sword or sharpest surgeon's scalpel can perform what a single word of God can accomplish. "For the word of God is quick, and powerful, and sharper than any two-edged sword, piercing even to the dividing asunder of soul and spirit, and of the joints and marrow, and is a discerner of the thoughts and intents of the heart," (Hebrews 4:12). Even the most formidable temporal power this world has to offer only pales in comparison to spiritual power, the everlasting power of God in His holy word.

God's word can seem so unassuming that its true power can be hard to discern. That's why our imaginations like to turn to more flamboyant and theatrical displays of power like those of the *Human Torch*. This is understandable but if you're into dazzling, staggering, stunning and astounding, you don't have to resort to graphic novels. Just turn to Psalm 29 if you want something truly mind-boggling. I can't recount it all here but let's just take a peek at verse 7 and the way it describes the power of God's word. "The voice of the LORD divideth the flames of fire." Wow, it's more powerful than a speeding bullet and puts even *Johnny Storm* to shame. Stay in the word, flame on!

Forget-Me-Not

Have you ever wondered where these little pale blue, pink or white flowers got their name? The official name is boraginaceae, its family classification, and myosotis is the genus. The latter is a Greek word meaning mouse ear which is descriptive of the shape of the leaves. There are many varieties as you gardeners probably already know. But where did it get its intriguing nickname, forget-me-not? There are various sources according to German folklore.

One legend has it that when God (actually Adam) was naming the plants, this small one cried out "Forget me not," and God purportedly replied, "That shall be your name." Another fable involving the Almighty had God handing out colors and nearly overlooking this little flower. When the flower cried out "Forget me not," God had just enough blue remaining to provide for the pale azure petals. As an aside, isn't it odd how inept and forgetful God is portrayed in these myths? One of the more imaginative traditions claims that a medieval knight was walking along a riverside with his lady and stopped to pick some of these flowers for her and fell into the water. He sank because of the weight of his armor but, before he drowned, he tossed the bouquet to her saying, "Forget me not."

I'm not into myths when it comes to matters of faith but stumbled onto this topic when I came across one of these dainty flowers pressed between the pages of a Bible. It was carefully preserved between the pages containing one of my favorite passages, John 8:31-32, "Then said Jesus to those Jews which believed on him, If ye continue in my word, then are ye my disciples indeed; And ye shall know the truth, and the truth shall make you free." It helped me to remember something very important.

The image of this little flower and the command to stay in the word popped into my mind during a special Lenten service. Why was it that I worshipped every Sunday and also in the middle of the week during Lent and Advent? And why did I go to Bible class continually and share devotions at home? Why did I listen to the same stuff over and over and over again? The answer came to me in the image of the tiny flower: I'm forgetful. I needed to refresh my memory again and again, especially with something as critically important as the gospel.

As I pondered, I realized there was more to this than just friendly reminders. I needed constant reassurance, the kind that could only come from God's word and promises. That was because my old, sinful nature never took a day off and that nasty, lying lion: Satan, remained constantly on the prowl seeking to make shipwreck of my faith by sowing the seeds of false doctrine. I knew that if I neglected so great a gift as God's word and sacraments, surely doubts and fears would crowd out my faith.

Consequently, I didn't mind hearing the same glorious message, the good news of the gospel, repeatedly. No matter how many times I heard a particular sermon or read a certain passage from the Bible, it always had the same wonderfully beneficial effect and often some heretofore undiscovered meaning. It strengthened me in mind and spirit and served to delight my immortal soul. It wasn't boring or repetitive but seemed every bit as delicious as a favorite meal. Who could ever get tired of pizza, wings, barbeque, a crisp, tangy salad, a banana split or thick, juicy steak?

Do you remember how the apostle put it in 2 Peter 1:10? He said, "Wherefore the rather, brethren, give diligence to make your calling and election sure: for if ye do these things, ye shall never fall." Amen brother, staying in the word is not a burdensome obligation but rather a great blessing and comfort! Thus, let us worship and study the word in all gladness keeping in mind God's great promise regarding our salvation in Philippians 1:6, "Being confident of this very thing, that he (God … John 6:29) which hath begun a good work in you will perform it until the day of Jesus Christ."

A Heavenly Diet

Dieting, health and fitness have become big business in our country. It's hard to watch TV without seeing an ad for Weight Watchers, Jenny Craig, Nutrisystem or Gold's Gym. Our national obsession with weight loss is deliciously ironic when you consider that in the 1970s academia issued dire warnings that we faced worldwide famine due to overpopulation.

Like today's preoccupation with climate change, the secular world fabricated the supposed population crisis to divert attention away from God's truths. Anyone who knew the Bible and trusted God's word realized that the world wouldn't come to an end through the deeds of mankind, whether fertility, pollution, industrialization or nuclear holocaust. God was surely laughing in derision at the so-called experts and their predictions of worldwide starvation when the exact opposite occurred. The same will happen with the people who have sounded the global warming alarm.

For the time being though, we've been left to ponder our expanding waistlines. You'd think the health and fitness trade would have declined as people achieved their goals of slimming down but business has continued to thrive on the basis of repeat customers because we, as dieters, are focused on the wrong solution.

There are two paths to follow and most of us have gone down the wrong road: the temporal expressway that caters only to our physical condition. It can lead to slim, trim, toned and tanned bodies for a while but winds up at a dead end. Eventually, our old natures take over and give into the temptations that abound. While there are some who are able to maintain their hard-fought gains through sheer will, even they must eventually face facts. Our bodies are destined for old age and death. Can we gain true satisfaction from having six-pack abs if there's a hollow void inside?

Let's consider the other route. Health and fitness can be a good pursuit if done the right way; God's way. To do so we need to focus on both our bodies and spirits. A healthy spiritual diet is actually much simpler to maintain since it consists solely of God's word in the Holy Bible. Listen to God's recipe for soul food in Psalm 34:8, "Taste and see that the Lord is good; blessed is the one who takes refuge in him," and also Psalm 119:103, "How sweet are your words to my taste, sweeter than honey to my mouth."

Then there's Hebrews 6:4-5, "Who have once been enlightened, who have tasted the heavenly gift, who have shared in the Holy Spirit, who have tasted the goodness of the word of God." And here's some dessert to top things off in 1 Peter 2:1-3, "Therefore, rid yourselves of all malice and all deceit, hypocrisy, envy, and slander of every kind. Like newborn babies, crave pure spiritual milk, so that by it you may grow up in your salvation, now that you have tasted that the Lord is good."

God's fitness program is equally simple. We should read, mark and inwardly digest Scripture on a daily basis and continue in the word faithfully (John 8:31). God, our heavenly trainer, says this about fitness in 2 Timothy 3:16, "All scripture is given by inspiration of God, and is profitable for doctrine, for reproof, for correction, for instruction in righteousness." He adds in 1 Corinthians 6:19-20, "What? Know ye not that your body is the temple of the Holy Ghost which is in you, which ye have of

God, and ye are not your own? For ye are bought with a price: therefore glorify God in your body, and in your spirit, which **a**re God's."

So, let's not worry about looking like Greek gods and instead shoot for the total package by building our bodies and spirits into living temples for the Holy Spirit.

Indoctrination

The word indoctrination usually carries a very negative connotation. It refers to the process of teaching someone to unconditionally accept a set of beliefs without question. In our country, this concept strikes us as un-American. We pride ourselves on free speech and the liberty to follow our own convictions as a matter of conscience in accordance with our constitutional rights. In this sense, indoctrination is anathema to us.

There have been many examples of indoctrination that we abhor. Reeducation camps in China and North Vietnam were infamous for brainwashing prisoners into accepting communist dogma through extreme measures including forced labor and even torture. This applied to dissident citizens as well as prisoners of war. People like Senator John McCain who suffered within the brutal confines of the Hanoi Hilton could attest to the latter. Shortly after his release, Otto Warmbier died as a result of the brutal treatment he received in North Korea.

Such gross violations of human rights are typically hidden from the public as much as possible but not always. Today we have all too often witnessed the worst form of indoctrination openly. Muslim fanatics have proudly displayed their nefarious deeds for all to see. It has hearkened back to the persecution of early Christians under Roman rule. Radical Muslims have employed the harshest, vilest means to force their warped ideology on others.

Christians, or infidels as they call us, must renounce our faith and accept the false god, Allah, and his prophet, Mohammed, or suffer death. This can come in the form of being beheaded, burned or drowned in a cage or tossed off a tall building. If confronted with this evil we have no choice but to be martyred as witnesses for Christ. God instructs us clearly in Matthew 10:28, "And fear not them which kill the body, but are not able to kill the soul: but rather fear him which is able to destroy both soul and body in hell." Denying Jesus can lead to damnation but suffering these horrible deaths for Christ's sake results in eternal life in heaven as merited by Jesus' atoning sacrifice.

After this disturbing opening, you may find this shocking but indoctrination can also be very positive, in the proper sense. Have you been confirmed as a teenager or later through adult instruction? If so, you've been indoctrinated. You went through a very structured process to adopt Christian teachings and, in a manner of speaking, were expected to do so without question.

Let me clarify because I'm sure you were given a chance by the pastor to ask lots of questions. Still, even though you were encouraged to ask about the word of God, you were expected to accept the authority and veracity of the Holy Bible without question. In this, you were like the Christians in Berea who heard Paul preach but then went back to make sure the words he spoke were consistent with Scripture (Acts 17:11).

When you think about your confirmation, you'll see how we can call this form of indoctrination good. When it came to His teachings, God instructed us to be of one mind (Ephesians 4:5). God implored us to undergo instruction in His word (Proverbs 22:6, 2 Timothy 3:16). Christ indoctrinated His disciples for three and a half years and encouraged them to stay in the word (John 8:31-32). He required our indoctrination as a necessary prerequisite for Holy Communion (1 Corinthians 11:29).

Most importantly, God wants us to be indoctrinated in His teachings for our salvation. He says in John 20:31, "But these are written, that ye might believe that Jesus is the Christ, the Son of God; and that believing ye might have life through his name." May we never forget the teachings of our confirmations and be fed continually through God's word.

Mission Impossible

Spreading the truth of God's creation account in Genesis seems like an episode of the old TV show *Mission Impossible*. The deck is stacked against us in a seemingly impossible fashion with the secular world, academia and media declaring evolution to be "settled science." Stating otherwise or even raising a simple question can bring heaps of scorn raining down on us as so-called flat earthers.

Our culture is so steeped in the ubiquitous Darwinian faith that even many Christians accept evolution as a fact even though there is no rational way to reconcile evolution with the truth of Scripture. If death preceded sin, then the Bible is a pack of lies and there is no need for a Savior. Evolutionists know this very well and gleefully undermine the very foundation of the faith, the authority of Scripture, while hordes of hapless Christians merrily indulge in the deadly opiate known as theistic evolution.

Here are just a few examples of what God has clearly revealed in His word about the truth of the Genesis creation account:

Nehemiah 9:6, "Thou, even thou, art Lord alone; thou hast made heaven, the heaven of heavens, with all their host, the earth, and all things that are therein, the seas, and all that is therein, and thou preserves them all; and the host of heaven worship thee."

Jeremiah 10:12, "He hath made the earth by his power, he hath established the world by his wisdom, and hath stretched out the heavens by his discretion."

Colossians 1:16, "For by him (Jesus) were all things created, that are in heaven, and that are in earth, visible and invisible, whether they be thrones, or dominions, or principalities, or powers: all things were created by him, and for him."

Revelation 14:7, "Saying with a loud voice, Fear God, and give glory to him; for the hour of his judgment is come: and worship him that made heaven, and earth, and the sea, and the fountains of waters."

How can we spread the truth in such a corrupt, hostile world? It seems impossible but with God all things are possible. We have a great example in God's faithful servant, John Mackay of Creation Research. He operates out of his home base in Australia but travels the world with his message of truth and hope.

John and all of his co-workers in Christ are out there every day doing the impossible by the power of the Holy Spirit working through the word. He provides a marvelous witness that brings science and history to bear in a way that confirms the Genesis account and draws scoffers, doubters and skeptics to hear and consider God's word of truth. One of John's fellow Aussies, Ken Ham of Answers in Genesis, is serving similarly right here in the United States.

You can learn from John and Ken by subscribing to their free newsletters. Simply visit their websites at Creation Research and AIG to sign up. You can sponsor one of John's seminars at your church. He can even arrange to take your group on a fossil dig. If you travel to Williamstown, KY just south of Cincinnati, you can walk the decks of a life-sized version of Noah's Ark at AIG's Ark Encounter and tour the nearby Creation Museum.

Donating to Creation Research and AIG offers a marvelous opportunity to support some of God's most gifted servants in spreading the truth of creation and God's saving gospel to people all around the globe. Now, if you accept this mission, expect miraculous results by the power of the Holy Spirit working through the word.

Super Power!

People strive for power and the more the better. Sometimes the powerless are fixated to the point of idolizing charismatic figures that misuse and abuse their power. How else can we explain our preoccupation with villains of every stripe: terrorists like Osama bin Laden, mobsters like John Gotti and evil despots like Hitler, Mussolini and Stalin? How about that crazy twenty-six-year-old gal that agreed to marry the late Charles Manson, the then eighty-year-old, incarcerated mass murderer? Perhaps the most dangerous and inexplicable flirtation with evil comes from the folks that delve into the occult or, worse yet, commit themselves to the service of Satan himself.

Power has a tantalizing lure that can seduce us if we're not careful. Don't we revel in the notion that today the United States is considered the only super power in the world? What is it that makes us a super power: wealth and military might? It's certainly no longer the moral high ground that we once occupied by the grace of God in Christ. When the real world fails to satisfy our thirst for power, don't we turn to our imaginations? We're fixated with fictional heroes endowed with super powers: Superman, Batman, the Incredible Hulk, Thor, the Green Hornet, the Fantastic Four, Aqua Man, Iron Man and my personal favorite the Flash.

The most ironic thing about this is that many of us pass at the chance to experience true power, supernatural power beyond anything this world can offer, real or imaginary: the power of Almighty God. He puts His omnipotent power at our disposal, right at our very fingertips. And yet, so many of us turn away to pursue the pitiful substitutes the world waves in front of us. Immense power, beyond anything we can imagine is right there for the taking in God's word, the Holy Bible. Think about it. God's omnipotent power is contained in the most convenient, easy-to-open package ever designed: Holy Scripture. Unfortunately, there it sits so often, unused and collecting dust. What a shame.

Even we Christians neglect this amazing opportunity all too often. Is it because we forget that God's word is the very source and essence of power?

Well, here are a few reminders to help us. Romans 1:16 states it so clearly, "For I am not ashamed of the gospel of Christ: for it is the power of God unto salvation to everyone that believeth; to the Jew first, and also to the Greek." God brought the universe and everything in it, including us, into existence simply by speaking the word. We're brought to faith or born again from above by the power of God's word (1 Peter 1:23). No other power on earth can perform this miracle.

Is there a greater miracle than resurrection from death? How did Jesus raise Lazarus from his tomb? As recorded in John 11:43, He merely spoke the words, "Lazarus come forth." But Jesus was present for that miracle, wasn't He? How can we rely on the word alone? Here's the proof positive from Christ himself in John 4:46-54. Let's recall the story of the wealthy, influential nobleman whose son was at the point of death. All of his wealth and power was useless in trying to save his son. So, he turned to the only sure hope and traveled from Capernaum to Cana to plead with Jesus. He asked Jesus to come back to Capernaum to perform the miracle and save his son but Jesus refused and tested his faith. The man believed by God-given faith when Jesus spoke the word. And what was the result? His son was restored by the word alone, spoken by Jesus from so far away at that very same hour.

Trust in the Lord. Take advantage of the incredible, miraculous, omnipotent power that He puts freely at our disposal. Let us turn to His word daily and continually in faith and trust.

The Book

What kind of answer would you get if you asked the average person on the street, "Have you read the book?" I'm guessing most would say, "What book?" A few might tell you about a novel they read recently, maybe something by James Patterson, Stephen King or perhaps J. K. Rowling. I'd like to think one or two might even mention one of my books. The results would be quite a bit different if you polled the members of a faithful Christian congregation. I'd be willing to wager that every last person would know you meant the Holy Bible.

Let's envision a different question: "What is the greatest book ever written?" This would open a whole new world of possibilities. Folks here in Missouri might name something by our favorite son, Mark Twain. Certainly, some would give the nod to William Shakespeare. Horror aficionados might go with Edgar Allen Poe's works. Undoubtedly, some of the classics would come up: Dante's *Inferno*, Homer's *Odyssey*, Tolstoy's *War and Peace*, *The Catcher in the Rye* by J. D. Salinger, Chaucer's *Canterbury Tales*, *Great Expectations* by Charles Dickens, Steinbeck's *The Grapes of Wrath,* George Orwell's *1984*, Herman Melville's *Moby Dick* or any number of Dostoyevsky's or Hemingway's novels.

Can any of these books or any others I've missed compare to the Bible? Think about it; it's not even close. In Isaiah 40:8, God's prophet made the case succinctly in a beautiful, poetic fashion, "The grass withers, the flower fades: but the word of our God shall stand for ever." It's true. No other book has anything near the staying power of the Holy Bible. It's at least 3,500 years old going back to the time of Moses and perhaps somewhere between 4,200 and 3,800 years old if Job was actually the first book written.

In either case, no other book chronicles the history of the earth and universe from the first day of creation some 6,000 years ago. That's because no other book was authored by the only eye witness to that stunning event: Almighty God. Think of the millions upon millions of books that mere men have written including the greatest classics of all time. Any books near the age of the Bible are long since out of circulation and most are out of existence except for rare ones collecting dust in museums. Yet, the Bible is still the most widely printed and read book in the entire world despite its age. It remains contemporary and incredibly relevant despite the passage of time. The Bible has been translated into every imaginable language on earth.

One other amazing characteristic sets the Bible apart and that is its veracity. Throughout history, scoffers and skeptics of every stripe have tried to undermine the authority of God's word but, in every case, time has shown the Scriptures to be God's verbally inspired and inerrant word, perfect and holy. No other religious book from the Koran to the Book of Mormon can make such a claim. That's why the Bible serves as the bedrock of our faith. It's God's plan of salvation; given to mankind for all time and miraculously preserved by God. Heaven and earth shall pass away but God's word in the Holy Bible will remain steadfast unto eternity.

They say that when it comes to riches, we can't take it with us. That is certainly true for everything in this temporal world. But, thankfully, we can and will take the greatest treasure with us from this life to the next. God's word shall stand forever.

Uncommon Sense

In today's high-tech world, we have to forfeit all ties to modern science in order to remain faithful, Bible-believing Christians, right? We must bury our heads in the sand and deny the obvious, correct? We have no choice but to eschew a preponderance of scientific facts and data in favor of myths and fables, true? People would like us to believe this but it is categorically false; a nefarious strategy aimed at silencing believers and cutting us off from public discourse.

Our detractors claim that we are wild-eyed fanatics who put faith before common sense. God, in His word, says otherwise. He says in Romans 1:20 that the truths of the Bible, including the Genesis accounts of creation and the flood, are apparent to anyone by looking at the world around us. It doesn't take anything but common sense to see it. "For the invisible things of him from the creation of the world are clearly seen, being understood by the things that are made, even his eternal power and Godhead; so that they are without excuse."

The Lord says in 2 Peter 3:5-6 that it's not Christians but rather the godless secular crowd worshipping at the altar of "settled science" that have their heads buried in the sand. "For this they willingly are ignorant of, that by the word of God the heavens were of old, and the earth standing out of the water and in the water: Whereby the world that then was, being overflowed with water, perished."

The Bible has always been way out in front of science. Here are just a few examples. Roe v. Wade was codified into law on the basis of a lie built on bad science. In 1973, one could attempt to argue on the basis of our then limited medical knowledge that a fetus was not a baby or a real person. In the decades following, there have been great advances in our understanding of DNA and diagnostic technology to see for ourselves, in the womb from conception, that the so-called blob of tissue is not an evolving guppy but a person with distinct characteristics and their full human genetic make-up.

Stubbornly defiant, the secular ideologues haven't changed their mind on abortion even though science is no longer on their side. They deny God and the truth at every turn. The same is true for the false notion that homosexuality is a genetic trait rather than type of behavior. Modern science has caught up with the Bible on this matter but to no avail. There is no gay human genome but the lie persists by willful ignorance.

There is nothing new under the sun. The Bible doubters have been playing this tune since early times. Scientific Bible bashers offered scathing criticisms of the numerous Old Testament accounts of the great and powerful Hittite Empire up until the late 1800s when archeological discoveries confirmed everything the Bible said about the heretofore unknown Hittites.

Bible-believing Christians are ridiculed as flat-earth proponents when, in fact, the Bible taught that the earth is spherical (Isaiah 40:22) long before modern science caught on. Not to be dissuaded, the doubters disingenuously claim that Isaiah was referring to a flat, pancake circle rather than a sphere.

How about NASA, those paragons of modern science? If they would have read and trusted in God's word, they wouldn't have wasted so much time and energy on putting those long legs on the lunar landing module. Do you remember how Neil Armstrong had to come down all those steps before taking his giant leap for mankind onto the moon's surface? The stilt-like legs were meant to compensate for all of the cosmic dust that should have accumulated if the universe was billions rather than thousands of years old. As it turned out, this was just another confirmation of a relatively young earth.

There are endless examples of where modern science and Scripture are amazingly consistent but scoffers still sarcastically question the veracity of God's word. They say that accounts of Jonah and the great fish and Joshua's long day are impossible. However, as a Bible believing Christian, I know that it's certainly possible that God slowed the earth's rotation to extend the length of that day in order to allow Joshua and the army of Israel to defeat Adoni-zedec and his coalition of nations.

The Bible is so precise and lays down so many markers that astronomers can even pinpoint that it was a Tuesday, July 22nd when this miracle occurred. Joshua's long day helps to explain how, despite all of our scientific know-how, we still can't get our calendar quite right due to the unaccounted day. Still skeptics say not so fast. They love to point out that astronomers have been able to calculate that Joshua's long day was forty minutes short and, thus according to them, God's word is not completely accurate.

My advice is that the skeptics read their Bibles further before mocking God. Then they might recall how God answered King Hezekiah's prayer for healing and fifteen more years of life and confirmed it by making the shadow go back on the sun dial of Ahaz by ten degrees. Amazingly, ten degrees is equal to forty minutes thus accounting for the full lost day of time.

Skeptics would rather change the subject than concede the point on Joshua's long day. Forget about Joshua and tell me how Jonah could fit through the throat of a whale. The skeptics have a point because most species of whales have an esophagus that is too small to accommodate a whole man. However, there is at least one type known as the mysticete whale that could get the job done. More specifically, the megaptera medosa or humpbacked whale family has no teeth and swallows its food whole. The largest variety known as the balaenoptera musculus or more commonly the sulfur bottom whale has been measured at ninety-five feet and six inches.

The largest recorded specimen was caught off the west coast of North America by the crew of the Norwegian whaler N. T. Nielson Alonso some years before it was sunk by a German U-boat in 1943. The air storage chamber in the whale's massive head measured fourteen feet long by seven feet across. These whales have been known to take objects too big to swallow and thrust them up into the air chamber. There are recorded cases of such whales swimming toward land into shallow water and ejecting their payload.

This does not necessarily prove the account of Jonah to be true but it shows it to be possible. Some theologians believe the term whale has been misapplied and that the correct English translation would be great fish. This would open up further possibilities and even the chance that God might have created a unique form of great fish specifically for His purpose in disciplining Jonah in such a dramatic way.

The most important thing to remember is that we don't have to forego science in order to remain Bible-believing Christians. If we approach things with an open mind, are patient and dig deep, we'll always find God's word in the Bible to be completely reliable. It will always stand the test of time. More importantly, it has real power, God-given power to create saving faith. At the end of the day, we don't trust the Bible because it stands up under scientific and historic scrutiny. Rather we trust it because it's God's inspired word of truth and His means of grace.

The Bambino, Beatles & Methuselah

Continuity is a thing of the past. Philosophically, that's an odd thing to say because continuity involves connecting the past to the present. But it's a valid point in the sense that we've lost touch with history, especially in the current generation where, with the aid of mercurial technological advances, things change so rapidly.

I love listening to the Beatles Station on Sirius XM and tried to bring my grandkids into my sphere of influence while riding in the car together. Much to my chagrin, they were largely oblivious to the greatest rock band in history. I tried to remedy the situation by sharing some of my Fab Four experiences. One day I exclaimed how *Please, Please Me* was the first Beatles 45 rpm I purchased in 1963. My personal recollections seemed to help them connect. Since then they've asked questions like, "Which Beatle died of cancer and which one was shot?"

This made me think about how a similar personal connection helped me when I was their age. My pediatrician was Hubert "Hub" Pruett. I couldn't relate to the old man until he told me about his past as a baseball player. Among other teams, he pitched for the St. Louis Browns and had a reputation for success against Babe Ruth. Of course, I had heard of the Bambino and seen old, black and white movies about him on TV. But hearing the firsthand account of someone who had hurled fastballs to the Yankee Sultan of Swat gave me a special perspective I could never have achieved on my own.

This got me to thinking of how different things must have been when people lived for incredible lengths of time. Although death reigned, the degenerative effects of sin hadn't advanced as far when our first parents, Adam and Eve, lived for 930 years (approximately 4,004-3,074 BC). Also, the environment, even though corrupted by sin, wasn't quite as harsh as after the worldwide flood of Noah's time. God's ancient mariner lived for 950 years. Here's the amazing part in the context of continuity. Even though Noah was born some 1,056 years after Adam and Eve or 126 years after they died, he was nearly their contemporary and had firsthand accounts of our first ancestors from his own "Hub Pruetts."

All of the other great patriarchs who preceded Noah had lives that overlapped with him and Adam and Eve except for Seth and Enoch. Here's the list along with the number of years they lived and number of years between Adam and Eve's creation and their birth: Seth (912/130), Enos (905/235), Cainan (910/325), Mahalaeel (895/395), Jared (962/460), Enoch (365/622), Methuselah (969/687), Lamech (777/874) and Noah (950/1056). This means that, for example, Enos was a contemporary of Adam and Eve for 695 years and also overlapped with Noah for the first 84 years of Noah's life.

Imagine how the oldest man on record, Methuselah, could have given first-hand accounts to Noah about how Adam and Eve walked with God in the Garden! Imagine the rich history Noah was able to pass on to his sons Shem, Ham and Japheth who founded the various tribes and nations of the world after the Flood and Babel dispersion! Although our average lifespan today is only about 76 years (81 for women), we can reclaim the incredible continuity of the patriarchs simply by turning to God's inerrant word in the Holy Bible where the history of our world is perfectly preserved.

Comfort, Peace, Promise and Prayer

Are You a Name Dropper?

I think we're all guilty of being name droppers from time-to-time because sometimes who we know is more important than what we know. In my high school days, I failed to secure a summer job with a can company after several tries until my brother's friend gave me a reference. When I returned, the surly hiring manager was poised to gleefully dismiss me again when I mentioned the name of the guy I really didn't know from Adam. Like magic, I was granted a brief interview, passed muster and was hired at about $4.00/hour more than the other summer jobs that were open to me.

Over the years, I've learned that things like this happen all the time. Have you ever been pulled over for speeding and dropped the name of a friend or relative to wriggle out of a ticket? Many times, I received preferential treatment based on my place of employment. There were discounts, better tee times, dinner reservations, ball tickets and all kinds of perks I never could have swung using my own name alone. Being a name dropper was essential in business. It was politely called networking.

Using personal connections can appear unseemly but it's not always a bad thing. Name dropping can be a great ice breaker in social settings. Have you ever been in an awkward situation struggling to make small talk with strangers? If you stumble upon a common acquaintance the mood changes in a heartbeat and the conversation just flows naturally. In terms of witnessing, I've found that discovering a common thread can help people become more receptive to hearing the gospel.

On the flip side, name dropping can come back to haunt us if we abuse the practice. Putting on airs can cause resentment or jealousy over what people may perceive to be unwarranted privileges. It can be extremely embarrassing too if you step over the line in taking undeserved liberties. Can you imagine using someone's name that you don't really know or with whom you've had a falling out and being exposed as a charlatan?

I guess that's why we're encouraged to practice humility. Do you remember the instruction offered in Luke 14:8-9? "When thou art bidden of any man to a wedding, sit not down in the highest room; lest a more honorable man than thou be bidden of him. And he that bade thee and him come and say to thee, Give this man place; and thou begin with shame to take the lowest room."

Yeah, name dropping can be good or bad. But there's one area where I'm as proud as punch to be called a name dropper. Jesus said in John 14:13-14, "And whatsoever ye shall ask in my name, that will I do, that the Father may be glorified in the Son. If ye shall ask any thing in my name, I will do it." Think about that. Isn't it amazing? We were enemies of God, deserving only to be cast into outer darkness. But instead, while we were yet sinners, Christ died for us.

Jesus not only paid the price we owed by suffering our punishment but also freely gives us all things.

Jesus encourages and even instructs us to use His name. What an incredible honor and privilege! The Lord God of the entire universe has given His very name to us and has promised that we can ask anything in Jesus' name and it will be given unto us. Talk about carte blanche! When someone asks you, what's in your wallet, you can confidently say I have the gold card to end all gold cards. By the name of Jesus, we can ask for and receive everything we will ever need, spiritual or temporal, in this life and the next. Let's be ever grateful and use it wisely.

Consolation Prize

To console someone means to offer them comfort in the face of a disappointment, setback or loss. A consolation prize is meant to soothe someone who failed to win. No one likes to lose but there is some solace and even pride in garnering a silver or bronze medal if someone else has captured the Olympic gold. However, there are times when receiving a consolation prize just feels like someone is pouring salt into our wounded pride.

Has anyone ever really been consoled by receiving a second-place trophy after being trounced in the Super Bowl? I think we've lost sight of the blessings that come with the agony of defeat. Doesn't failure produce motivation and determination? Has anyone ever made it to the top without experiencing hardships along the way? Would victory ever taste so sweet if it came without sacrifice, hardship and suffering along the way? Would *Rocky's* eventual victories have been as enthralling if he hadn't first lost to Apollo Creed and Clubber Lang and suffered so grievously when his friend Apollo was killed by the Russian champ, Ivan Drago?

In our misguided society, we've gone so far off track that we've tried to eliminate the need for consolation altogether. Everyone gets a trophy for participating. No one is crowned champion for fear of leaving others dejected. Everyone is a winner baby!

Thank the Lord that, in His realm, consolation is still and will always be very much in vogue. Listen to what His inspired Apostle, Paul, had to say on the subject in 2 Corinthians 1:3-7. "Blessed be God, even the Father of our Lord Jesus Christ, the Father of mercies, and the God of all comfort; Who comforts us in all our tribulation, that we may be able to comfort them which are in any trouble, by the comfort wherewith we ourselves are comforted of God. For as the sufferings of Christ abound in us, so our consolation also abounds by Christ. And whether we be afflicted, it is for your consolation and salvation, which is effectual in the enduring of the same sufferings which we also suffer: or whether we be comforted, it is for your consolation and salvation. And our hope of you is steadfast, knowing, that as ye are partakers of the sufferings, so shall ye be also of the consolation."

Faith Food — Steve Stranghoener

It's a well-known fact from Scripture that we as Christians can expect to suffer all manner of tribulations in this life. Both our losses and victories in this world are tainted with sin and corruption. Our struggles are not occasional; they are daily. Our outlooks would be completely fraught with despair if there was nothing beyond this temporal existence in our lost and fallen world. Quite literally there would be no consolation.

Have you ever tried to console someone who lost a loved one who was clearly and unabashedly an unbeliever? There is no tougher task. It's an impossible situation where the comforter is left to offer hollow, meaningless, disingenuous platitudes. How much different is it when you know that the dearly departed was secure in the one true Christian faith? It's as far away as the east is from the west or as stark as a crimson stain on white wool. As pointed out in the aforementioned, inspired passage, it helps to have suffered similarly in offering comfort to the afflicted.

There is one consolation prize that truly is just as valuable as the first-place trophy. Look at us. We're so pitiful that we couldn't even enter the race on our own power. We were dead in our trespasses and sins. We were slaves to our worst enemies: sin, death and Satan. The gun sounded and we couldn't move an inch to get out of the starting blocks. But, miracle of miracles, a champion stepped in to run the course for us. Jesus Christ lived the perfect life we couldn't lead, suffered all manner of temptation without sinning and in humility was beaten, tortured and nailed to a cross. Then He claimed the ultimate, all-time, cosmic win and God sealed His victory in His triumphant resurrection.

Inexplicably, Jesus didn't keep the trophy for Himself. Instead, out of sheer grace, mercy and love, He added all of our names to that trophy. We are victors in Christ just as if we competed and won that contest. This is one consolation prize that truly offers comfort and so much more. Thus, we can humbly and joyfully declare, we are the champions; we're number one in Jesus Christ, our Lord and Savior. Won't it be glorious to be a part of the victory parade when our Champion returns?

Cool as a Cucumber

Where did this idiom come from and what does it mean? One of the earliest references I could find dated all the way back to 1610 in a play titled *Cupid's Revenge* wherein the writer referred to a certain woman as being cold as a cucumber.

Not a reference to body temperature, the subject term is used to describe a person's attitude as imperturbable in spite of dire circumstances. Put another way, it captures the temperament of one who is able to remain calm in the midst of a storm. Supposedly, cucumbers are able to maintain a temperature on the inside that is about twenty degrees cooler than the surrounding, ambient temperature. If you're a gardener, perhaps you can verify this claim.

In any case, I think there's an application that we Christians can take to heart. We live in a crazy world where our circumstances might easily lead us to nervously pace the floor. There are so many things that could cause us to lose sleep: natural disasters, economic woes, political upheaval, diseases, famine, terror and wars. On a personal level, we can experience pain, sorrow, illness, uncertainty, disappointment and danger around every corner. As if that were not enough to rattle us, Christians are often subject to peculiar pressures aimed at robbing us of our composure. Even in the United States with our Godly heritage and constitutional protections, it seems that Christians are regularly singled out for scorn and persecution.

Despite seemingly having targets on our backs, the Bible assures us that we can remain cool as cucumbers. That's because as Christians we can see past the trouble and view things in a better light. It says in 2 Corinthians 5:7, "For we walk by faith, not by sight." With our spiritual lenses firmly in place, we can calmly and confidently repeat the reassuring refrain from 2 Corinthians 4:8-9, "We are troubled on every side, yet not distressed; we are perplexed, but not in despair; Persecuted, but not forsaken; cast down, but not destroyed." Our peace and assurance are grounded on this sure foundation of Revelation 19:6, "The Lord God omnipotent reigns." Jesus proclaimed as recorded in John 16:33, "These things I have spoken unto you, that in me ye might have peace. In the world ye shall have tribulation: but be of good cheer; I have overcome the world."

We can remain calm in the midst of the storm because we have the long view of eternity at our disposal and the perfect example to follow. Satan roars like a lion on the prowl and does his best to steal away our peace and salvation but he can harm us none. Jesus Christ defeated sin, death and the devil for us. The final victory has already been won and we can look forward to eternity in a better, perfect world. It's a sure thing that has been confirmed in the resurrection of our Lord and Savior.

We can look to the example that Christ set while He walked this earth. Jesus slept peacefully in a boat when a storm overtook them. His apostles were terribly frightened and awoke Jesus but the Lord calmly rebuked the wind and the waves (Mark 4:38). Christ was as cool as a cucumber, so to speak, in all that He did including His death on the cross. No one has ever faced such harrowing circumstances: rejection, mocking, torture, crucifixion and the wrath of God toward all sinners for all eternity. Yet, He faced the Jewish mob, Pilate and the Bulls of Bashan with dignity and unshakeable confidence. God please bless us to serve as His faithful witnesses until He returns to fulfill all things.

It's Just Not Fair!

Have you ever uttered these words in frustration and anguish? Or have you at least entertained this dark, brooding thought in your mind? C'mon, let's be honest. I think most of us have done this more times than we can count. We're only human, right?

Do any of these thoughts sound as familiar to you as they do to me? *Officer, I was barely exceeding the speed limit. I can't drive thirty miles per hour without keeping my foot on the break. And anyway, didn't you see all those other cars that were zipping by me? Why is it that the referee only throws a flag when I retaliate? Didn't he see that other guy poke me in the eye and chomp down on my finger first? Why do I have to wait in line at the grocery store behind that guy using food stamps that I, Joe Taxpayer, paid for anyway? Why do I have to spend my hard-earned money while he gets a free ride? The teacher gave me a B-minus after all the hard work I put into this project. Suzy got an A and she didn't do anything but ride my coat tails.*

How about some of these gems? *Lumbergh wants me to work on Saturday again? This is the third weekend in a row. I'm getting audited; why me? My health insurance coverage got cancelled, I had to switch doctors and my premiums are going through the roof under Obama-care. Why am I getting stuck? I didn't vote for the guy. Our troops are putting their lives on the line for us every day and all our government can do is tie their hands behind their backs with ridiculous rules of engagement that protect the enemy while putting our guys and gals in harm's way. It's just not fair!*

The list could go on and on. Many of our complaints are self-centered and self-serving. Others are completely legitimate. Who's working for whom anyway? Do we report to those scalawags in D. C. or is it still supposed to be a government of, by and for the people?

When it comes to our self-interests and personal well-being, we have a finely-honed sense of justice. But what's good for the goose is not always good for the gander. Our moral outrage has its limits and our best intentions can be tainted by jealousy, greed, pride or worse. I'm no different. It's all part of our Old Adam; our sinful human natures that continue to cling to our corrupt flesh even after we've been born again from above. It's always been that way since the fall, hasn't it? Take Psalm 73:3 for example, "For I was envious at the foolish, when I saw the prosperity of the wicked."

Thankfully, when these feelings overtake us we can turn to God's word for wisdom, peace, humility and meekness. For example, once when I was sulking I turned to John 1:1-14 and read about the wondrous fulfillment of God's Old Testament gospel promises in the birth of Jesus Christ. Something about the tenth verse really hit me. "He was in the world, and the world was made by him, and the world knew him not." This blew me away as I pondered the truth. Jesus

Christ, as part of the Holy Trinity, created the entire universe and everything in it (Colossians 1:16). The Lord has total power and authority over heaven and earth (Matthew 28:18). Jesus is coming back to execute final judgment on the last day in earth's history (Revelation 14:7).

Multitudes of us who are deserving of hell and damnation will be spared from this judgment because of Christ's righteousness which He earned through His perfect life and death on the cross. He bore the hell of God's wrath we deserved and then imputed His perfect righteousness to us sinners. And yet, the world knew him not. Jesus was despised, denied, mocked, tortured and killed by us. The creatures murdered the Creator.

Why didn't He destroy us? Why didn't He make us pay? We utterly rejected Him but He didn't deny us or desert us. Instead of punishing us He died for us. Now I submit to you, it's just not fair! Eternal thanks and praise to God that it's just not fair. It is something far different. It is the essence, epitome, origin and source of love; God's great, undeserved, unconditional love for us. The next time I start feeling like I didn't get a fair shake, I hope the Lord will sanctify me and allow me to stop complaining and instead proclaim, "Praise the Lord for He is good and His mercy endures forever!

Quantity and Quality

Usually these two terms are expressed in contrast as if there is a necessary trade-off between quantity and quality. For example, it is presumed that if you go to an all-you-can-eat buffet, the quality of the food will be inferior to a fine restaurant. I think we'd all like to have our cake and eat it too but is it reasonable to expect a choice filet like we might get at Ruth's Chris Steakhouse when we're putting on the feedbag at Old Country Buffet? Simple economics would say no. But then again, God's economy runs quite differently than ours.

Let's turn to Ecclesiastes for some Godly wisdom. Some modern scholars claim otherwise but we know the author is wise King Solomon based upon the text. The theme of this book is vanity. No, it's not addressing our contemporary understanding of vanity, that is, someone who is consumed with superficial looks. Instead it's talking about the utter foolishness and uselessness of dwelling on temporal or earthly things which are referred to over and over as things under the sun.

In the fifth chapter it scoffs at the futility of amassing earthly fortunes for vain pleasure rather than practical usefulness. Here is how Solomon puts it in verses 11-12, "He that loves silver shall not be satisfied with silver; nor he that loves abundance with increase: this is also vanity. When goods increase, they are increased that eat them: and what good is there to the owners thereof, saving the beholding of them with their eyes?"

In verses 16-17, we hear the plight of the miserly that seek pleasure in amassing wealth for wealth's sake but live joyless, pitiful lives in spite of their largesse. I think verse 15 sums it up best, "As he came forth of his mother's womb, naked shall he return to go as he came, and shall take nothing of his labor, which he may carry away in his hand." Haven't we heard this somewhere before? In our common vernacular we like to say about earthly wealth, "You can't take it with you."

Right now, some of us may be wondering, is that all there is? Does Solomon have anything else to offer besides an admonishment against the love of money? Yes, there's much more. Verses 18-20 capture his sage advice concisely, "Behold that which I have seen: it is good and comely for one to eat and to drink, and to enjoy the good of all his labor that he taketh under the sun all the days of his life, which God giveth him: for it is his portion. Every man also to whom God hath given riches and wealth, and hath given him power to eat thereof, and to take his portion, and to rejoice in his labor; this is the gift of God. For he shall not much remember the days of his life; because God answers him in the joy of his heart."

Wow, that says a lot, doesn't it? First, we're encouraged to enjoy the fruits of our labor. We don't need to be miserly or worry about where our next meal is coming from. That's because it's God that provides for our needs. God gives us our portion, our perfect portion, sized just as we need it. We don't have to worry if we have a little or a lot. God provides for our needs as His gift to us.

Here's the most important part. God's gifts are not just temporal. He takes care of all our needs both temporal and spiritual. And which is most important? It's the latter, of course. This life is short but eternity is forever. We won't much remember our short stay here but our hearts will be filled with joy forever, both now and unto eternity through the salvation of Jesus Christ. So, in God's economy we can have our cake and eat it too. He provides the very best for all our needs; top choice, A-1, in just the right proportion. And He pours out His grace, mercy, forgiveness, faith, peace and love so richly and abundantly. Thank the Lord for He is good!

Godly Economics 101

Life seems awfully complicated sometimes, especially when we lean on our own understanding. Finance and economics can be doubly confusing. If you don't believe me, just try to make sense of the stock market. Is your portfolio diversified enough? What is the right mix of stocks, bonds and treasuries? Do I need to tweak the ratio between foreign, domestic, small and large cap investments? A lot of us probably give up since our net worth isn't substantial enough to fret over. We trust that our 401k and pension, if we have them, and Social Security will get us through retirement. For now, food, clothing and a roof over our heads are our primary concerns. If we are able to save, it usually takes a financial advisor to help us navigate our way to our golden years.

Here's the good news though. God says there is no need to worry. The inspired Apostle Paul tells us in Romans 8:32, "He that spared not his own Son, but delivered him up for us all, how shall he not with him also freely give us all things?" Said another way, God asks, since I've sacrificed my own beloved Son to secure your eternal well-being, don't you know that I will surely see you through this brief life too?

Still we have our doubts when we don't know where our next paycheck is coming from or our credit cards are maxed out trying to keep the wolves at bay. But these are exactly the times when we need to trust in God and take heart in His promises. God never guarantees us earthly riches or a trip down easy street but we must stop and think. Although none of us surely has received anywhere near all the things we want, have we ever gone without the things needed to sustain us in this life?

While we can certainly trust in the Lord's promises, as sinful human beings we are prone to weakness, doubt and fear. Thus, it is natural, according to our old natures, to worry about our economic well-being when things get dicey. When such fears arise, we should turn to God's word in the Holy Bible and take a lesson in Godly economics. He has such a wonderful way of making things divinely simple. In Proverbs 15:16-17 we read, "Better is little with the fear of the LORD than great treasure and trouble therewith. Better is a dinner of herbs where love is, than a stalled ox and hatred therewith." In other words, money isn't everything. Affluent people often have very troubled lives in spite of their wealth. Those with meager means are richer indeed than loveless people who have squirreled away a fortune devoid of faith and hope.

Here's one more lesson from Proverbs 11:24, "There is that scatters, and yet increases; and there is that withholds more than is meet, but it tends to poverty." Someone who has little but shares what they have with others gains wealth untold while the miser who hoards every penny has a soul that suffers nothing but poverty. I like this passage because it transcends earthly economics. God's economy is a spiritual one that will survive eternally after this old, corrupt earth and all its vaunted treasures have been destroyed forever.

We don't need temporal wealth to be charitable. We can be destitute and still scatter the seeds of faith found in God's inspired, inerrant, life-giving word. Doing so will build up unimaginable treasures in heaven, all to the glory of God. Don't ever consider bartering with the devil for temporal wealth, power and pleasures in this brief life. They are here today and gone tomorrow. Take hold of an infinitely better deal that will last for all eternity. It will cost you nothing; it's absolutely free, by the grace of God.

Sticks and Stones

Do you remember reciting this idiom as a child when some other little kid hurled an infantile insult your way? The charge might have been ratfink, cry baby, fat, ugly, skinny or sissy. In reply your defiant repartee might have been, "Sticks and stones may break my bones but words will never hurt me." True in a sense, this was a good way to teach kids not to react to name calling. Hey, what does it hurt, right? Now, if they threw a rock at you or clubbed you with a tree branch, that might do some real damage.

Looking back from this side of adulthood, most of us have developed a very different take on things. The pendulum has swung wildly in the other direction in the age of political correctness. Has a day gone by where we haven't heard about some kind of lawsuit being filed because someone has been offended by someone else's language?

It seems like hyper-sensitive, self-absorbed "snowflakes" have made a habit of demanding apologies for something someone else said. And many times, the offending party was guilty of nothing more than telling the truth. They've done so under the watchword of tolerance but in our society today, tolerance has become a one-way street. People might tolerate you as long as you agree with them. If not, you better look out. And don't even think about spouting that "hateful" Christian nonsense and don't dare bring up the Bible!

Faith Food — Steve Stranghoener

We live in a crazy, topsy-turvy world. So, what's the remedy? Should we go back to our seemingly saner sticks-and-stones mentality of childhood or do the contemporary secularists have a point that words really do matter? Let's turn to God's word for some guidance in Psalm 118:1-9. "O give thanks unto the LORD; for he is good: because his mercy endures forever. Let Israel now say, that his mercy endures forever. Let the house of Aaron now say, that his mercy endures forever. Let them now that fear the LORD say, that his mercy endures forever. I called upon the LORD in distress: the LORD answered me, and set me in a large place. **The LORD is on my side; I will not fear: what can man do unto me?** The LORD taketh my part with them that help me: therefore shall I see my desire upon them that hate me. It is better to trust in the LORD than to put confidence in man. It is better to trust in the LORD than to put confidence in princes."

Wow, isn't that great? In effect, God is saying the exact opposite of sticks-and-stones. Physical punishment is of no effect because persecution, beatings, torture and even death have no impact on us ultimately for God will and does deliver us from all of these things. What's the worst that anyone can do to us in this world? Yeah, they can kill us. But temporal death means nothing to God. God can and will resurrection us from the first death. The proof positive is in the resurrection of Jesus Christ, our Lord.

On the other hand, words really can harm us or help us. In Galatians 1:8-9, God offers a stern warning to avoid false teachings that contradict His true gospel message. He warns us about false Christs (Matthew 24:23) and our chief adversary the devil who is on the prowl like a roaring lion (1 Peter 5:8) whose primary weapon is deception and twisting the truth of God's word (John 8:44).

But if we cling to God's word, nothing can harm us for we are eternally His. God says that if we continue in His word the truth will make us free (John 8:31-32). He tells us that His word is the source of our faith and salvation (John 20:31). In Ephesians 6, He depicts His word as the one offensive weapon at our disposal in His arsenal in battling Satan. So, there you have it. Don't worry about sticks-and-stones. Pay attention to words instead and especially cling to the word of God.

The Ultimate Body Guard

Did you ever see the 1980 film, *My Bodyguard*? It was kind of a quirky, charming little movie about a shy, nerdy kid named Clifford Peache, played by Chris Makepeace (appropriate name), who was plagued by a high school bully named Moody, played by a young Matt Dillon. Clifford was misused and abused to no end by tough guy Moody until he enlisted the help of a giant kid named Ricky Linderman played by Adam Baldwin. Linderman was an enigma. The hulking high schooler could have been a gridiron star or hoops phenomenon but instead chose to remain an outcast.

Linderman was sullen and quiet almost to the point of being reclusive. No one even dared to bother him because of his size and reputation. As false rumor had it, he purportedly killed his own brother in cold blood. Moody and his gang extorted other kids like Clifford by claiming to offer protection from Linderman. Ricky was a complete loner until desperate Clifford mustered the courage to approach him with a proposition.

Enterprising Clifford convinced Linderman to serve as his personal bodyguard. Revenge was sweet when sadistic Moody attempted to resume tormenting poor Clifford only to have Linderman turn the tables on him. Through the course of events, Lindeman came out of his shell and he and Clifford developed a true friendship. Unfortunately, things turned sour for the pair when Moody one-upped Clifford by hiring his own second who was even tougher and bigger than Linderman. Of course, in the end, Clifford learned to stand on his own two feet in refusing to back down from Moody's bullying.

Ah, if only life could be as easy as it seems in the movies. Unfortunately, real life doesn't always turn out like a Hollywood script. The good guys don't always win and sometimes the bullies prevail with injustice holding sway over the just. This applies to believers and unbelievers alike but in truth it is we

Christians who are more likely than not to get the short end of the stick in a worldly sense.

Christ told us it would be this way. In Matthew 10:22 He warned, "And ye shall be hated of all men for my name's sake." Furthermore, in Luke 21:12 Christ told His followers, "But before all these, they shall lay their hands on you, and persecute you, delivering you up to the synagogues, and into prisons, being brought before kings and rulers for my name's sake." Jesus revealed the harsh truth that we will not be spared even from death as Paul cautioned in Romans 8:36, "As it is written, for thy sake we are killed all the day long; we are accounted as sheep for the slaughter."

There is a bright side to this though. The good news is that, no matter what happens, no matter how bad things get temporally, we win in the end. It's a classic underdog story that is better than anything Hollywood ever concocted. Maybe we should call it the Ultimate Bodyguard story because the guy who has our backs is tougher than anyone Moody could ever enlist. Even Satan himself with all of his power cannot hold a candle to our heavenly bodyguard.

Jesus Christ is in our corner, the ultimate bodyguard. Just look at the way He deals with our enemies, both temporal and spiritual. "He delivers me from mine enemies: yea, thou lifts me up above those that rise up against me: thou hast delivered me from the violent man," (Psalm 18:48). "For the LORD your God is he that goes with you, to fight for you against your enemies, to save you," (Deuteronomy 20:4). "But the salvation of the righteous is of the LORD: he is their strength in the time of trouble," (Psalm 37:39).

There's more. "What shall we then say to these things? If God be for us, who can be against us?" (Romans 8:31). "For I am persuaded, that neither death, nor life, nor angels, nor principalities, nor powers, nor things present, nor things to come, nor height, nor depth, nor any other creature, shall be able to separate us from the love of God, which is in Christ Jesus our Lord," (Romans 8:38-39). "But Jesus beheld them, and said unto them, With men this is impossible; but with God all things are possible," (Matthew 19:26). So, bring it on Moody! As for you, Satan, we have one little word, Jesus. He's our Ultimate Bodyguard.

Sweet & Sour

In today's politically correct world, slapstick comedy is no longer in vogue. Still I can't help busting a gut when I see old clips of Moe, Larry and Curly or Shemp. I also can't refrain from chuckling at the sight of a baby tasting a slice of lemon for the first time. Some might label this as cruelty but it's still hilarious to see the startled look on their unsuspecting, contorted faces.

What was God thinking when He made lemons so sour? Surely, He had sugar simultaneously in mind when He conceived the pucker-prompting, yellow fruit. Combine the two with cold, clear water and our taste buds are delighted with a refreshing summertime treat like no other.

Life is much more like a basket of lemons than a bowl of cherries. So often it seems like our sour experiences outnumber the sweet ones by a wide margin. There's sadness, sickness, guilt, pain, deception, betrayal, greed, poverty, tragedy, disaster, injustice and, worst of all, death. Sometimes our troubles and afflictions can be so overwhelming as to even challenge our faith. On occasion we're even driven to ask "Why God, why me?"

We know that God is not out to kill us even though as despicable sinners we're admittedly deserving. He said so through His prophet Ezekiel (33:11), "Say unto them, As I live, saith the Lord God, I have no pleasure in the death of the wicked; but that the wicked turn from his way and live." Still in times of travail it's hard not to wonder and doubt.

Here's the good news. No matter what kind of temptations and troubles Satan throws our way, we can be completely confident in God's grace, mercy and love. Yes, God will chastise us and allow certain consequences to come to bear in our lives but only for our eternal good. God is not the author of evil. His primary concern for each and every one of us is our eternal salvation. God went beyond death to offer assurances of His good intentions in temporal matters too through Jeremiah in Lamentations 3:31-33, "For the LORD will not cast off for ever: But though he cause grief, yet will he have compassion according to the multitude of his mercies. For he doth not afflict willingly nor grieve the children of men."

God is our perfect, loving Heavenly Father. Everything He allows into our lives is meant to work together for our temporal and eternal good. He tells us in Hebrews 12:7, "If ye endure chastening, God deals with you as with sons; for what son is he whom the father chastens not?" God's true intentions are clearly stated in 1Timothy 2:3-5, "For this is good and acceptable in the sight of God our Savior; Who will have all men to be saved, and to come unto the knowledge of the truth. For there is one God, and one mediator between God and men, the man Christ Jesus." Yes, God is constantly turning our lemons into lemonade. His sweet grace and mercy are constantly turning our sour sinfulness into perfect refreshment; the living water that slakes our thirst now and forever.

Super Glue

When we're in the throes of winter, our hearts are warmed by the distant echo of the thud of baseballs popping into catchers' mitts and the crack of bats as line drives are launched in the balmy climes of Florida. When the rite of Spring Training is underway, it buoys our resolve to outlast February's bitter chills in the Midwest.

Baseball, America's past-time, can be a breath of fresh air and a source of unity in the midst of all the fractious divisions that have been tearing us apart as a nation in recent years. This holds true in St. Louis like no place else. We are Cardinal Nation and here opening day at Busch Stadium might as well be a national holiday. I think the sense of unity that comes with every new season of Cardinal baseball is what makes it so special to St. Louis. It binds us not just in the here and now but across generations.

I used to delight in talking baseball with a much older brother in Christ named Henry who has since gone home to heaven. I loved to hear him share firsthand memories of Cardinal heroes that I only knew from the pages of history. He recounted the triumphs of old-timers like Enos "Country" Slaughter who won the 1946 World Series for the Cards by scoring the winning run in game seven by way of his famous mad dash against the Red Sox.

Every Cardinal fan is connected to Cardinal Nation by that most sacred Cardinal red thread, Stan "The Man" Musial. I got to see him play one time at old Sportsman's Park in his last season, 1963. I was eight years old and it was my first game in person. We beat the Cubs 8-0 and Ol' Number 6 hit one clear out of the stadium. I was so hoarse from cheering that I couldn't talk the next day. Later in life, I even got to have lunch with him one time. Now that was a thrill! I've passed these memories on to my children and, hopefully, they in turn will be able to share them with their kids.

There's another thread that binds us together even tighter and closer. It's practically invisible and barely noticeable to the naked eye. However, this thin, ethereal thread provides the strongest bond in the entire universe. There is no power on earth that can break it. This one is red too but a different shade. It's a scarlet thread dyed in the crimson blood of Jesus Christ, our Lord and Savior.

The power of this thread is so magnificent it bonds us like brothers and sisters with people we've never met; people who lived some 6,000 years ago and others who haven't even been born yet. And long after the Cardinal's baseball team ceases to exist, even after this earth and the entire universe are gone forever, the scarlet thread that bonds all believers in Christ will remain unto all eternity.

Here's how this bond is described in Ephesians 4:1-6, "I therefore, the prisoner of the Lord, beseech you that ye walk worthy of the vocation wherewith ye are called, With all lowliness and meekness, with longsuffering, forbearing one another in love; Endeavoring to keep the unity of the Spirit in the bond of peace. There is one body, and one Spirit, even as ye are called in one hope of your calling; One Lord, one faith, one baptism, One God and Father of all, who is above all, and through all, and in you all."

For now, even when we're in the midst of winter's bitter cold, let's think warm thoughts of opening day and revel in the simple blessings of unity that baseball can bring. And in a much higher way, let's take heart in the indescribable joy that exceeds anything this world has to offer, giving praise and thanks to God for our Savior, Jesus, who draws us near to Him in a miraculous, inseparable way with all believers for all eternity; the super glue of blood-bought salvation.

Time Flies

People say that time flies when you're having fun. The relativity of time is an odd phenomenon. The second hand on a clock at the front of a classroom can seem frozen to children during their daily lessons but recess passes by in a blur. Office clocks advance at a snail's pace during the week but the clocks in our homes spin wildly on the weekends. Things really slow down when we're eagerly anticipating an upcoming special event like a birthday party, favorite holiday, baby's birth or family vacation but hit warp speed when the day actually comes.

Our life clocks play tricks on us too, don't they? As kids we can't grow older fast enough. It seems to take an eternity to hit important milestones like getting our first driver's license. As young adults, we long to move ahead as fast as possible in achieving our goals. *When will that next promotion come?* We strive for an early retirement someday but the good life we envision seems impossibly beyond our reach. Then, just like that, someone flips a cosmic switch and we reel off the years at a mind-boggling pace. *Who is that stranger staring back at me in the mirror with all those wrinkles and gray hairs? Oh, wouldn't it be great to be young again?*

Sometimes the spiritual realm seems no better when it comes to the relativity of time. We know by faith that heaven is our home but our old natures can still make us slaves to the inconsistency of times and seasons. When we're young, we can suffer from the dangerous illusion that death is of no concern since we think we have plenty of time left. As the years pass and we become more cognizant of our mortality, we may try to slow things down through healthy dieting, exercise and miracle drugs. At the end, we may want to speed things up as our lives are consumed by pain and suffering. Throughout life we pray and pray but oftentimes our prayers become a lesson in patience.

Thankfully, we can always find peace in God's promises. They are a sure thing. But even God's prophetic word can cause major anxiety if we let our concept of time get in the way. Take for example one of God's shortest, simplest and most powerful promises that Christ made to us in Revelation 22:20, "Surely I come quickly." This is most certainly true but still the day can't seem to come soon enough when we look at the pitiful nature of this corrupt, sin-sick world with all its injustice, suffering and death.

However, God reminds us through 2 Peter 3:8, "But, beloved, be not ignorant of this one thing, that one day is with the Lord as a thousand years, and a thousand years as one day." We can rest assured that, as He did with Christ's first coming in the fullness of time, Jesus will return at just the right, precise and perfect moment. Thus, we need not be clock watchers but rather should stay focused on Christ alone and continue in His sure, life-giving word.

Stewardship and Service

Two Natures of Members

Each and every believer is a unique individual with a distinct personality and characteristics that set them apart from every other human being on the planet. We each have our own lives, separate families and friends, responsibilities and vocations. Every Christian has their own interests, likes, dislikes, hobbies and pastimes. Yet we're all members of the Body of Christ, voluntarily assembling together as brothers and sisters. Thus, we all have something wonderfully special in common; one Lord, one faith, one baptism (Ephesians 4:5).

In some ways, in a spiritual sense, we're even closer than blood relatives. Isn't that what Jesus meant in Matthew 12:48 and 12:50? "But he answered and said unto him that told him, who is my mother? And who are my brethren? For whosoever shall do the will of my Father which is in heaven, the same is my brother, and sister, and mother."

Given this special bond, we should be blessed with a singleness of purpose when we join together within a congregation. Yet, as members of such a body we often find ourselves pulling in different directions. That's because as Christians, regardless of our voluntary and God-pleasing affiliations, we all have two natures. There's our old sinful nature and the new man in Christ.

Here's how the Apostle Paul put it so aptly in Romans 7:19-25, "For the good that I would I do not:

but the evil which I would not, that I do. Now if I do that I would not, it is no more I that do it, but sin that dwells in me. I find then a law, that, when I would do good, evil is present with me. For I delight in the law of God after the inward man: But I see another law in my members, warring against the law of my mind, and bringing me into captivity to the law of sin which is in my members. O wretched man that I am! Who shall deliver me from the body of this death? I thank God through Jesus Christ our Lord. So then with the mind I myself serve the law of God; but with the flesh the law of sin."

As members within a church body, still afflicted by the Old Adam with the corruption of sin clinging to our flesh, we're subject to the same pitfalls that tarnish our lives outside a congregation. We can be petty, selfish, jealous, spiteful, greedy, hateful and downright difficult. Thus, there never has been and never will be a congregation completely free of trouble and strife. Nevertheless, we continue to assemble together in order to receive untold blessings through worship, word and sacrament ministry and true Christian fellowship. We know that these priceless blessings are available nowhere else on earth outside the Body of Christ.

Ironically though, we regularly fail to conduct the work of the church as Christ would have us do. While we put money in the plate as cheerful givers and attend worship and Bible study regularly, we take much for granted. Somehow, we think things happen by magic.

There are a lot of miraculous things that happen in church such as faith being imparted to a helpless little baby through baptism and forgiveness being poured out to us freely in the bread, wine, body and blood of Holy Communion. But certain practical matters require a little elbow grease and commitment. Someone has to pick up those donuts and brew the coffee. A faithful servant has to wash the communion cups and refill them with wine. Somebody has to pay the bills and keep track of donations. Who will make the call when the furnace or air conditioner goes out? The list goes on and on because there's a lot involved in operating a church.

This is where our two natures as members come into play. I'm not trying to lay a guilt trip on anyone or twist any arms. I'm just stating a fact; something I know to be the truth because I fall prey to my own sinful nature over and over again at my church as well as in every facet of my life. Sometimes, I think *Hey, let somebody else do it. I'm doing everyone a big enough favor just by making an appearance in worship services or Bible class. I don't have time for anything else; I'm a busy guy.* I can be lazy, self-centered and ungrateful even after all that Christ has done for me, an undeserving sinner. But then, thankfully, by the power and grace of God, sometimes we can overcome the Old Adam and pitch in, not out of guilt or obligation but thankfulness and love of Christ.

Do you ever find yourself, as a member of the Body of Christ, caught up in the Pauline struggle between your new nature and the "Chief of Sinners?" When the new nature prevails do you ever find yourself wondering, what can I do to serve the Body of Christ out of love and gratitude? With me, that Old Adams still creeps up and tries to pull me back down that slippery slope into the slough of despond. I'm great at making excuses. *What can I do? I'm not qualified? I might mess up and disappoint someone, maybe even the pastor. Hey I'm new to the congregation and I'm sure they don't want rookies helping out. No, I better play it safe and stay on the sidelines.*

Don't let the Old Man drag you down. If the urge to serve grabs you, go with it. Don't worry about what to do. There's plenty of meaningful work to go around. Don't worry about whether you're qualified. God loves to use broken tools like Paul, King David, Moses, Peter, you and me. No one will criticize you for trying since they're much more likely to give you a hand up in helping you to serve. There's a long list of things we can do to serve our brothers and sisters in Christ in a practical way. We can help in spiritual matters such as teaching, mentoring, assisting the pastor or evangelizing. However, even the simplest tasks can be of meaningful service and bring great satisfaction. All will bring glory to our great, gracious, loving God.

Time, Talent & Treasure

When it comes to supporting Christ's church, I've often caught myself thinking of treasure while forgetting about time and talent. Maybe it was an update in the church bulletin or the treasurer's reports I received at a church board meeting. *Oh my, receipts are trailing needs again; is the sky going to fall?* I've found it hard not to fall into this trap sometimes because, simply put, the bills must be paid. Scripture also offers reminders that we need to support the ministry with monetary gifts. In that sense, it's a good thing for us to pay attention to budgets and focus some time and attention on financial matters.

However, we can run afoul if we turn this into a burden; a worrisome, gut-knotting obligation that can breed resentment. God doesn't want us to fret over the church's financial needs but rather offers us the opportunity to give as a blessing and source of joy. It's a wonderful way for us to worship Him and show our gratitude and thanksgiving for all the gifts, spiritual and temporal, that He has showered on us.

When our attitude is gratitude, it makes all the difference in the world. Just look at the gift offerings of Abel and Cain. One was given joyfully and lovingly and the other grudgingly. In Cain's case, this led to bitterness, faithlessness and spiritual shipwreck. God was not pleased by Cain's reluctant offering. But

Abel's heartfelt gift was received joyously. God doesn't need our money. Everything we have is His anyway, right? God will not lose any of His elect regardless of whether we give a dollar or a dime.

God doesn't need our money but rather wants our love and gratitude. He wants us to be happy. He said so in 2 Corinthians 9:7, "Every man according as he purposes in his heart, so let him give; not grudgingly, or of necessity: for God loves a cheerful giver." It brings joy to God and His faithful servants when people give willingly out of thankfulness. Look at the gratitude Paul had for the Church at Philippi for their faithful, loving support of his ministry (Philippians 4).

If God doesn't want us to fret over red ink why do we need financial reports and constant reminders? Well, God still wants us to be good stewards and sometimes that requires a little bean counting on our parts. Think about the parable of the talents in Matthew 25. Just like the lord in that parable, God is greatly pleased when we use good stewardship to manage and grow the gifts He has provided to us. Thus, it's good to use the wisdom God has given us to apply good accounting practices in stewardship but, most importantly, we should do so cheerfully and joyously as ones who have been granted a great privilege. And at the same time, we should do so confidently as ones who walk by faith and not by sight knowing that God will provide for all our needs as He sees fit (Genesis 9:3, 2 Peter 1:3).

With God's good guidance we can thus be good stewards of the treasure He's afforded us but we shouldn't overlook time and talent. We're also given the great privilege of serving God and His church through the use of the gifts of time and talent with which He has equipped us (Ephesians 4:7-15). Thankfully, we don't have to be preachers, teachers; eloquent orators or highly skilled professionals to participate in the building of God's kingdom. God delights in using us flawed human beings in accomplishing His good purposes. God has a place for all of us in His service.

We don't have to be wealthy to serve God and His people. For that matter, we don't have to possess some special skill like a doctor, lawyer, business person, musician or educator. God calls us but also equips us. We may not even recognize the value of the talent and time with which God has blessed us. It may be our physical strength and endurance or patience, empathy, dedication, craftsmanship, cooking skills or any other number of qualities. Just ask your fellow church members and opportunities to serve will abound. Pray to God and He will bless you and equip you for a calling that will bring much joy and satisfaction.

Faith Food   Steve Stranghoener

Kingdoms of the Left and Right Hand: God, Government and Society

Devouring Their Young

Rodney Dangerfield had a fabulous career as a comedian due mostly to his self-deprecating humor summed up in his tagline, "I get no respect!" He also had a bit of Don Rickles in him and could deliver some funny barbs to others around him. For example, in the movie *Caddy Shack* he took one look at Judge Smails' disgusting grandson Spaulding and unleashed this zinger, "Now I know why tigers devour their young!" I think he meant to say lions but it got a big laugh anyway. Actually, the thought of some animals devouring their offspring is no laughing matter. Some sharks, wolf spiders, chickens, salamanders, polar bears and even cuddly hamsters are among the members of the animal kingdom known to sometimes cannibalize their offspring.

This must cause a lot of people heartburn since our world is so filled with overzealous animal lovers. Don't get me wrong. I love animals too and find them fascinating as part of God's creation. But I try to keep things in the proper perspective when it comes to animals and humans. Too often today, misguided people put the welfare of animals above that of people, the pinnacle of God's creation. They ascribe human-like attributes to animals and want to afford them with equal rights. Some even claim that killing an animal for any reason equates to murder and should be adjudicated accordingly. Thus, PETA and other animal extremists must face a terrible conundrum when they hear about an animal eating its own offspring. The same can't be said for Bible-believing Christians who know that the entire creation has been corrupted by sin.

Progressive animal lovers can exhibit such compassion toward a helpless lion cub when threatened with death by a hungry or jealous male member of the pride. Yet, they sense no hypocrisy when the same standard isn't applied to human beings. Just imagine if Congress passed a law making it legal to abort puppies. Liberal heads would explode. There should be the highest moral outrage when a helpless baby is torn apart in its mother's womb during an abortion. However, this evil, horrific practice of infanticide is vigorously defended as a woman's choice in exercising her rights over the sanctity of her own body. Never mind the baby's separately functioning body, soul and right to life. Even the downright devilish procedure of a late-term termination of life including the gut-wrenching atrocity of partial-birth abortion is hailed as somehow part of a nobler, higher cause.

Understandably, most people feel shock, grief and dismay at the sight of a cute, cuddly polar bear cub having its life violently snuffed out by its sire. Then why doesn't everyone feel the same or worse when a baby is murdered in the womb with the consent of its own mother? Forget Roe v. Wade. Medical science has long since exposed the lie that served as that unconstitutional travesty's foundation and now every sane person knows that a baby in the womb at any stage of development is a person with a complete DNA code. When a killer shoots a pregnant woman and both the mother and baby die, the perpetrator is charged with two murders, not one. Yet, as a nation we continue to devour our own young; some sixty million lives lost since Roe v. Wade.

Why is this issue still embroiled in bitter controversy today? The answer is simple. There can be no compromise between good and evil. Abortion is murder and it is evil. Any time we grow tired of the battle we must remember this is not a live-and-let-live proposition. We can't succumb to a compromise that dignifies legalized murder of helpless human beings. Whenever we need our courage restored, we only need to turn to Scripture and remember this sobering warning from our Lord and Savior in Matthew 18:6, "But whoso shall offend one of these little ones which believe in me, it were better for him that a millstone were hanged about his neck, and that he were drowned in the depth of the sea."

All Men Evolved Equally?

Something struck me as odd when I listened on March 26, 2014 as President Obama addressed an EU audience in NATO's headquarters in Brussels, Belgium about Russia's annexation of Crimea. He made a point about how Russia's actions were in stark contrast to our Western ideals of liberty, freedom, representative democracy and self-determination. This quote summed up his speech nicely. "And those ideas eventually inspired a band of colonialists across an ocean, and they wrote them into the founding documents that still guide America today, including the simple truth that **all men, and women, are created equal.**"

This struck me as odd even though these words echoed our Declaration of Independence, "We hold these truths to be self-evident, that all men are created equal, that they are endowed by their Creator with certain unalienable rights; that among these are life, liberty and the pursuit of happiness." It surprised me since the President, like secularists in our nation and Western Europe, firmly believed in the "settled science" of evolution. True to form though, he left out a reference to our Creator. Also, he referred to the colonists as colonialists; a negative connotation.

Whether evolutionary theory is science or just an alternate expression of faith is a debate for another day. Nonetheless, isn't it strange, even bizarre that a secularist and evolutionist would claim that all men and women were **created** equal? How could we be created if we've arrived here through evolution; a process of random chance that is the antithesis of intelligent design? Did the President use the term "created" as just the cavalier application of literary license?

That wouldn't make sense because I'm sure evolutionists would like to avoid the term created altogether if possible but that would be most difficult in this context thanks to the precise terminology of our Founding Fathers. The best excuse secularists might offer is that the Founders loosely used the term "created" to imply evolution; a concept beyond the scientific limitations of the 18th century. However, this would be pure sophistry aimed at blurring the clear intentions of the Framers.

Consider this. If you think we've evolved rather than being created by the ultimate intelligent designer, our Creator God, how on earth could you claim that we're all equal? Evolution is a deadly, bloody, tooth and claw struggle where natural selection vanquishes the weak and favors the strong. We supposedly all started from single cells in primordial goo and the race was on. After eons of death, extinction and supposed transformation from one kind of being to another, we've reached a point in time where humans for the moment just happen to be at the pinnacle of the evolutionary hierarchy. If we were all created or evolved equally wouldn't there be one perfectly homogenous species?

Even if evolutionists could account for the diversity of other creatures still in existence today, which happens to be completely consistent with the Genesis account of creation, they would still need to explain the human species. Could we all really be equal on the basis of evolution? This would be impossible since we would all be at different points of superiority or inferiority on our evolutionary paths. Thus, the theory or faith of evolution is diametrically opposed to our founding principles. The two cannot coexist in logic or intellectual honesty.

Isn't it amazing though how the ideals we as Americans all hold so dear are perfectly consistent with the truth of Scripture? "So, God created man in his own image, in the image of God created he him; male and female created he them," (Genesis 1:27). "This is the book of the generations of Adam. In the day that God created man, in the likeness of God made he him," (Genesis 5:1). "I have made the earth, and created man upon it: I, even my hands, have stretched out the heavens; and all their host have I commanded," (Isaiah 45:12). "Have we not all one father? Hath not one God created us?" (Malachi 2:10).

We're obviously not equal according to the naked eye. We all have different gifts and abilities (1 Corinthians 12). Yet, we are all equal in the eyes of God. He has the ability to look beyond the superficial, to peer into our hearts and ponder our souls. He loves us all equally as His children in spite of our many transgressions. He sent God the Son to pay the price for all of our sins, each and every one of us, equally and totally. He created us in His likeness and image. Thus, He is the only one with the authority to declare us equal and to endow us with certain unalienable rights. If we forsake God for the lie of evolution, we forsake all.

Faint Not!

This world is a horrible place. We see the evidence all around us. It invades our living rooms through the incessant, 24/7 news cycle and shatters our peace daily. Immorality is lauded in all its ugly forms such as sexual perversion, violence and hatred. The world is an upside-down place where confusion reigns to the point where one can be ostracized or even suffer threats by suggesting that perhaps, just maybe, boys should use the boys' bathroom. Genocide against millions of helpless babies is codified into law and championed as a just and noble cause. Christians seem to be fair game for every manner of persecution and injustice. False religions are fostered and coddled, including those that resort to coercion and even terror to advance their evil aims.

We don't belong in a world like this. God says so in 1 Peter 2:9, "But ye are a chosen generation, a royal priesthood, an holy nation, a peculiar people," and 2 Corinthians 6:17, "Wherefore come out from among them, and be ye separate." Yet, here we sit, as the hymn *I'm but a Stranger Here* says, strangers in a foreign land longing for the Lord's return. We don't know when Judgment Day will come but surely all the signs foretold in Matthew 24 and elsewhere say we're approaching the end of the age. God teaches that these signs have been apparent to one degree or another in every generation including Noah's (Matthew 24:37) but also cautions that no one but Him knows when that hour will come (Matthew 24:36).

In Philippians 1:2, Paul lamented like us but knew there was a purpose for his time here, "For to me to live is Christ, and to die is gain." How then are we to complete our race here? Are we required to conquer this sinful, old world? As the Lord tells us in John

18:36, the answer is clearly no in a temporal sense, "Jesus answered, My kingdom is not of this world: if my kingdom were of this world, then would my servants fight, that I should not be delivered to the Jews: but now is my kingdom not from hence." Christ has already declared us to be citizens of His heavenly realm but has left us here as spiritual warriors to spread the gospel and make disciples.

Should we then serve out our term here in dread like reluctant Foreign Legionnaires? No, God has equipped us perfectly for His good purposes and is always with us. Thus, we can go about His business with wonderful assurances like these. "I had fainted, unless I had believed to see the goodness of the LORD in the land of the living," (Psalm 27:13). "Do all things without murmurings and disputes: That ye may be blameless and harmless, the sons of God, without rebuke, in the midst of a crooked and perverse nation, among whom ye shine as lights in the world," (Philippians 2:14-15). May God bless us to make the most of our time here in building His heavenly kingdom joyfully, all to His glory and honor alone.

Whoppers

What comes to mind when you hear the term whoppers? For a fishing enthusiast it might bring visions of hooking a trophy-sized bass. For movie goers it probably conjures concession stand reminiscences like Junior Mints or Jujubes. I never understood the concept behind the colorful but rock-hard Jujubes. Perhaps they were designed by dentists to increase their business. They seemed better suited for throwing than eating. One couldn't say the same for Whoppers though. The marble-sized balls were coated in milk chocolate that melted in my mouth to reveal an inner core of deliciously delectable malted milk centers that could be crunched for instant gratification or patiently savored as they slowly dissolved.

As much as I used to enjoy a trip to the theater as a kid for a movie, popcorn, soda and candy, "whoppers" no longer reminds me of the sweet confection any more. Instead, it brings to mind the common colloquialism for tall tales or, put more bluntly, big, fat lies. I'm not talking about hyperbole or any other literary vehicle such as those employed by the likes of Mark Twain in imparting his legendary wit and wisdom. When I think of whoppers today, I'm talking gross prevarication. Today our world is caught up in some of the biggest whoppers imaginable; conceived, nourished and propagandized by politicians, educators, the media and so-called scientists who are hell-bent on replacing Christianity with faith of another sort: the religion of secular humanism.

This phenomenon is as old as Christianity. Paul had to reprove false teachers in his inspired epistles to the Church at Corinth. Ponder the stark warnings he issued about false gospels in Galatians 1:8-9. During His earthly ministry, Jesus warned us about false Christs (Matthew 24:24) and Peter cautioned us about our chief adversary, the devil, who he said was on the prowl like a roaring lion seeking to devour us (1 Peter 5:8). We're told in Revelation and elsewhere in the Bible how in the final days the great Antichrist will use deception and false doctrine as his chief weapon in attacking Christ's church.

Although we shouldn't be surprised by what is happening today, I'm still taken aback by the foolishness of men. The lies being swallowed hook, line and sinker are ludicrous. Sadly though, this happens when people turn away from the word of God in the Bible. God foretold as much in 2 Timothy 4:3-4, "For the time will come when they will not endure sound doctrine; but after their own lusts shall they heap to themselves teachers, having itching ears; And they shall turn away their ears from the truth, and shall be turned unto fables."

Speaking of cunningly devised fables (2 Peter 1:16), there are three big whoppers that have been foisted upon us today by Satan's purveyors of secular humanism. Please note how they stand in stark contrast to the clear teachings of the Bible.

Whopper 1: There is no God. The universe came into being out of nothing via an inexplicable big bang and then slowly, over millions of years, life appeared and evolved by sheer chance. Blobs eventually produced apes which somehow turned into men.

God says, "So God created man in his own image, in the image of God created he him; male

and female created he them," (Genesis 1:27). "I have made the earth, and created man upon it: I, even my hands, have stretched out the heavens, and all their host have I commanded," (Isaiah 45:12).

Whopper 2: This one follows from Whopper 1. Since there is no Creator God and mankind evolved from the animals by chance, it's okay to kill unborn babies through abortion. It's not a human being with an immortal soul. It's just a blob of fetal matter.

God says through King David, "Behold, I was shapen in iniquity; and in sin did my mother conceive me," (Psalm 51:5). "Thine eyes did see my substance, yet being imperfect; and in thy book all my members were written, which in continuance were fashioned, when as yet there was none of them," (Psalm 139:16).so

Whopper 3: If you accept Whoppers 1 & 2, then you must have a cause to follow; an object of your secular humanist faith. You must save the planet from mankind! The air we exhale (CO_2) and that plants thrive on is not a naturally occurring element essential to life but is a pollutant created by mankind and the capitalist system. It must be eradicated at all costs, even if it impoverishes billions and destroys life as we know it. Or else, the world will come to an end at the hand of evil mankind through climate change.

God says, "While the earth remaineth, seedtime and harvest, and cold and heat, and

summer and winter, and day and night shall not cease," (Genesis 8:22).

Just three little lies. That's all it takes to undermine faith. There is no middle ground since either the secularists are correct or God is right. No lukewarm compromise will help but the answer to this dilemma is simple. We can trust the word of man, the ever-changing winds of doctrine, or stand on the truth of God's word, the Holy Bible. Only the latter is perfectly trustworthy and completely reliable (John 17:17).

Government: From Bloated to Blessed

Authority has come under attack in our country today. Citizens have always been a bit wary of law enforcement but healthy skepticism has been replaced by open warfare where police officers are regularly killed assassination-style. Parents and educators have been unfairly shackled by politically correct, screwball moralists who have virtually made proper discipline a crime. Sometimes even authorities have undermined authority. Mayors and governors in so-called sanctuary cities and states have openly defied federal law and refused to cooperate with Immigration and Customs Enforcement (ICE) officials. Often, the safety, security and well-being of American citizens have been sacrificed to benefit illegal aliens, some whom have committed other criminal acts including felonies.

To be fair, government officials have too often earned the disrespect of citizens. Corruption has been all too common and far too many bureaucrats have acted more like masters than servants of the public. Justice seems to have been turned on its head with perpetrators treated as victims. Somewhere along the line, we lost track of the purpose of good government.

God and not man established government to serve His good intentions. As He revealed in Romans 13, God established governments to keep the peace that we might receive His blessings. He offered this advice in verses 1-4 about the attitude we should have toward authority. "Let every soul be subject unto the higher powers. For there is no power but of God: the powers that be are ordained of God. Whosoever therefore resists the power; resists the ordinance of God: and they that resist shall receive to themselves damnation. For rulers are not a terror to good works, but to the evil. Wilt thou then not be afraid of the power? Do that which is good and thou shalt have praise of the same: For he is the minister of God to thee for good. But if thou do that which is evil, be afraid; for he bears not the sword in vain: for he is the minister of God, a revenger to execute wrath upon him that doeth evil."

We seem to have a conundrum since God has taught us to respect governmental authority and adhere to the law but our government has turned its back on God in many ways. Does God want us to remain faithful by kowtowing to a godless government?

Thankfully, our dilemma isn't without precedent. Tax collectors in Jesus' time cheated the people to fill their own coffers but God still inspired Paul to write Chapter 13 of Romans which included instruction to pay taxes. This wasn't because God excused the sins of the publicans. Jesus gave clear instruction to government officials regarding His expectations for them in Luke 3:12-14. "Then came also publicans to be baptized, and said unto him, Master, what shall we do? And he said unto them, Exact no more than that which is appointed you. And the soldiers likewise demanded of him, saying, and what shall we do? And he said unto them, do violence to no man; neither accuse any falsely; and be content with your wages."

We're all sinners including elected officials, government bureaucrats and citizens alike. However, that doesn't change God's good intentions in establishing governments to promote peace and order. God's underlying purpose is to provide for our eternal well-being. When carried out in accordance with His commands, government allows for the gospel of salvation to flourish. Even when governments stray from God's instructions, His providence in spiritual matters will prevail.

Thankfully, we still live in a country where we can approach the government for redress of our grievances. Thus, we should obey the law and work within the system to promote good governance while keeping our priorities in order with God always first. Thank God for a President who recognizes we worship God and not government.

Failure of Leadership

On November 26, 2014, my thoughts turned inexorably to the events of the prior two days which were filled with rioting, violence, looting and wanton destruction here in St. Louis and all in the name of justice. We stared anarchy squarely in its malevolent face. I tried to reflect on the situation and looked to God to make some sense out of it all. I had no doubt that He would accomplish His good purposes, despite the senseless mayhem, because He declared in Romans 8:28, "We know that all things work together for good to them that love God, to them who are the called according to his purpose."

A young man was tragically killed, on the basis of forensic evidence and eyewitness testimony, as a consequence of his own action in attacking an officer of the law. Still some refused to recognize the facts of the case and stubbornly insisted that Michael Brown was murdered by an overzealous cop filled with racial animus. Many of them seemed to be driven by frustration, anger and hatred that stemmed from deep-rooted problems stretching beyond Ferguson, Missouri. These forces threatened to tear apart the seemingly fragile fabric that bound us together as a nation and people.

While searching for answers, I wondered how things went so far afield. The obvious answer seemed to be a lack of leadership. Our President and Attorney General first called for peace and calm and in the next breath expressed understanding for the frustrations the "protesters" felt toward the justice system. They rationalized the senseless, totally inexcusable behavior of lawless rioters and thus only encouraged more such despicable behavior. At the same time, we were left to ponder why our Missouri Governor declared a state of emergency a week in advance only to leave the National Guard on the sidelines during the first night of rioting when so many businesses and lives were indiscriminately destroyed. It all made no sense whatsoever.

Although there was no doubt that government obfuscation played a part in this debacle, I felt we needed much more than just a change in leadership. The root cause of our nation's woes was that we had turned our backs on God. This was no small matter considering from whence we started. Going back to the Pilgrims who came over on the Mayflower in 1620, it was indisputably evident that our nation was founded on Christian principles and God's word in the Holy Bible. This was true for the colonists and our Founding Fathers who hammered out the Declaration of Independence, our Constitution and the Bill of Rights.

While tolerant of other peoples and religions, we were undoubtedly a Christian nation and were outspoken in that regard. Since then we've undergone a long process aimed at replacing the true religion of Jesus Christ with a false, pagan religion known as secular humanism which elevates the creature above the Creator. The truth has never mattered because the wicked one behind this movement was and is Satan; a liar and the very Father of Lies.

As a case in point, we've heard much from liberal progressives about the separation of church and state in justifying endless attacks on Christianity. The term separation of church and state appeared nowhere in the Declaration of Independence, Constitution or Bill of Rights. It was a phrase used by Thomas Jefferson in 1802 in a letter to the Danbury Baptist Church to assure them the government would not force a particular Christian denomination's doctrine upon them. The "wall of separation" was intended to be a protection for churches against the government and not vice versa. My how things have changed!

Despite our seemingly insurmountable troubles, my fears and frustrations faded as I recalled all of the blessings that God had bestowed upon us and through us as a nation. God promised that all things are possible with Him including turning Ferguson and all our other tragedies around to grant us new life, peace, faith and joy. Even the horrendous bloodshed of the Civil War produced new blessings of freedom and liberty.

America has been through incredible difficulties throughout our history but God's providence has always shown through. At this tenuous time when we appear to be woefully divided along racial and political lines, we need to turn back to the source of our nation's strength and good fortune; the word of God in the Bible. I pray that God will re-establish our trust in government by restoring it to His good purposes as outlined in Romans 13. That is, to promote good and discourage evil.

Lord please help us to put aside our old, sinful natures and the hatred and petty differences we so often dwell upon; divisions caused by our preoccupation with inane, superficial distinctions like race and gender. Dear Father, please bless us with the true unity of one Lord, one faith, one baptism (Ephesians 4:5). And most importantly, God please bless us with love toward one another; the kind of selfless, unconditional love that motivated you to send Jesus to the cross to pay the price for our sins. Please grant us faithful, God-fearing leaders who will look to you and your word for guidance. Draw us all near to you and show us the way so that this might be a blessing to us and many others, all to your glory and honor alone.

Marriage: Back to Basics

Marriage is a hot topic for debate today. It sounds like bad math but husbands and wives are two thirds of the marriage equation. That's because a marriage is made up of three persons: husband, wife and Jesus Christ. Some might think this is an outdated equation since non-Christians marry and many Christians don't have a clue about Jesus being the third party in a marriage. To confuse matters further, a lot of people won't even accept that the bonds of marriage are reserved exclusively for one man and one woman. We really do need to go back to the very basics, God's basics, to understand marriage.

God has offered considerable guidance about His institution of marriage in the Bible but, for the sake of brevity, a couple of proof passages should suffice. In Genesis 2:24 God declared, "Therefore shall a man leave his father and his mother, and shall cleave unto his wife: and they shall be one flesh." Jesus reinforced and expanded upon this in Matthew 19:4-6, "And he answered and said unto them, Have ye not read, that he which made them at the beginning made them male and female, And said, For this cause shall a man leave father and mother, and shall cleave to his wife: and they twain shall be one flesh? Wherefore they are no more twain, but one flesh. What therefore God hath joined together; let not man put asunder."

Inspired by God, Paul left nothing to question in 1 Corinthians 7:1-2, "Now concerning the things whereof ye wrote unto me: It is good for a man not to touch a woman. Nevertheless, to avoid fornication, let every man have his own wife, and let every woman have her own husband." The Apostle Paul summed things up precisely; God established marriage as one man and one woman in union with their loving God and Savior.

God's authoritative word is abundantly clear on this subject but unfortunately many people don't put much stock in the Bible. People who scoff at God's wisdom might argue that the only thing that matters is that two people, of any gender, love each other. They might erroneously add that sexual orientation isn't a behavior or a choice but instead is a genetic trait and homosexuals are born that way. We can challenge their logic by asking if pedophiles should be able to marry children. They will likely reply in an indignant tone, "Of course not!" We can then really throw them for a loop by challenging them, "How can you be such an intolerant bigot?"

Please note that, at this point, we might have to duck, pick them up off the ground or at least help them to shut their gaping jaws. When they've regained their composure, we should calmly explain that if sexual preference is a genetic trait, then we can't blame pedophiles for their inborn sexual preference and denying them the right to marry in accordance with that preference would be a violation of their civil rights.

This sounds crazy and it is but the parallels are undeniable. Perhaps this might open some eyes and give them some pause. Some might even consider the truth that marriage was instituted by God from the very beginning between one man and one woman to serve God's good purposes and intentions for us. Regardless of popular opinion that shifts like the wind, the best approach is always to get back to the basics. That is, the basic truth of the Holy Bible; God's authoritative, inspired and inerrant word.

The Last Child

My pastor who is a sci-fi buff gave me a copy of an obscure, made-for-TV movie entitled, *The Last Child*. I was too polite to say thanks but no thanks and reluctantly accepted his gift. I thought about tossing it into a chest full of old DVDs never to be seen again but knew that he would ask me about it sooner or later. Thus, I forced myself to pop it in the Blue-Ray player but kept my index finger near the fast-forward button.

I felt my misgivings had been justified when I saw it was made in 1971 when I was a sophomore in high school. The production quality was even a little shabby for back then. The film was grainy and the acting was pretty poor. I laughed at the credits which included Aaron Spelling as the producer. He gave us TV classics such as *The Mod Squad*, *Charlie's Angels* and *Beverly Hills 90210*. The movie's star, Michael Cole, was a member of the *Mod Squad* and the cast also included Ed Asner of the *Mary Tyler Moore Show* and Van Heflin, a real old-timer in his last film role. A funny thing happened as my finger hovered over the FF button. The movie drew me into the plot and captured my imagination. I realized why my pastor, an intellectual sort, held this low budget flick in such high regard.

The Last Child depicted the United States at some point in the future as a country given over to Big Brother and a set of draconian laws aimed at stemming the tide of overpopulation. Couples were only allowed to have one child and acute medical care was withheld from anyone over sixty-five. The Millers, Alan and Karen, were expecting their second child after the death of their first child. They were on the lam because their first child had lived for fifteen days or five days past the legal limit that would have allowed them to conceive again. Consequently, they were supposed to report to Population Control for the baby to be aborted. They were assisted in their escape by Karen's brother, Harry Guardino, who grudgingly cooperated even though he was a government bureaucrat who could lose his job and Van Heflin as an old, retired Senator who was in jeopardy since he was well past sixty-five.

One thing that sucked me into this small screen drama was the novelty of it all. Back in 1971 when our American cultural revolution was kicking into high gear, there were very few vocal people in the loyal opposition, especially in Hollywood. This movie was actually pro-life in terms of both abortion and euthanasia, although they missed the mark in portraying Canada as a sanctuary for traditional beliefs regarding the sanctity of life.

Another thing that kept me glued to the set was wonderment at how far they missed the mark on certain things. The premise of the movie bought into Malthusian philosophy hook, line and sinker. Thomas Malthus was an 18th century philosopher who theorized that the earth could not sustain its rate of population growth. This was rehashed and popularized by Stanford professor Paul Erlich in his 1968 tome, *The Population Bomb*, which predicted mass starvation in the 1980s due to overpopulation and scarcity of resources. Of course, both men and all of their acolytes were completely wrong. Perhaps we could excuse them for not seeing how technological know-how in agriculture would more than allow the world to keep pace with population growth. But if only they had read their Bible they would have known that God would provide somehow since He instructed us from the very beginning to "Be fruitful and multiply," (Genesis 1:28).

It was rather funny and sad to think how much wasted energy and bloated rhetoric went into the imaginary population crisis. This made me think how we'd more recently hatched another mythological crisis, climate change, in order to justify all manner of misguided policies. Again, we've ignored the simple truth of God in Genesis 8:22 where it's easy to see that climate change is the least of our worries, "While the earth remaineth, seedtime and harvest, and cold and heat, and summer and winter, and day and night shall not cease."

While clueless in some regards, *The Last Child* was incredibly prescient in other ways. Population Control was able to track the Miller's movements through the use of ID cards that had to be scanned to conduct any kind of simple transaction from buying a burger to purchasing a train ticket. Importantly, the plot centered on the sanctity of life in issuing a bold warning against the dangers of abortion and euthanasia. Above all, I think its greatest achievement was the underlying message, one that has proven to be true, that the greatest threat to our freedom and life as we know it is the menace of big government.

The hyper-bureaucracy depicted in the movie, the Population Control Agency, is no match for the government intrusion we're experiencing in our country today through the IRS, NSA, Homeland Security, EPA, HHS, FDA, VA and Department of Education to name a few. As reflected in socialist programs like Obamacare and Common Core, government elites and bureaucrats want to control every facet of our lives from cradle to grave and completely supplant the Lord and Giver of Life while revoking our unalienable constitutional rights that have been endowed to us by our Creator.

This is not an anti-government rant. I'm a firm believer in the purpose of government as described in Romans 13. Therein God explained that He has set up governments to suit His good purposes, namely to promote good and thwart evil and ultimate provide for a safe environment where the gospel can be proclaimed. But as long as governments are run by sinful human beings, we need to remain vigilant. That's what our Founders had in mind with our Constitution and the balance of power between the three branches of government. Ours is a government of, by and for the people and is designed to make the best of government while keeping our representatives in check.

I'm glad I watched *The Last Child*. It taught me something about our world today and reminded me of our duty as citizens and Christians. That is, we need to honor the God-given authority of the government and do our best to help them carry out their duties while always remembering from whence the authority came; God Almighty.

The Tax Man Cometh

Sometime around the glorious joy of Easter we're faced with fear, foreboding and loathing. That's when Uncle Sam digs even deeper into our pockets. The tax man cometh, we're doomed! Of course, my tongue is planted firmly in cheek because nothing in this world can diminish the unending joy of Christ's Easter resurrection: God's immutable seal of approval of our new life and salvation. In all seriousness though, the tax deadline does raise some interesting questions of a spiritual rather than fiscal nature. Why do we loathe the tax man but gladly give to the best of our ability when an usher passes the plate in church?

Dreading the tax man didn't start with the IRS. The same foreboding existed in ancient times as recorded in the Bible. Matthew served as a tax collector when Jesus first approached him (Matthew 9:9). Chapter 9 also revealed that Jesus was criticized by the Pharisees for accepting a dinner invitation from Matthew. They asked why He would sit down to eat with sinners. Matthew was considered not only a sinner like the rest of us but one deserving particular scorn as a tax collector among the Hebrews. Why was that? He was just doing his job, wasn't he?

Well, in those days and in that part of the world, a tax collector like Matthew stood for everything distasteful to the Jews. He represented not only the Jewish Tetrarch but consequently the Roman Empire since Judea and Galilee were client states of Rome. As if that wasn't enough, Matthew was probably corrupt like many tax collectors given that he was able to throw lavish dinner parties. The Jews resented paying what amounted to tribute to the oppressive Roman government but really chaffed when corrupt bureaucrats skimmed off the top to satisfy their own greed.

Things haven't changed much over the centuries. How did that line from the Beatles' song *Tax Man* go? The tax man said to the tax payer after taking ninety-five percent off the top, "If five percent appears too small, be thankful I don't take it all." In contemporary America, has anyone ever thanked the IRS after filing a tax return or volunteered to be audited? They haven't generated much good will by feeding the government's voracious appetite for higher and higher taxes at our expense. Sometimes they've even abused their vast power by intimidating people of opposing political viewpoints.

Shouldn't we have been happy to support our American government every April 15th? Hasn't it been a good thing when we've paid our taxes to build and maintain our infrastructure and provide for our common defense? Viewing things in such a positive light has been difficult because our government has grown so bloated. So many government programs have turned out to be unnecessary, wasteful and, in some cases, objectionable. We've lost control of how our hard-earned tax dollars are spent. Congress has left many tax payers with the impression that they think taxes are their money and not ours. Thus, we've naturally adopted the same sour attitude that the ancient Jews had toward tax collectors.

Thankfully though, we've had a completely different perspective in spiritual matters. When we've given to Christ's church, we've done so cheerfully. That's because we've realized our money is His anyway and every good gift is from above (James 1:17). The money we've put into the plate has gone to serve God's good purposes and especially His highest cause: the spreading of the gospel of Christ. The return on investment has been enormous, priceless.

God's economic system is completely different than ours. He preaches service and humility rather than self-promotion. Christ gives us everything for free; not only life's provisions but everything we need spiritually in this life and the next unto eternity. "For ye were as sheep going astray; but are now returned unto the Shepherd and Bishop of your souls," (I Peter 2:25).

Our wealth and glory are not ours and they are not just temporal. Thus, we can truly be cheerful givers in all thankfulness and humility. "Humble yourselves therefore under the mighty hand of God, that he may exalt you in due time," (I Peter 5:6). Do we need further convincing? Just look at Matthew's transformation or Paul's or so many others. God is the tax man that gives rather than takes. He gives all eternally.

Mother Hen

Mother's must feel like Rodney Dangerfield these days since it seems they so often get very little respect. Feminists look upon stay-at-home moms with a certain disdain prompting them to wonder, *what did I do to deserve such scorn*? That's how mixed up our world has become, belittling mothers for devoting their lives, full-time, to their highest calling. Nevertheless, thankfully we still set aside a special day to honor our mothers. With that in mind, would you ever celebrate by referring to your mom as a mother hen? It sounds like an unflattering comparison. Surely, there's a better way to fete our dear mothers.

Isn't it strange that we've come to the point where praising motherhood seems like such a difficult task? If only we had the wisdom of Adam. He knew the score. When God blessed him with female companionship, Adam immediately bestowed great honor upon her with the name Eve as recorded in Genesis 3:20. "And Adam called his wife's name Eve; because she was the mother of all living." Of all the responsibilities he could have highlighted, he chose to identify her primarily in the role of motherhood.

There are many reasons to respect virtuous women as enumerated in Proverbs 31. "Her price is far above rubies. The heart of her husband doth safely trust in her, so that he shall have no need of spoil. She will do him good and not evil all the days of her life. She seeks wool, and flax, and works willingly with her hands. She is like the merchants' ships; she brings her food from afar. She rises also while it is yet night, and gives meat to her household and a portion to her maidens. She considers a field, and buys it: with the fruit of her hands she plants a vineyard. She girds her loins with strength, and strengthens her arms. She perceives that her merchandise is good: her candle goes not out by night. She lays her hands to the spindle, and her hands hold the distaff. She stretches out her hand to the poor; yea, she reaches forth her hands to the needy. She is not afraid of the snow for her household: for all her household are clothed with scarlet. She makes herself coverings of tapestry; her clothing is silk and purple. Her husband is known in the gates, when he sits among the elders of the land. She makes fine linen and sells it; and delivers girdles unto the merchant. Strength and honor are her clothing; and she shall rejoice in time to come. She opens her mouth with wisdom; and in her tongue is the law of kindness. She looks well to the ways of her household, and eats not the bread of idleness. Her children arise up, and call her blessed; her husband also, and he praises her. Favor is deceitful, and beauty is vain: but a woman that fears the LORD, she shall be praised."

It sounds like contemporary women have nothing on their ancient counterparts since their plates seemed quite full. This litany of duties in Proverbs 31 reminds me of that 1980 perfume commercial, "I can bring home the bacon, fry it up in the pan, and never let you forget you're a man; 'cause I'm a woman, Enjoli." Yet, out of all of these varied responsibilities, one stands out: motherhood.

Even Jesus Christ afforded special honor to motherhood when He used this comparison to express His undeserved, unconditional love for us, His wayward children, including even those who rejected Him. "O Jerusalem, Jerusalem, thou that kill the prophets, and stone them which are sent unto thee, how often would I have gathered thy children together, even as a hen gathers her chickens under her wings, and ye would not!" (Matthew 27:37). Hmmm, maybe the term mother hen is appropriate after all. I wonder if I can get that on a greeting card.

Unconventional Wisdom

To the world, conventional wisdom represents the truth. It is the consensus that has been reached, at a given point in time, by the "experts" of the day and accepted by most people. Often this occurs without much critical thought or careful analysis, even when the conventional wisdom undermines core beliefs that have been held for a lifetime. This type of truth is subject to continuous revision with the passing of time; being tossed to and fro by the winds and waves of doctrine that can change course with mercurial speed.

The purveyors of conventional wisdom often tell us that this truth has been arrived at by historical fact or settled science without a shred of evidence to back it up. Those of us who challenge or question conventional wisdom are not counseled with patient logic and reason but rather are ostracized through personal attacks laced with vitriolic invectives. We are labeled flat earthers, haters, extremists, racists and such.

True wisdom is anything but conventional these days. God tells us in Proverbs 1:7 that "The fear of the LORD is the beginning of knowledge." The Lord counsels us in John 17:17 that if we want the truth, there's only one reliable source; His word, the Holy Bible. These two world views are at loggerheads. The secular world casts dispersions on the authority of Scripture and elevates human reason to the pinnacle. However, God puts it this way in Proverbs 16:22-25, "Understanding is a wellspring of life unto him that hath it: but the instruction of fools is folly. The heart of the wise teaches his mouth, and adds learning to his lips. Pleasant words are as a honeycomb, sweet to the soul, and health to the bones. There is a way that seems right unto a man, but the end thereof are the ways of death."

We've seen this struggle played out in so many facets of life in recent times and not only in secular matters but within the church at large as well. Examples have included evolution, abortion, the so-called separation of church and state and even something as seemingly straightforward as the definition of terrorism. While the Jihadists have declared war on us, we've been told that Islam is a religion of peace. Beheadings of Americans in the name of Allah have been deemed workplace violence. President Obama once lectured us that the self-labeled Islamic State in Iraq and Syria was neither a state nor Islamic. Don't worry about Jihadists or the economy. Plastic straws are the real menace!

One example has illustrated better than most how conventional wisdom and God's inconvenient truth are diametrically opposed. Amidst all of the chaos in this world; economic hardships, terrorism, corruption, mass migration and widespread, bloody persecutions and genocide, conventional wisdom has claimed that the greatest danger we face is climate change. This has become the folly of so many people who have made it their life's passion, leading them on quixotic crusades. It truly has become a case of Nero fiddling while Rome burns.

Here's what God said about the matter in Genesis 8:22, "While the earth remaineth, seedtime and harvest, and cold and heat, and summer and winter, and day and night shall not cease." Which view reflects what we've seen before our very eyes? The latter has been proven true by any objective measure. Seasons have changed and the climate trends have shifted back and forth between colder and warmer periods. But man-made CO_2 hasn't threatened us with the end of the world.

The enviro-maniacs who have pushed their false doomsday religion must admit that, regardless of where you stand on climate change, mankind has had very little impact in the matter. If cornered by facts they will reluctantly concede that, if we enacted every cockeyed idea they've proposed; ideas that would destroy our economy and way of life as we know it, it would only lower the amount of CO_2 in the atmosphere by one or two percent. That kind of change has occurred naturally in minutes with just a few volcanic belches like we've witnessed in recent years.

Yet, conventional wisdom has reigned and the word of God has been shunned by the intelligentsia. It shouldn't matter that they've tried to belittle us with unflattering labels. We've been called by God to bear witness to His timeless truth regardless of any pressure. When conventional wisdom is used as a cudgel against us we should remember the words of Psalm 119:99, "I have more understanding than all my teachers: for thy testimonies are my meditation."

Faith Food   Steve Stranghoener

Seeing the World Through Spiritual Lenses

Generating Profit

Profit has become a dirty word in our country today. Identity politics have pitted the so-called rich against the so-called poor in a class warfare that has caused some to question the very basis of our free-market, capitalist society. As a business guy, I've completely rejected this socialistic nonsense. To me, profit has remained simply the ability of a business to produce a surplus by providing goods or services while generating revenues greater than operating costs and expenses. Some have argued that too much profit is a bad thing. I've countered, that's why we have competition. If someone wanted to charge exorbitant prices, a competitor would come along to protect consumers and keep the competition in line. That's always been the beauty of a free and open marketplace.

Some have conceded this point in a temporal sense but have come back to condemn filthy profits from a spiritual perspective. They've pointed out that Jesus asked, "For what shall it profit a man, if he shall gain the whole world, and lose his own soul?" (Mark 8:36). There's no denying that Christ gave profit a negative connotation in this passage but it should be examined in a broader scriptural context. This was in keeping with the lesson of 1Timothy 6:10 that the **love** of money and not necessarily money alone is the root of all evil. God wasn't condemning profit in general but rather the misplaced priority of making money at the expense of seeking one's spiritual well-being.

When I've taken a deeper dive into the Bible, it has revealed that profit is not necessarily a bad thing, even in God's economy. Profitability has often been presented in a positive light in spiritual matters. For example, "Thus says the LORD, thy Redeemer, the Holy One of Israel; I am the LORD thy God which teaches thee to profit, which leads thee by the way that thou should go," (Isaiah 48:17).

Furthermore, "And if thy right eye offends thee, pluck it out, and cast it from thee: for it is profitable for thee that one of thy members should perish, and not that thy whole body should be cast into hell," (Matthew 5:29). "Even as I please all men in all things, not seeking mine own profit, but the profit of many, that they may be saved," (1 Corinthians 10:33). "Meditate upon these things; give thyself wholly to them; that thy profiting may appear to all," (1 Timothy 4:15). "For they verily for a few days chastened us after their own pleasure; but he for our profit, that we might be partakers of his holiness," (Hebrews 12:10).

God has shown that profit can be incredibly positive in spiritual matters when we keep our priorities in order; in line with God's plan. God profited mankind by creating an endless surplus for our benefit. Our Savior, Jesus Christ, possessed an endless supply of righteousness that He made available to us through His all-availing, atoning sacrifice on Calvary's cross. The whole world was justified by Jesus. We have been made rich indeed by the infinite profit God has bequeathed to us, His heirs, through Jesus Christ. He has also arranged to secure our profits and multiply them daily through His word. May we ever continue in His word, exulting in the profit won for us by Jesus and nurtured through His Holy Bible; our treasure trove of spiritual profitability.

Invisible Things

Like Christians since the 1st century, we confess the Nicene Creed and recite this opening line, some of us by memory, "I believe in one God, the Father Almighty, Maker of heaven and earth and of all things visible and invisible." The first part of that last phrase makes sense for, as the old adage goes, seeing is believing. The last part seems more troublesome. What exactly does this mean?

Has your mind ever wandered while speaking these words? Be honest, have you ever thought about the *Invisible Man*, just for a fleeting moment? Hollywood brought H. G. Wells' classic novel to life on the silver screen in 1933 with the inimitable Claude Rains as the lead. As iconic horror film monsters go, Rains' invisible madman ranked right up there with Boris Karloff's *Frankenstein*, Bela Lugosi's *Dracula* and Lon Chaney, Jr's. *Wolf Man*. Folks much younger than me would more likely recall Kevin Bacon's menacing portrayal in *Hollow Man*. In my opinion, while the 2000 remake outstripped the original in high-tech special effects, it didn't match the lasting dramatic impact of the 1933 version.

But such was the stuff of fantasy. Is that what we've alluded to when we've confessed the Creed, a mere flight of fancy? No, my friends, it's been something much deeper, a matter of faith. Jesus pointed this out in John 20:29, "Jesus saith unto him, Thomas, because thou hast seen me, thou hast believed: blessed are they that have not seen, and yet have believed." Christ's lesson for us was simply this: there is a spiritual realm that transcends the temporal world we see. The Lord has repeatedly reminded everyone, as He did in ancient Jerusalem when he appeared before Pilate, "My kingdom is not of this world," (John 18:36).

So again, what are these invisible things that we profess to believe in? Just to name a few, there are angels, both good and evil, Satan, hell and heaven. Most importantly, we believe in the Triune God: Father, Son and Holy Spirit. We can't see Jesus in a temporal sense but we connect with Him spiritually every time we read His word in the Holy Bible and commune at His table.

The invisible things of which our Lord and Savior spoke should be a great comfort to us. Listen to these words of assurance from 2 Corinthians 4:17-18 and be joyful, "For our light affliction, which is but for a moment, works for us a far more exceeding and eternal weight of glory; While we look not at the things which are seen, but at the things which are not seen: for the things which are seen are temporal; but the things which are not seen are eternal."

Although Claude Rains is long dead and gone, his portrayal of transparent Dr. Jack Griffin still delights and entertains a few through the magic of film but, like everything else in this old world, is destined to fade into obscurity and eventually total destruction when Jesus returns in judgment on the last day. However, the invisible things of God will continue on unto eternity, including our immortal souls that will eventually be fitted with transformed, glorified bodies in Christ's now invisible kingdom of grace. Imagine our amazement and joy when these invisible things are revealed and we dwell in God's heaven and see the Lord face-to-face.

Life's Love/Hate Relationship

Jesus warned us in John 12:25, "He that loves his life shall lose it; and he that hates his life in this world shall keep it unto life eternal." Did this mean that the Lord expected us to muddle through this life with dour faces, draped in sackcloth and ashes and hating our earthly existences? I dare say not because God also told us in Ecclesiastes 3:13, "And also that every man should eat and drink, and enjoy the good of all his labor, it is the gift of God." There must be more because I don't think God wanted to leave us confused while pondering whether we can enjoy the good things in life without risking hellfire.

We have all probably fretted over this at some point because of the danger involved. We're reminded of what happened to poor Demas. Paul lamented to Timothy in his second epistle 4:10, "Demas hath forsaken me, having loved this present world." It appeared that Demas, once a faithful follower, forfeited his eternal salvation in favor of enjoying his earthly life. Likewise, as recorded in Matthew 19:16-23, a rich young man spurned Jesus' life-giving advice because he was so enamored with worldly treasures.

But surely God didn't want us moping around like sad sacks, right? As Ed McMahon used to say to Johnny Carson, "You are correct, sir!" And as Leslie Nielson exclaimed in his famous parody, *Airplane*, "Don't call me Shirley!" Sorry, I couldn't resist. But in all seriousness, our earthly lives have been filled with God's blessings and the Bible has offered many exhortations for us to approach this life joyfully.

The inspired Apostle Paul clarified the matter in Romans 12:21-26. "For to me to live is Christ, and to die is gain. But if I live in the flesh, this is the fruit of my labor: yet what I shall choose I wot (know) not. For I am in a strait betwixt two, having a desire to depart, and to be with Christ; which is far better: Nevertheless, to abide in the flesh is more needful for you. And having this confidence, I know that I shall abide and continue with you all for your furtherance and joy of faith; That your rejoicing may be more abundant in Jesus Christ for me by my coming to you again."

Paul understood Christ's meaning in John 12:25 so clearly that he sincerely exclaimed he would rather die and be with the Lord in heaven than continue living in this world. He knew full well that nothing in this life, even the best it had to offer, could come close to comparing to the eternal glories of heaven. Yet, he remained committed to living his hard and sometimes tortuous life while rejoicing. That's because, even though he lacked wealth or sometimes even basic comforts and often faced persecution and the direst of circumstances, Paul knew he was blessed to do the work of building the Lord's kingdom.

Paul realized how much better off he was after his amazing transformation on the road to Damascus. Although stripped of his former power, luxuries and comforts, Paul was able to proclaim this glorious truth in Romans 8:18, "For I reckon that the sufferings of this present time are not worthy to be compared with the glory which shall be revealed in us." Let us rejoice and take heart too, living life to the fullest as servants while remaining eternally focused.

Money Isn't Everything

I've long been a firm believer in free market capitalism, hard work, Horatio Alger and the American Dream so I wouldn't want to bash success and wealth. However, God has offered warnings about affluence. For example, in Matthew 19:24 He advised, "It is easier for a camel to go through the eye of a needle, than for a rich man to enter into the kingdom of God." Did this mean we should all take a vow of poverty to ensure our salvation? No, God didn't say it was **impossible** for rich people to be saved but warned it could be very difficult with misplaced priorities.

Faith Food   Steve Stranghoener

God has dispensed His wealth to His people freely and accomplished many of His good purposes through the temporal gifts He has showered on us. However, God cautioned in 1 Timothy 6:10 against falling into the trap of making money into our god, "For the love of money is the root of all evil: which while some coveted after, they have erred from the faith, and pierced themselves through with many sorrows." Yeah, that was the rub. If we allowed the pursuit of temporal wealth to crowd out the true spiritual treasure of God-given faith, then we'd put ourselves in great peril.

Through Timothy, God encouraged us to strike a healthy balance. He wanted us to work hard as providers and count our blessings in thankfulness and joy but also cautioned us to remember from whence all blessing flowed. God's wise counsel to set our priorities in accordance with His word and will has benefitted countless people through the ages.

Perhaps more than any other nation, the United States has been synonymous with amassing great wealth as idealized in the American Dream. Yet, we've also been blessed to embrace God's wisdom. Sometimes we've captured the truth of Scripture in old adages familiar to everyone. For example, who hasn't heard the phrase you can't take it with you? This was surely rendered from Christ's parable in Luke 12. The foolish rich man got caught up in building bigger storehouses for his possessions without realizing that he would die that very night.

Faith Food — Steve Stranghoener

God has offered a lot of good counsel to help us keep our priorities in order with spiritual matters of faith and salvation far outweighing anything this material world has to offer. We've often taken God's good advice and boiled it down into our common-sense lexicon. Don't worry, be happy could be a footnote to Matthew 6:25-26, "Therefore I say unto you, Take no thought for your life, what ye shall eat, or what ye shall drink; nor yet for your body, what ye shall put on. Is not the life more than meat, and the body than raiment? Behold the fowls of the air: for they sow not, neither do they reap, nor gather into barns; yet your heavenly Father feeds them. Are ye not much better than they?"

If a cynic read our subject line he might argue, money isn't everything, it's the only thing. But how many people have gained incredible wealth in this world only to make shipwreck of their faith or find out in the end that money couldn't buy happiness? Some incredibly rich people have wound up miserable because they got their priorities out of whack. Some have even fallen so deep into despair that they've committed suicide.

God expressed the truth of this devotion's subject in Proverbs 16:8, "Better is a little with righteousness than great revenues without right." If we have amassed few possessions and little wealth but have been blessed with Christ's righteousness as a free gift, then we've attained greater riches than the wealthiest person in the world. Christ's righteousness has secured the treasures of heaven for us which far exceed anything imaginable in this sin-sick world. Thank you, Lord, for having provided for all of our needs in this life but even more so for having lavished us with eternal gifts beyond our wildest imaginations.

Evangelism

Faith Food Steve Stranghoener

The Greatest Speech Ever (Part 1)

What would you say if someone asked you to name the greatest speech of all time? To make the choice even more difficult, let's exclude the words of our Lord and Savior and limit this to sinful human beings. Whoa, that's a tough one! I don't know if I could break it down further than a top ten.

Hmmm, let's see, how about using Martin Luther's most famous speech? On April 18, 1521, Luther addressed the Imperial Diet of the Holy Roman Empire in the German city of Worms in response to charges by Pope Leo X and Emperor Charles V with his life hanging in the balance. They wanted him to recant his teachings which restored the gospel and launched the Protestant Reformation. After much trepidation and prayer, he courageously and valiantly refused to change his position unless convinced otherwise through Holy Scripture and closed with these famous words, "I stand here and can say no more. God help me. Amen."

I'd also have to include Washington's Farewell Address recounting his twenty years of God-blessed, faithful public service even though it was delivered in the form of a letter dated September 19th, 1796. While we're on the subject of American Presidents, how could I forget Lincoln's Gettysburg Address on November 19, 1863 or his Second Inaugural Address on March 4, 1865 wherein he famously referred to God's divine providence in guiding him in leading the nation through the Civil War?

We could take a quick trip across the Atlantic to hear the echo of Winston Churchill's Blood, Sweat & Tears speech before the House of Commons when he replaced Neville Chamberlain as Prime Minister of Great Britain on May 13, 1940. It is said he borrowed the "Blood, Toil, Tears and Sweat" phrase from Italian Revolutionary Giuseppe Garibaldi and Teddy Roosevelt. Still, he was quite stirring in facing down the threat of Hitler while the Nazis were ravaging Europe and bombing London relentlessly.

After the end of WWII, with the Nazis and other Axis Powers vanquished, a new threat arose in the form of communism. Again, Churchill confronted the menace head on by comparing communist oppression of liberty and freedom to a great Iron Curtain descending on Eastern Europe and Russia. He threw down the gauntlet against communism in Fulton, Missouri at Westminster College and it resounded around the globe. President John Kennedy took up this same fight and went to the heart of the Iron Curtain in decrying the Berlin Wall in his famous speech of June 26, 1963 wherein he proclaimed "Ich bin ein Berliner." Then Ronald Reagan put the final nail in the Soviet coffin on June 12, 1987 when he challenged Mikhail Gorbachev to "Tear down this wall!"

Okay, we have two more to go to round out the top ten. Martin Luther King's I Have a Dream speech of August 28, 1963 in Washington D. C. galvanized a nation by proclaiming that we should judge people by the content of their character rather than the color of their skin.

Finally, one of my personal favorites is General George S. Patton's inspiring speech to the 3rd Army before the bloody Invasion of Normandy in 1944. It was actually a series of three speeches even though it was immortalized as one in the 1970 movie, *Patton*, wherein George C. Scott raised the roof with the gigantic American flag emblazoned behind him.

What's that; I've left one out of the top ten? What about a little comic relief you ask? Okay, I'll give you that one. Who could ever forget John Belushi's impassioned, albeit offbeat, rousing address to Delta House as frat boy John "Bluto" Blutarsky when he posed the question "Was it over when the Germans bombed Pearl Harbor?"

Well, there you have it, the top ten plus one for good measure. Wait, I can almost hear some of you complaining. That's because I didn't really answer the question. Even with Martin Luther on the list, there still seems to be something lacking. Now that I think of it, there is one speech that tops them all and should be pegged as the winner; the greatest speech of all time. Stay tuned for the exciting conclusion.

The Greatest Speech Ever (Part 2)

Now, where were we? Oh yes, I attempted to answer the question of what was the greatest speech ever given by a mere human. I tried to weasel out of this tough assignment with a list of ten. There was Martin Luther, George Washington, Abraham Lincoln (twice), Winston Churchill (twice), John F. Kennedy, Ronald Reagan, Martin Luther King, Jr. and General George S. Patton. I tacked on fictional frat boy John "Bluto" Blutarsky's misguided rant for a little comic relief.

I gave this a lot of thought in the interim. At first, I was torn between two but then excluded Peter's sermon on Pentecost since he was so greatly aided by the Holy Spirit and no one recorded the full text. The winner also got an assist from the Holy Spirit but it wasn't quite as flashy with the tongues of fire and all and it was documented in great detail. Drum roll please. The greatest speech ever given was Stephen's Defense as recorded for us in the Book of Acts.

We don't have the space here but I would strongly encourage you to please read Acts 6 & 7 rather than depending solely on this brief commentary. As a backdrop, there was trouble in Jerusalem. The Greeks were miffed at the Hebrews because the former felt their widows were being neglected. The early church had a labor shortage and the Apostles had their hands full with their primary responsibility, the ministry of the word. Thus, they appointed elders to assist them with other duties.

One of the first such men was Stephen, a man full of faith and the Holy Ghost. Stephen was greatly blessed and, as we're told in Acts 6:8, "Stephen, full of faith and power, did great wonders and miracles among the people." Unfortunately, some of the Jews were falling back into old habits and took offense at Stephen and the gospel of Christ. They were still clinging to works righteousness and Old Testament ceremonial law. We're told that they could not fairly and honestly dispute the wisdom and truth of Christ that Stephen spoke so instead brought forth false witnesses to charge him with blasphemy. It was a set-up much like Christ faced with Pilate at the hands of the Jews. There was a young man in the mob named Saul who would later become the great Apostle to the Gentiles.

Saul and the Jews meant business. Stephen knew that he faced a horrible death if he persisted but he did not waver. He launched into the entire history of the Hebrews. Although his words may have seemed harsh, he only spoke the truth and, you know what they say; sometimes the truth can hurt. Stephen chronicled how God kept His promise of the Messiah even though Israel sinned repeatedly by backsliding over and over again into idolatry and unfaithfulness.

It was quite a recap. If you ever want a brief primer on Old Testament history and don't have time to read through Genesis and Exodus, just peruse Acts 7. It was like God's *CliffsNotes*; simply wonderful stuff. It begged the question though. Did Stephen recite the Hebrews' sorry record to rub their noses in it? No, it was nothing of the sort. He had a kind and loving purpose. Stephen loved them so much that he took drastic measures at great personal peril to awaken their consciences and draw them to repentance and salvation.

Unfortunately, they resisted the Holy Spirit. Stephen closed with this final attempt to reclaim them in verse 52, "Which of the prophets have not your fathers persecuted? And they have slain them which shewed before of the coming of the Just One (Jesus Christ); of whom ye have been now the betrayers and murderers." They were so stubborn and hard-hearted that they gnashed on him with their teeth. This was where the Holy Ghost stepped in and opened the heavens for Stephen to see a vision of the glory of God with Jesus standing at His right hand. Stephen proclaimed the vision but they covered their ears and, in a rage, grabbed him and took him outside the city to stone him to death.

Being pelted to death with dozens of stones was a horrible way to go but, by the power of the Holy Ghost, Stephen's courage and faith never flagged. As the vicious carnage engulfed him, Stephen followed Christ's example and cried out, "Lord Jesus, receive my spirit." His final words as recorded in Acts 7:60 also echoed his Savior, "And he kneeled down, and cried with a loud voice, 'Lord, lay not this sin to their charge.' And when he had said this, he fell asleep." Even as he was being unfairly charged, cruelly punished and stoned to death, Stephen gave the perfect witness. He asked forgiveness upon his murderers.

Did anyone take this to heart and repent. I'm not sure. However, we know what happened to Saul Paulus on the Damascus Road and everything the Lord accomplished through His servant thereafter. Yes, I've ranked Stephen's Defense as number one in my book. It was not just the content of his speech but the context and incredible circumstances under which it was delivered. It was a miraculous speech, literally. Praise God and the power of His Holy Spirit which equipped Stephen for such matchless devotion and faithful service.

Calling All ...

"Calling all cars, calling all cars, be on the lookout for ____," you fill in the blank. How many times have we heard this phrase repeated in old movies or television shows? Perhaps it was the Untouchables and Elliot Ness trying to track down Al Capone, Frank Nitti or some other bootlegger during the Roaring Twenties. Maybe it was former Texas Ranger Frank Hamer on the trail of Bonnie and Clyde. Or perhaps it could have been dogged G-man Melvin Purvis leading the manhunt for John Dillinger. In any case, the theme was always the same. When law enforcement was faced with a menacing threat to the public safety, maybe even public enemy number one, they called on everyone to pitch in and get the job done.

God kind of did the same thing didn't He? However, it didn't have anything to do with law enforcement. In fact, it was pretty much the exact opposite. Rather than handing down punishment to law breakers, God commuted our sentences. In doing so, God didn't turn a blind eye to the law. He provided a substitute who paid the terrible price required by His perfect justice so that we wouldn't have to suffer the punishment we deserved. God-incarnate came to earth in the person of His Son, Jesus Christ, and atoned for our sins, covered us in His perfect righteousness and secured our salvation and eternal life in heaven.

God's treatment of sinners was radically different from the old-time lawmen immortalized in popular American culture but His call to action was similarly ubiquitous. God memorialized His Great Commission in Matthew 28:18-20, "And Jesus came and spake unto them, saying, All power is given unto me in heaven and in earth. Go ye therefore, and teach all nations, baptizing them in the name of the Father, and of the Son, and of the Holy Ghost: Teaching them to observe all things whatsoever I have commanded you: and, lo, I am with you always, even unto the end of the world. Amen."

This calling was issued by our Lord and Savior, Jesus Christ, not to some of us or many of us but to **ALL** of us. This has led most of us to manufacture all sorts of reasons to avoid our God-given responsibility. *I just don't have the time. I'm not very good at speaking publicly. I'm too shy. Hey this can be dangerous. I might make someone mad. That's the pastor's job.*

Excuses, excuses; we've made a million of them but we've wasted our time because God didn't offer any exemptions when it came to evangelizing. This has been a problem since day one including Old Testament times. God has always called on His people to spread the good news of His plan of salvation. For example, He declared through His prophet in Micah 4:2, "And many nations shall come, and say, Come, and let us go up to the mountain of the LORD, and to the house of the God of Jacob; and he will teach us of his ways, and we will walk in his paths: for the law shall go forth of Zion, and the word of the LORD from Jerusalem." God prophesied that His gospel would be spread by word of mouth from Jerusalem to all nations, including us Gentiles (see also Isaiah 49:6 & 22, Isaiah 52:10, Hosea 2:23 and Malachi 1:11).

The risen Christ confirmed the fulfillment of these prophesies and explained the simple yet profound and essential reason for the Great Commission in Luke 24:46-48, "And said unto them, Thus it is written, and thus it behooved Christ to suffer, and to rise from the dead the third day: And that repentance and remission of sins should be preached in his name among all nations, beginning at Jerusalem. And ye are witnesses of these things."

We really need to change our mindsets when it comes to evangelizing. First, it's not a burden but an incredible privilege. God could spread the good news of salvation in any number of ways. His power is limitless. Yet, he calls us to be his humble servants in getting the word out ... wow!

It's important to note that God's Great Commission doesn't require us to be fancy, flowery or verbose. His message is simple; repentance and remission of sins. We're sinners in need of a Savior and God provides salvation to us in the person of Jesus Christ. Thus, we should repent of our sins and put our faith and trust in Jesus Christ. That's easy enough, right?

Rather than worrying or making up excuses, let's take up the task enthusiastically and joyfully and go forth under the banner of each one, reach one. If each of us shares the simple message of Christ's salvation with a friend, neighbor, co-worker, relative, acquaintance or even a total stranger, God will do the rest. God provides the message, God provides the power and God equips us, protects and guides us. All He asks us to do is get the word out. It's a very simple and easy task but one with such rich rewards to the hearer and messenger. Calling all Christians, calling all brothers and sisters in Christ ... let's spread the good news of our Savior, Jesus Christ.

Bad Company

When I was in college back in the early 70s, one of the more popular rock bands named themselves *Bad Company*. They really pushed this theme by calling their first album and one of their biggest early hits *Bad Company*. It sounded appropriate for their front man, Paul Rogers, who had a distinctive, husky voice that growled out the simple lyrics to their melodic tunes. I suspect the name was aimed at cultivating a bad boy image to attract young listeners but, by rock 'n roll standards, they seemed quite tame, especially when compared to the punk rockers that sprang up later in that same decade like Johnny Rotten and Sid Vicious. I guess the lesson was to not judge a book by its cover but rather to discern a tree's goodness or lack thereof by the fruit it bore.

Recalling *Bad Company* reminded me of an interesting conundrum we often face as Christians. Jesus instructed in His Sermon on the Mount not to judge other people on the basis of their sins since we're sinners too. However, He also taught us throughout His Bible in places like Galatians 1:8-9 to carefully examine people's doctrine and avoid false teachers. Likewise, Jesus preached that His kingdom is not of this world and cautioned us against getting too caught up in temporal matters. Yet, at the same time, He made a point of coming into this world, taking on human flesh, experiencing our infirmities and temptations and all without sinning (Hebrews 4:15) and purposefully mingled with sinners despite being roundly criticized by Jewish religious leaders.

Our Lord's commands have sometimes seemingly put us at odds with ourselves. He instructed us to remain separated from the world and simultaneously called for us to go and make disciples of all nations.

Martin Luther addressed the problem this way, "Be **in** the world but not **of** the world."

Paul handled this puzzlement with aplomb when he encountered the problem among the congregation at Corinth. He offered this stern advice in 1 Corinthians 5:9-13, "I wrote unto you in an epistle not to company with fornicators: Yet not altogether with the fornicators of this world, or with the covetous, or extortioners, or with idolaters; for then must ye needs go out of the world. But now I have written unto you not to keep company, if any man that is called a brother be a fornicator, or covetous, or an idolater, or a railer, or a drunkard, or an extortioner; with such an one no not to eat (fellowship). For what have I to do to judge them also that are without? Do not ye judge them that are within? But them that are without God judges. Therefore, put away from among yourselves that wicked person." To paraphrase in modern parlance, Paul warned that keeping bad company will lead to bad morals.

Was Paul then separatistic? Nothing could be further from the truth. Although he called a spade a spade and didn't shy away from condemning sin, no one did more to spread the gospel among sinful human beings like you and me. Paul was **in** the world but not **of** the world. He went to extraordinary lengths and suffered mightily to speak to power and preach the truth to sinners of every stripe; from those in prison to emperors and rulers. So, we should follow his example. We should avoid the rotten and vicious of the world that might corrupt our morals but we must rub elbows with bad company sometimes to spread the gospel while never compromising God's principles.

Be Careful What You Ask For

I thought about making the title of this devotion I Dare You but wanted to offer encouragement rather than sounding confrontational. Would we like to see God's kingdom expand and grow? What if it only involved one lost soul? I'm sure every Christian would offer a resounding yes to the first question.

As for the second, I hope we would have the same reaction as the shepherd mentioned in Luke 15:4-5 and pray accordingly, "What man of you, having an hundred sheep, if he loses one of them, doth not leave the ninety and nine in the wilderness, and go after that which is lost, until he finds it? And when he hath found it, he lays it on his shoulders, rejoicing."

That said, why did I offer a warning in the title? Many times, I've prayed for opportunities to witness and God has always answered affirmatively, invariably much sooner than I anticipated. I've been amazed at the response but really shouldn't have been surprised since God assured us in James 5:16 that, "The effectual fervent prayer of a righteous man availeth much." He went even further in Mark 11:24, "Therefore I say unto you, whatsoever things ye desire, when ye pray, believe that ye receive them, and ye shall have them." Praying for an opportunity to witness for Christ in particular has yielded marvelous results because such petitions have clearly conformed to God's will as stated in the Great Commission of Matthew 28:19-20.

Sometimes I've suffered from cold feet when the Old Adam in me has whispered, *Wasn't the Great Commission meant for evangelists?* Although technically true, in God's plan this work wasn't reserved for pastors, professional evangelists or a special church board or committee. We've all been called as evangelists, commissioned by the LORD to do the work of spreading the gospel and building His kingdom one soul at a time.

We need not have any fear because God has equipped us perfectly for this purpose. We're not required to have a special degree, theological training or certain type of personality. We're only asked to share the simple good news of what Jesus personally means to us with others as friends reaching out to friends. As simple messengers we're not tasked to succeed. God has promised that His Holy Spirit will do the heavy lifting of creating faith through His word.

So, will you give it a try? Will you heed God's call and just ... well ... GO ... and make disciples? Pray to our Heavenly Father and ask Him for an opportunity to share and I guarantee that you won't be disappointed. Somehow, some way, God will cause you to cross paths with a friend, relative, co-worker, acquaintance or complete stranger who needs to hear the gospel. God will equip you for the job in His perfect way.

The wonderful thing about evangelizing is not just in knowing the blessings being imparted to the object of our attention. It also offers a great gift to us. Every time God provides us with such a privilege, He fills us with incredible satisfaction and joy in realizing that He is willing to use us, His broken tools, for the most important task of making disciples.

Fear Factor

While fishing recently, I couldn't help but recall that old TV show called the *Fear Factor* as I baited my hook with a squirming night crawler that oozed liquid goo. The show's contestants competed for big money by taking dares that played upon some of our worst fears: heights, claustrophobia, drowning, fire and dangerously high speeds. Some of the most disgusting challenges featured slimy, reeking creatures that the guys and gals had to consume in whole or part. For example, one competition required the guests to chow down on pig innards and another had live worms on the menu. It was sometimes so vile that people couldn't keep their stomachs down. Now that was what I'd call entertainment, NOT!

As bad as they were, *Fear Factor* challenges paled in comparison to today's real-world problems: war, famine, terrorism, deadly diseases, natural disasters and violent crime. We've all been touched by these horrible maladies or known someone who has fallen prey to them. When faced with the threat of fascism and the reality of world war, President Franklin Roosevelt quelled the fears of Americans by assuring them that "There is nothing to fear but fear itself." He encouraged everyone to meet the threats America faced head on rather than succumbing to fear.

Christ had to address the fear factor with His followers two thousand years ago. He warned of the persecution they'd face for His name's sake but assured them that He would always be with them in spirit. The persecution of Christians has continued unto the present, even in the United States. We've all heard of the stories of persecution being ratcheted up in our country. Bakers and photographers and such have been run out of business for standing on God's word. Even pastors have faced legal threats for speaking the truth of God's word on controversial topics like gay marriage.

Most of us haven't faced life's worst ordeals personally or even silly but disgusting dares like the ones dreamed up on the *Fear Factor*. The vast majority of us haven't even faced harsh persecution for our faith. However, every Christian has dealt with some level of fear. I think we've all felt some trepidation in answering God's call to carry out His Great Commission.

Sometimes I've found it tough to speak up and share the truth of the gospel. *What will people think? They might laugh at me. They might criticize me, or worse. Can't I just practice my faith in my own personal way within the safe confines of my home and church? Why should I rock the boat? Why put myself in harm's way?* When such fears have gripped me with this bad train of thought, God has offered me encouragement through His word of promise. For example, Jesus offered this eternal assurance to us in Luke 12:8, "Also I say unto you, whosoever shall confess me before men, him shall the Son of man also confess before the angels of God."

Christ never wanted us to be fraidy cats hiding in the shadows. He told us to get out there and spread the good news and put it all into perspective this way in Luke 12:4-5. "And I say unto you my friends, be not afraid of them that kill the body, and after that have no more that they can do. But I will forewarn you whom ye shall fear: Fear him, which after he hath killed hath power to cast into hell; yea, I say unto you, Fear him." Thusly, Jesus encouraged us not to fear Satan and his minions who can only harm us temporally. He said the one we should really fear is God who controls our eternal destiny.

It should be noted that, in the aforementioned passage, God referred to a different type of fear; we could call it reverence instead. As for that other type of temporal fear, God said, in effect, we have nothing to fear but fear itself. Here's how he stated this in 1 Timothy1:7-8. "For God hath not given us the spirit of fear; but of power, and of love, and of a sound mind. Be not thou therefore ashamed of the testimony of our

Lord, nor of me his prisoner: but be thou partaker of the afflictions of the gospel according to the power of God."

We have nothing to fear because God has promised He has our backs. For example, He offered this assurance in Romans 10:13, "For whosoever shall call upon the name of the Lord shall be saved." By the power of God in Christ, we can face all of our fears, even the fear of temporal death. Christ has already conquered death for us and removed its sting. Death hath no more dominion over us.

In the Spotlight

Do you like to be in the spotlight, the center of attention? When a new store opens somewhere, they sometimes place spotlights in the parking lot to light up the night sky and draw new customers from miles around. If you've ever attended a Broadway play or even enjoyed a production at the local repertory theater, you've probably seen how the stage lights can be used to focus the audience on the talents of a single cast member. Sometimes the light can be harsh, like when the beam from atop a prison wall is used to track down an escaping convict. Being somewhat of a ham, I must admit to enjoying center stage now and then but, as I've matured, I've developed more of an affinity for the peaceableness of being inconspicuous, off in the wings.

God has a lot to say about light. From His perspective, it can seem like we should seek the limelight continually. In 1 John 1:7 we're told to walk in the light and in 1 John 2:10 we're told to abide in the light if we love our brother. In 1 John 1:5 we're told expressly that God is light.

Hiding in the shadows is frowned upon with darkness so often being equated with evil, "But if thine eye be evil, thy whole body shall be full of darkness," (Matthew 6:23). Ephesians 5:11 adds, "And have no fellowship with the unfruitful works of darkness, but rather reprove them." Ephesians 6:12 echoes this theme, "For we wrestle not against flesh and blood, but against principalities, against powers, against the rulers of the darkness of this world, against spiritual wickedness in high places." In Matthew 4:16, God tells people not to sit in darkness but step out into His marvelous light.

Still, it strikes Christians as unseemly to clamor for self-aggrandizement since we're supposed to go about the Lord's business in meekness and humility. "Humble yourselves therefore under the mighty hand of God, that He may exalt you in due time," (1 Peter 5:6). God cast the sanctimonious Pharisee in a bad light when he made a show with his public prayers only to be abased while the contrite, humble sinner who prayed meekly was justified (Luke 18:14).

To sort out this dilemma, let's shed some light, pun intended, on the subject by turning to Matthew 5:16. "Let your light so shine before men, that they may see your good works, and glorify your Father which is in heaven." God wants us to reside in the light but a different kind of light. He doesn't want us turning the spotlight on ourselves. As sinners, we can't point the way by pointing to ourselves. No matter how good an example we try to set, the light will always expose our dark underbelly; our corrupt, sinful human natures.

Rather God wants us to be mirrors reflecting His marvelous light so that others can see Him in and through us. As James so aptly points out, our faith bears the fruit of good works and not vice versa. By letting God's light shine through us, we are truly doing good work; God's work of sharing the gospel and pointing others to our Savior.

So, let us seek the spotlight to illuminate what God means to us and what He has done for us and everyone through the atoning sacrifice of Jesus Christ. Good works are those that are conducted out of love to benefit others and bring glory not to ourselves but to the One who deserves all the credit for our forgiveness and salvation: Jesus.

Literally Wrong

God warns us in Matthew 7:15 to beware of false prophets, especially those that come in sheep's clothing. This means that we sometimes have to be warier of people posing as Christians than atheists and secular humanists who attack brazenly. False teachers often mimic Satan, the Father of Lies, who even tried to tempt Jesus Christ in the wilderness by twisting the word of God.

Here's an example of such subterfuge that someone posted on, of all places, a website for Confessional Lutherans. They claimed that Christians shouldn't evangelize today because Christ only issued His Great Commission in Matthew 28:18-20 to the Apostles. This has long been a favorite tactic of sophisticated false teachers. They have often cherry picked a single passage of Scripture and given it a narrow, literal interpretation where a broader or more figurative meaning was intended.

Under God's inspiration as recorded in 2 Peter 1:20, the Apostle warned against private interpretation and thus set forth the Godly principle that, when the Bible's meaning is in question, we should always let Scripture interpret Scripture while relying on the full counsel of God. With that in mind, I easily deconstructed the false doctrine noted above by taking a deeper dive into the Holy Bible. For example, Christ promised in Acts 1:8 that, "Ye shall receive power, after that the Holy Ghost is come upon you: and ye shall be witnesses unto me both in Jerusalem, and in all Judaea, and in Samaria, and unto the uttermost part of the earth." As we know from Scripture, not only the Apostles but all believers in attendance received the Holy Ghost on Pentecost.

I found many other examples. Jesus addressed not just the Apostles but multitudes during His Sermon on the Mount when he stated in Matthew 5:16, "Let your light so shine before men, that they may see your good works, and glorify your Father which is in heaven."

Under God's inspiration, Peter instructed all followers thusly in 1 Peter 3:15, "But sanctify the Lord God in your hearts: and be ready always to give an answer to every man that asks you a reason of the hope that is in you with meekness and fear."

In Philippians 2:14-16, Paul offered these instructions to all the believers in Philippi, "Do all things without murmurings and disputing: That ye may be blameless and harmless, the sons of God, without rebuke, in the midst of a crooked and perverse nation, among whom ye shine as lights in the world; Holding forth the word of life; that I may rejoice in the day of Christ, that I have not run in vain, neither labored in vain." He offered similar instructions to all the believers in Colossae in Colossians 4:5-6, "Walk in wisdom toward them that are without, redeeming the time. Let your speech be always with grace, seasoned with salt, that ye may know how ye ought to answer every man."

I could go on but instead, for the sake of time, one passage from 1 Peter 2:9 put the final nail in this coffin of deceit, "But ye are a chosen generation, a royal priesthood, an holy nation, a peculiar people; that ye should shew forth the praises of him who hath called you out of darkness into his marvelous light." Everyone has been called by God into the priesthood of all believers to spread the good news of salvation in Jesus Christ.

I pray that God will continue to equip, guide, bless and protect us as His witnesses, His evangelists to this lost and fallen world so that many blood-bought, immortal souls might be saved by the power of His Holy Spirit working through the word.

Opportunity Knocks

The earlier devotion titled *Be Careful What You Ask For* offered a somewhat tongue-in-cheek warning against asking God for opportunities to witness. My cheeky humor aside, I offered this caution not as a joke but rather a serious reminder to be prepared because God will always respond to such appeals and, in some cases, with stunning swiftness. We shouldn't be surprised because Jesus told us clearly in Matthew 21:22, "And all things, whatsoever ye shall ask in prayer, believing, ye shall receive." Believing is a key word, meaning that we should trust in God and conform to His will in our prayers.

In Matthew 6, Jesus gave us specific instructions on how to pray including the Lord's Prayer. Therein He said in verse 10, "Thy kingdom come, Thy will be done in earth, as it is in heaven." The Lord went into even greater detail at the end of Matthew 28 with His Great Commission for us to go and make disciples of all nations. Is it any wonder then when God has responded affirmatively to our prayers for opportunities to witness? I've come to expect it but still am delighted and amazed at God's faithfulness in dispensing such blessings.

Recently, I prayed for an opportunity to witness as I embarked on my daily walk. I had only strolled about a quarter mile from my house when a car pulled up alongside me and the passenger, an older man, opened the window and asked, "Are you the author?" This took me aback because I've pursued my craft in virtual anonymity. I responded, "I am **an** author." Apparently, he knew me well enough to say, "Don't you write Christian mysteries?" I nodded somewhat mystified until the man said his friend, the driver who I didn't recognize, claimed to be an old neighbor from where we used to live.

He asked where he could buy my books and I steered him to Amazon. Unfortunately, he had no computer with access to our digital world. Consequently, I offered to sell him one from my personal stock if he cared to stop by my house sometime. He then informed me that he would be returning home to Arizona in a couple of days. Finally, I said he could stop by in about forty-five minutes after I finished my walk, if he liked.

As I continued on my way, I pondered because I knew this was no happenstance encounter but had been guided by God. Plodding along, I wondered if God had answered my prayers to help me spread His word through my calling as a writer. It seemed an odd way to boost my marketing efforts; to send an old man from Arizona without access to a computer.

By God's providence, my new friend Donn met me when I returned home from my walk. I let him in and we had a conversation for about forty minutes. He turned out to be a brother in Christ and we enjoyed building each other up in the faith but I couldn't see God's purpose in our chance meeting.

Then it happened. He told me his friend and my former neighbor had a problem. He had lost his mother recently and blamed God. Donn worried about his friend's faith being in jeopardy but confessed that he had been unable to counsel or help him. Ah ha, the light bulb came on! I gave Donn an extra copy of my book, *Straight Talk About Christian Misconceptions* for his forlorn friend and highlighted the chapter that addressed how the bad things in our lives are not punishments from God since God sent His Beloved Son Jesus to pay the price for our sins.

All of a sudden, my lack of temporal success as an author didn't seem to matter so much. I felt blessed to be used in this special way to help one suffering soul be comforted by the gospel. Now, whenever I've prayed thusly, I've learned to listen for that wonderful sound of God's opportunity knocking.

Love

Why Am I Here?

Debating the theory of evolution versus God's creation account in Genesis has led to some interesting questions. Several times, I've been confronted by this one: *Why am I here?* This made sense when coming from an evolutionist since they've been taught that the earth, universe and mankind all originated randomly by mere chance and thus one's purpose in life was subject only to self-determination. Pondering this question also made sense for Christians since, as we believe and teach, everything including us came about intentionally by God's power and will. We could argue until the cows come home about our origins and perhaps even win such a debate on the basis of logic, science and history but it would be pointless if we couldn't explain why God put us here.

Whether talking to a skeptic or believer, I've often pointed to the Great Commission in Matthew 28:19-20 since it clearly outlines our main, God-given purpose in life to spread the gospel and make disciples. While this satisfied Christians, it rang hollow with non-believers. Human reason could not grasp why God would create people simply to witness to other people. What's in it for God they've asked? And why did He create people in the first place since, being God, He knew they would fall away into sin?

These were good questions that deserved an honest answer. What motivated God in the first place? The only way to provide a valid reply was to first turn to God's word in the Holy Bible. Oddly enough, I found the answer by looking forward rather than backward. In Revelation 4, God provided an amazing view of heaven and the church triumphant; offering endless praise to the Lord. Verse 11 offered an incredible insight into the mind and motivation of God. "Thou art worthy, O Lord, to receive glory and honor and power: for thou hast created all things, and **for thy pleasure they are and were created**."

That was the quid pro quo that had eluded me! God created us and all things for His pleasure. While skeptics may not have accepted this truth, they could certainly understand God's motivation. We, His creatures, brought pleasure to God as a child does to his father but in a much higher way.

In addition to providing a clear, logical answer to a compelling question, this approach also provided a path to present the gospel. God created us because it pleased Him despite knowing that we would fall away into sin and separate ourselves from Him for all eternity. Because it pleased Him and He loved us dearly, God came up with a plan before the foundation of the world to reconcile us to Him through Christ to suit His great pleasure for all eternity.

God stated His intentions plainly in Hebrews 12:2, "Looking unto Jesus the author and finisher of our faith; who for the **joy** that was set before him endured the cross, despising the shame, and is set down at the right hand of the throne of God." God revealed the same cosmic quid pro quo, His motivation for saving us. God in the person of Jesus Christ endured the cross and wrath of the Father in the hell that we deserved in exchange for infinite joy; the joy of being reconciled to us, His cherished children who were made in His own image.

Friend or Foe?

Like a military sentry at a dark, lonely outpost, some people have had a tough time distinguishing friends from foes. Christians have suffered from this problem too, even in spiritual matters. That's why Christ warned us to beware of false prophets who come as wolves in sheep's clothing (Matthew 7:15). Many Christians have suffered dire consequences and even jeopardized their faith by failing to heed this warning. Does this mean we should exhibit the same friend-or-foe wariness in temporal matters?

We've all faced adversaries where doctrinal disputes had no part in the matter. As a case in point, have you ever been involved in a family feud that has lasted for weeks, months or even generations. The Hatfield's and McCoys embodied hillbilly hatred at its worst. However, such animosity hasn't been limited to mountain folk. William Shakespeare captured this truth in his timeless classic, *Romeo & Juliet*. The Capulets and Montagues were just as consumed by stubborn, mean-spirited and foolish bitterness and it didn't end well.

Whether fictional or real, the odd thing about such blood feuds was that the reasons often got lost over time. Maybe it started out with an offense or insult and festered and grew from there. There was an episode of the *Andy Griffith Show* that brought this to light in a humorous way. It's the one where young Hannah and Josh woke Andy in the middle of the night desiring to be married. Unfortunately, she was a Wakefield and he was a Carter and their families were involved in a long running feud.

Andy tried to solve the dilemma by seeking to uncover the root cause of the dispute. It turned out that no one on either side could recall. They were fighting just because, well, they'd always been fighting as far back as anyone could remember. Andy employed Solomon-like wisdom to force the feuding fathers to ponder whether it was worth losing their son or daughter to keep the foolish feud roiling.

The Bible chronicled a feud that has persisted unto today. In a time of doubt and weakness, Abraham and Sarah took matters into their own hands in trying to produce the child God had promised to them. Sarah enlisted Hagar, her much younger Egyptian maid, to take her place. Ishmael, the child Hagar conceived with Abraham, became the father of many nations, the Arab peoples, but was not the child of promise. The covenant was fulfilled by God when Abraham and Sarah conceived Isaac.

God warned that, as a result of Abraham's and Sarah's unfaithfulness, there would be an ongoing conflict involving the brothers and their descendants. In Genesis 16:12 God said, "And he (Ishmael) will be a wild man (stubborn like a wild donkey); his hand will be against every man, and every man's hand against him; and he shall dwell in the presence of all his brethren."

We've seen how things have turned out. The Arabs and Islam which they spawned haven't been able to get along with their neighbors or themselves. It has been a perpetual state of conflict with no end in sight despite the outside world's interminable peace efforts. The repeated attempts to promote peace between the Palestinians and Israelis have been futile. They've ignored the only source of true peace: faith in the Savior of the world, Jesus Christ.

Skeptics might argue that Christ was more intractable than the Hatfields and McCoys or even the Palestinians and Israelis. I would concede this to be true in a sense. Jesus declared in Matthew 12:30, "He that is not with me is against me." This certainly didn't leave any room for debate or compromise. The Lord said in effect, my way or the highway. But Jesus said this in reference to spiritual matters and God's one and only plan for our salvation, not temporal disputes.

Jesus had a completely different approach to dealing with our fellow human beings, friend and foe alike. In Luke 6:29 Christ said, "And unto him that smites thee on the one cheek offer also the other." And listen to what he advised in Matthew 5:44, "But I say unto you, Love your enemies, bless them that curse you, do good to them that hate you, and pray for them which despitefully use you, and persecute you."

These seemingly contradictory approaches; one a hard, inflexible line and the other an olive branch, were both offered out of undeserved, unconditional love. In the first instance, Jesus issued a stern warning concerning matters of faith and doctrine. Throughout Scripture He warned about false teachings because they could rob us of our God-given faith. False doctrine was the brain child of our worst enemy, Satan, whom God warned us to avoid like a roaring lion that was seeking to devour us.

Christ set the perfect example in resolving this friend or foe conundrum. Jesus gave no quarter to our worst foe, Satan. But when it came to us, He took the opposite approach. We were God's enemies by nature after the fall into sin. There was nothing good in us; we were desperately wicked through and through (Jeremiah 17:9). Yet, God did not punish and banish us as we deserved. Instead He poured out the most extravagant, unconditional love possible. Jesus took our place, bore our punishment on the cross and, in exchange, imputed His perfect righteousness to us in order to reconcile sinful man to God (Romans 5:8).

So, here's the bottom line in hillbilly parlance. If someone comes to you preaching false doctrine, treat them like a revenuer sneaking up on your still. But in all other matters, treat our fellow sinners, even our worst enemies, like long, lost cousins and fix up a batch of possum stew, uh, that is, feed them some sweet, sweet gospel.

Can't Buy Me Love

While they were adored by teens when the movie and album *A Hard Day's Night* were released in 1964, the Beatles were already in their early twenties. Still, they were very young to be offering advice about love. However, the fledgling Beatles actually issued a very profound morsel of philosophy in the last song on side one. Paul McCartney wrote, "I don't care too much for money, money can't buy me love."

On the surface, it was an uncomplicated assertion that was about as straightforward as the simple, effortless melody that accompanied their catchy tune. Nevertheless, the Fab Four hitched a ride on a rocket ship to fame and fortune that showered all of them with fabulous wealth, unbridled celebrity and unprecedented influence as cultural icons. Four working class lads from Liverpool made it to the big time.

Despite their youthful inexperience, they had the wisdom to realize that there were some things in this world much more valuable than anything money could buy. For example, have you ever wondered how much you would be willing to pay to restore your health if you were incapacitated by an incurable, crippling disease? Have you thought about what treasure you might relinquish to restore the life of a lost loved one?

Cynics have said baloney, it would be a lot easier to find love if you were loaded with cash like the Beatles. If the truth be told, someone could buy plenty of friends and even companionship if they were wealthy enough like that old billionaire who married blond bombshell Anna Nicole Smith. Did she love him or was it his money? I think the Beatles were spot on that all the money in the world couldn't buy true love when eighty-nine-year-old J. Howard Marshall married twenty-six-year-old Anna in 1993. He died after fourteen months of marriage.

How did the Bible define love and was there a monetary value attached? In John 15:13, God put things as simply and straightforward as Paul McCartney in *Can't Buy Me Love*: "Greater love hath no man than this, that a man lay down his life for his friends." Have you ever cared enough for someone to sacrifice everything, even your own life to save them? What would you expect in return?

Perhaps we would suffer death for a spouse, child or other loved one but would we lay down our lives for our worst enemies? That's what Christ did for us. Jesus demonstrated a unique kind of love that could not be procured at any price. So many people have been frustrated in trying to find such love by looking in all the wrong places. God summed up where our pursuit of true love should always start in three little words in 1 John 4:8, "God is love."

Many have tried but no one has ever earned God's love. That's because, as the song implied, no amount of money, good works, devotion or even prayers could procure God's love. That's because God's love, undeserved and unconditional, has always existed and has been offered to all of us completely for free. This may sound too good to be true but God affirmed as much in 1 John 4:10, "Herein is love, not that we loved God, but that he loved us, and sent his Son to be the propitiation for our sins".

Jesus died for us on that bloody cross while we were yet sinners, his sworn enemies. He only asked one thing in return and gave us the power to do it: "And thou shalt love the Lord thy God with all thy heart, and with all thy soul, and with all thy mind, and with all thy strength: this is the first commandment," (Mark 12:30). We all deserved God's wrath and punishment as sinful human beings with hearts prone to wickedness. But instead, God showered us with His love. That's why we've been able to follow God's first commandment and declare our love for Him; because He first loved us.

Endless Love

The 1981 Franco Zeffirelli film, *Endless Love*, was a modest box office hit at best but the soundtrack's signature song by Lionel Richie and Diana Ross rose all the way to number two on the pop charts that year behind Kim Carnes' *Betty Davis Eyes*. It became so popular that eventually Billboard Magazine named this tune as the greatest song duet of all time. This wasn't really surprising considering the combined talents of the two megastars and the enduring appeal of the song's theme.

Unfortunately, the concept of endless love has sometimes seemed like nothing more than a pipe dream under the harsh light of reality. After watching a mushy chick flick, my wife recently declared, "It's too bad those initial feelings of love can't last forever." I felt a little deflated and wondered what had happened to the unbridled, giddy, head-over-heels emotions that once gripped us. Sure, we still loved one another but no longer went gaga over each other like lovesick teens. What happened; did our hormones give out or was it the curse of the Righteous Brothers as captured in their biggest hit, *You've Lost that Loving Feeling*?

We should have seen this coming based on the wedding day warning we received from our prescient pastor. He started on a high note with 1 Corinthians 13, the love chapter, with key passages like verse 14, "Love is patient, love is kind. It does not envy, it does not boast, it is not proud." Then he reminded us about the challenges to come. He rightly cautioned that our initial feelings of endless love would be buried under an avalanche of daily challenges such as financial burdens, stress, disagreements and all manner of hardships. He said that's why marriage required a commitment before God and many witnesses to honor the bond of matrimony in good times, bad times, sickness and health.

Thankfully, the message didn't end on a sour note. He proclaimed the good news that there was a source of endless love but encouraged us to look outside of ourselves. He declared that a good marriage required three parties: the bride, groom and Jesus Christ. He shared how our Savior made endless love possible because "God is love," (1 John 4:16); the very source and essence of love.

Our pastor wisely stated that looking for endless love or even permanent and consistent love from any human being, even a spouse, was a fool's errand. The harsh truth was that even the best we had to offer each other as human beings would come to an end; until death do us part. But he joyfully proclaimed that God's love was perfect, unconditional and forever, stretching out from before the world began and beyond Judgment Day unto all eternity.

Some people have foolishly complained that heaven will be boring. They've wondered how anything could last forever. But they've missed a crucial point. Once in heaven, we will no longer be burdened by the constraints of time but instead, like our Lord and Savior, will exist forever with no death awaiting. We will live in His presence and our feelings for Him will be infinitely more thrilling and intense than anything we've felt in this life; from our first crush to the joy of our wedding day. However, we don't have to wait. While yet in this temporal world, through Jesus Christ and His word of promise, we can experience the endless love that will enthrall us unto life everlasting in the new heavens and earth where we will dwell face-to-face with our Lord, God and Savior.

Summer of Love

Were you around in 1967? It was labeled as the Summer of Love due to a fledgling movement that centered in the Haight-Ashbury district of San Francisco. The 1950's beatniks morphed into the 1960's hippies and touched off a social revolution founded on drugs, sex and rock 'n roll. Adherents labeled the unbridled sexual immorality they promoted as free love. Mind altering drugs fueled the whole thing as pied pipers like Timothy Leary encouraged young people to "Turn on, tune in and drop out."

Far from a loving message, the so-called flower children aimed to end conformity and break down societal institutions like capitalism, church, marriage and the family. Music played a big part in popularizing this movement. Jimi Hendrix's song, *If 6 was 9*, was illustrative of the times. Although it gained fame later in 1969 as part of the sound track for the movie *Easy Rider*, it was actually released in 1967. While I enjoyed Jimi Hendrix's music and marveled at his immense talent and creativity, the lyrics to *If 6 was 9* reflected a mixed-up view of the world.

Completely self-centered, the singer proclaimed that he didn't care if the mountains fell into the sea or all the hippies cut off all their hair since, as he put it, "Dig, 'cos I got my own world to live through, and I ain't gonna copy you." He summed up his philosophy of life thusly by expressing disdain for white collared conservatives who he felt put him down by wagging their plastic fingers at him; "But I'm gonna wave my freak flag high, high; wave on, wave on."

Many summers have passed since 1967 and many people have come to adopt the twisted concept of love as espoused by the flower children. In fact, the radical nonconformity of the late 1960s has largely come to represent the norm. As a society, we've been transformed to where I believe it's imperative that we recalibrate the meaning of love by looking to God; the source and very essence of love. Unlike the hippies of Haight-Ashbury, God has always been a conformist when it comes to love as clearly revealed in 1 John 2:3-5, "And hereby we do know that we know him, if we keep his commandments. He that saith, I know him, and keeps not his commandments, is a liar, and the truth is not in him. But whoso keeps his word, in him verily is the love of God perfected: hereby know we that we are in him."

God's love is completely different from the love this world has to offer. Wouldn't it be wonderful to experience a new, totally transformative summer, fall, winter and spring of love based on God's word of truth as reflected in 1 John 4:9-10? "In this was manifested the love of God toward us, because that God sent his only begotten Son into the world, that we might live through him. Herein is love, not that we loved God, but that he loved us, and sent his Son to be the propitiation for our sins."

Are You a Hater?

Today, if someone doesn't go along with conventional wisdom, even if it reflects a false narrative, they are often tagged by unflattering labels. If you don't buy into the nonsensical, false religion of evolution, you're a flat-earther. If you think that climate change is an ideology that depends on fabricated data and intellectual coercion rather than objective scientific methodology, you're a climate denier. If you adhere to the biblical teaching that marriage was instituted by God for the exclusive union of one man and one woman, you're a homophobe. In all cases, you're likely to be slapped with the one-size-fits-all pejorative moniker of hater. That's what it has come down to in our woefully divided society. If you disagree with the liberal elite, you are swiftly banished as a hater. There's no discussion or debate. The sentence is swift and final: hater.

I don't really mind. I'm proud to display the label hater. No, I don't hate gay people, evolutionists or enviromaniacs. They are people just like me and we're all miserable sinners regardless of where we reside on the political spectrum. While I may not like their policies and feel the right and obligation to speak out against them, I cannot judge them as fellow human beings.

Here's how Jesus put this during His Sermon on the Mount in Matthew 7:1-3, "Judge not, that ye be not judged. For with what judgment ye judge, ye shall be judged: and with what measure ye mete, it shall be measured to you again. And why beholdest thou the mote (speck) that is in thy brother's eye, but considerest not the beam that is in thine own eye?" I'm in no position to judge anyone on the basis of their sins since I'm a sinner too. I can evaluate the fruit of the tree, someone's behavior, but I can't judge others as though I'm above the law and without my own transgressions.

No, I'm not advocating hatred toward anyone. That would be giving into my sinful nature and violating the Fifth Commandment. What I willingly and faithfully hate is evil, including my own sin. I'm only following God's example because He is a hater in that regard. While we are sinners, He is perfect and holy (Psalm 18:30) and cannot tolerate sin in any measure. God has terrible wrath toward sin. At the same time, God is love (1 John 4:8), the very source and essence of love.

Thankfully for us, God satisfied His perfect justice and poured out His wrath over our sins completely upon Himself when He sacrificed His beloved, perfect Son, Jesus Christ. "For he hath made him to be sin for us, who knew no sin; that we might be made the righteousness of God in him," (2 Corinthians 5:21). This was truly the love of God made manifest that He redeemed us at such a terrible price in spite of our sins and the just punishment we so richly deserved.

So, don't be afraid of being called a hater for gladly conforming to God's word and will. By doing so, you're showing true Christian love. God commands as much in Psalm 97:10, "Ye that love the LORD, hate evil: he preserves the souls of his saints; he delivers them out of the hand of the wicked." If we love the sinner but hate the sin, God will preserve us from any persecution we may face, even being called haters.

Prized Possessions

What is your most prized possession; your house or car? Maybe a precious family heirloom comes to mind. Whatever it is, I'll bet it's something of great worth; monetarily or perhaps just in sentimental value. Did you receive it as a gift or work long hours and save for many years to afford it?

Turning to the other end of the spectrum, is there something despicable or disgusting you'd like to shed if you could? Do you own a rusty rattle trap of a car that you can't wait to trade in on a new one? How about that musty, old couch in the basement that's crawling with dust mites? Could it be that lazy neighbor next door that has let his house run down to the point where it's hurting the value of your home? Worse yet, is there a bully that threatens you constantly and makes you a nervous wreck?

Where does God stand on this subject? Out of His entire creation, what do you think is the most prized possession of the Almighty God of the universe? Can you believe it's you and me? This sounds pretty crazy considering God's treasure chest includes everything;

the sun, moon, stars, planets galaxies and all that is therein. Nevertheless, it's true. God makes it perfectly clear in the Holy Bible over and over. Think about it. God values us above anything and everything in His vast, infinite universe, including His holy angels.

Scripture says it, so we must accept it but still it begs the question. Why does God place such an incredible value on us? It's simply mind-boggling, especially when the Bible also clearly teaches that we have no worth. In fact, we're less than worthless. As poor, miserable sinners and rebellious enemies who hate God by nature, how can He value us at all? Why doesn't He dispose of us like that smelly couch in the basement or give us the bum's rush like we would do to our nasty neighbor or mortal enemies if we could? It's summed up in one little Hebrew word, segulah.

Segulah is a prized possession that isn't loved because of its value but rather has great value because it is loved. Does God love us because of our value to Him? First of all, we can't take any credit for our relationship with God because He chose us as His people rather than vice versa (Deuteronomy 7:6-8, John 15:16). Furthermore, we can't claim He chose us because of any intrinsic value or merit in us. The opposite is true as revealed in Romans 5:8, "But God commendeth his love toward us, in that, while we were yet sinners, Christ died for us."

Despite knowing this, we still fall over the same stumbling block that tripped up so many in ancient Israel by thinking much more highly of ourselves than we should. God doesn't choose us to be His witnesses because of something good in us but instead places great value on us in spite of our sinfulness. God captures the meaning of segulah so clearly and wonderfully for us in Malachi 3:17, "And they shall be mine, saith the LORD of hosts, in that day when I make up my jewels; and I will spare them, as a man spares his own son that serves him." God makes us His jewels or His cherished possessions out of love.

In the Greek language of the New Testament, the word for peculiar is used to describe us as unusual, prized possession or treasures. It's expressed this way in 1 Peter 2:9, "But ye are a chosen generation, a royal priesthood, a holy nation, a **peculiar people**; that ye should shew forth the praises of him who hath called you out of darkness into his marvelous light." We're the same as the ancient Israelites in that God chooses us and not the other way around. We're peculiar or valued as His chosen, adopted children because of His love for us.

We were lost in total darkness before God called us to be His prized possessions. We deserved to be cast into hell for all eternity under the just wrath of God but out of grace and mercy He didn't punish us as we deserved. Instead God gave us the incredible, priceless gift of eternal salvation that we most assuredly did not merit.

If we ever doubt the good news of God's salvation, the depth of His love or value He has placed on us, we should remember this. The heavens and earth, which were once good and perfect but then corrupted by our sin, will be consumed in fervent heat and destroyed. Yet, we will remain as His children and will dwell forever with Him in the new heavens and earth that He will create. The rest will be tossed out but not us and the holy angels He has deigned to serve us. Our Heavenly Father really does value us more than anything else in this world.

To Know Him is to Love Him

A while back, Philippians 1:9 popped up when I turned the page on my calendar, "And this I pray, that your love may abound yet more and more in knowledge and in all judgment." It struck me as odd. I thought *what does knowledge have to do with love?* The more I pondered, the more befuddled I became since relying on head knowledge rather than God-given faith would be a dangerous, heretical error. Early Gnostics went astray by emphasizing personal religious experiences rather than relying on God's means of grace.

Faced with this conundrum, I turned to Proverbs 1:7, "The fear of the Lord is the beginning of knowledge: but fools despise wisdom and instruction." This helped because I needed to understand what knowledge meant in order to apply it to love. How did fear play into the equation? Fear seemed such a far cry from love.

I tried to see things from God's point of view through His word by connecting the dots of love, knowledge and fear. An imponderable from man's perspective made perfect sense when seen through the lens of the Bible. The fog lifted when I substituted the word reverence for fear. I was able to see why God cautioned against fearing men while encouraging fear of Him. He stated it this way in Matthew 10:28, "And fear not them which kill the body, but are not able to kill the soul: but rather fear him which is able to destroy both soul and body in hell."

The latter didn't refer to Satan but rather to Almighty God. This wisdom, this healthy fear was considered a good thing for it promoted goodness, kindness and obedience in us as Paul exhorted in 2 Corinthians 7:1, "Having therefore these promises (adoption by God and salvation as noted in the preceding chapter 6), dearly beloved, let us cleanse ourselves from all filthiness of the flesh and spirit, perfecting holiness in the fear of God."

As I began to understand and embrace this notion of love stemming from knowledge, I couldn't keep an old tune from creeping into my head. Have you ever heard a pop song by the Teddy Bears from 1958 called *To Know Him is to Love Him*? The refrain says "To know, know, know him is to love, love, love him and I do."

If this song was recorded well before your time and you don't have access to YouTube, perhaps you've heard of a founding member of the Teddy Bears, Phil Spector. He's was a well-known producer responsible for some of the biggest pop hits by some of the biggest stars of the last fifty years. He was also the guy convicted of shooting and killing a female companion in his mansion in 2003.

Music trivia aside, Paul under inspiration from God addressed sinfulness in Romans 3:18 by tying it back to fear of the Lord or the lack thereof, "There is no fear of God before their eyes." By this he meant to teach that fearing God in the right way was a blessing that produced good fruit by the sanctifying power of the Holy Spirit but lacking such fear was a grave error that would only lead to destruction.

This seemingly circuitous path led me to see that to know God the Savior is to love Him. And the best way to know Jesus was to find Him in His word, the Holy Bible. "But these are written, that ye might believe that Jesus is the Christ, the Son of God; and that believing ye might have life through his name," (John 20:31). Knowing this and everything Christ has done to procure our salvation at such a price, how could we not love Him? "We love him, because he first loved us," (I John 4:19). I couldn't keep that old melody out of my head, "To know, know, know Him is to love, love, love Him and I do, yes I do."

Puppy Love

Do you remember what it was like to be madly in love? No, I don't mean lust. That's a self-serving emotion. I'm talking about being head over heels about someone where you simply wanted to be near them all the time and your heart ached whenever you were apart. Back then you would have eagerly done anything and even risked life and limb for your gal or guy without giving it a second thought. Maybe it was springtime and perhaps you were in your teens or twenties.

If you've been married to that person for a long time, have you lost that loving feeling? You know what I mean. The pilot light may still be flickering but the intense bonfire has likely been tamped down by the harsh realities of life: dirty diapers, alarm clocks, mortgages, endless bills, chores and the inevitable march toward old age.

Wouldn't it be great if we could feel that romantic fervor forever and go through life on cloud nine with the object of our affection? Unfortunately, even the most devoted couples fall short. We could learn a lesson from our dogs, couldn't we?

There's a reason why dogs are known as man's best friend. Our furry K-9 companions never seem to lose their tail-wagging devotion. They don't criticize the way we look or behave. Fido jumps for joy and lavishes us with slobbery kisses no matter how many pounds we've put on or gray hairs and wrinkles we've amassed.

Maybe we've given the term puppy love a bad rap since a pup's love isn't frivolous or foolish but instead seems to be virtuous in its unconditional nature. Then again, even a dog can turn on its master if it is abused enough. Unfortunately, our sin-corrupted world can ruin even the purest form of love in a temporal sense.

Thankfully, there is one love that transcends everything in this world. Jesus' passion for us far exceeds anything we've ever experienced, humanly speaking. God's love for us in Jesus is amazing beyond comprehension. To put God's mercy and grace in perspective, consider this. Even a dog will bite the hand that feeds it if provoked enough. However, we treated our Lord and Savior like a dog … no, much, much worse than a dog with shameful mocking, brutal beatings, vicious torture and crucifixion.

Yet the Master never turned on us mongrels. He didn't even punish us. Astonishingly, He willingly suffered the horrific punishment we deserved and at the same time asked our Heavenly Father to forgive us. His ardent passion for us has remained unchanged for some 2,000 years and will remain just as intense unto eternity.

So thankfully, we can remain madly in love forever. The key is to make Jesus Christ the object of our affection rather than fleeting things in this sin-sick world. The secret to true love is revealed by God in 1 John 4:15-17: "Whosoever shall confess that Jesus is the Son of God, God dwells in him, and he in God. And we have known and believed the love that God hath to us. God is love; and he that dwells in love dwells in God and God in him. Herein is our love made perfect, that we may have boldness in the Day of Judgment: because as he is, so are we in this world."

ian Food | Steve Stranghoener

Grace

Faith Food   Steve Stranghoener

Oil and Water

When two things just don't go together or sometimes when two people just can't seem to get along, they are often compared to oil and water. Have you ever tried to mix oil and water? I attempted this and found it virtually impossible. I wondered why and pulled this simple explanation from the web.

"Oil and water don't mix because oil is made up of non-polar molecules while water molecules are polar in nature. Because water molecules are electrically charged, they get attracted to other water molecules and exclude the oil molecules. This eventually causes the oil molecules, or lipids, to clump together."

Jesus used a similar analogy in Mark 2:21-22. "No man also sews a piece of new cloth on an old garment: else the new piece that filled it up taketh away from the old, and the rent is made worse. And no man puts new wine into old bottles: else the new wine doth burst the bottles, and the wine is spilled, and the bottles will be marred: but new wine must be put into new bottles."

What was Jesus talking about? What didn't go together? As he often did, Jesus was using familiar, earthly elements to make a spiritual point. The examples He used made complete sense to the people of those days and still carry a clear meaning for us today if we use our heads a bit.

Faith Food — Steve Stranghoener

In our throw-away society we often toss out old garments and buy new clothes instead. But let's say we've torn a hole in our most precious and comfy pair of jeans or favorite tee shirt to which we've grown so attached. We wouldn't throw out such treasures, would we? Of course not; we'd try to repair them. But no one would sew a dark blue patch onto some light blue denims. And even if we found a perfect color match for our old, faded orange tee shirt, we wouldn't use a new piece of cloth for the repair. New and old cloth shrinks at different rates in the dryer. In no time the new cloth would stretch and tear away from the old leaving a bigger hole than before.

The wine example is a little tougher since we typically use glass bottles today rather than wine skins. But think about the fermenting process. It creates a lot of gas bubbles that generate pressure. You know that if you've ever popped a cork on a champagne bottle. The new wine that Jesus speaks of is grape juice that is still fermenting. Old wine skins aren't resilient and robust enough to expand with the pressure of fermentation. Putting new wine in old wine skin bottles will cause them to burst leaving nothing but a terrible mess.

We know that Jesus wasn't trying to teach us about sewing, wine making or packaging. He had a spiritual lesson in mind. Early believers were confusing the Old and New Covenants and specifically deeds of the law versus the gospel. Jesus was cautioning them and us about works righteousness. Christ warned that clinging to the law and works righteousness while trying to claim the gospel promise was very dangerous and would lead to disastrous results. He likened works righteousness and the gospel to that day's oil and water paradigm. He wanted to warn that justifying ourselves, even in a tiny little part, was no more possible than mixing oil and water. "Christ is the end of the law for righteousness to everyone that believeth," (Romans 10-4).

I went back to the web and read further and found another fitting analogy in the article's conclusion.

"But all is well that ends well

With the advanced technologies, we have detergents and soaps that help in cleaning the grime and oil from both our body and utensils. So, do not worry, let chemistry play its parts while we will play ours!"

In regard to our salvation, we play no part. We're saved by grace through faith alone which is a gift from God (Ephesians 2:8-9). So, part of the analogy doesn't apply but there is a marvelous, miraculous, spiritual cleaning agent that can cleanse us from every spot of sin. It is the blood of Jesus Christ; the most powerful detergent in the world that can turn our crimson stains to pure white and remove our transgressions as far away as the east is from the west. Let us offer our thanks and praise to God Our Father for sending His Son, Jesus Christ, the Lamb of God to take away the sins of the entire world.

Righteous Work

There are really only two religions in this world: works and grace. We are blessed with this glorious truth, "For by grace are ye saved through faith; and that not of yourselves: it is the gift of God: Not of works, lest any man should boast," (Ephesians 2:8-9). Yet God also tells us through James 2:24, "Ye see then how that by works a man is justified, and not by faith only." This apparent contradiction delights Bible doubters and false teachers and causes consternation for some believers but there is an easy explanation. We simply need to put the horse before the cart and not vice versa and look to the Holy Scriptures for the answer.

Before being born anew from above (John 3:5), we were all dead in our trespasses and sins (Ephesians 2:1). Thus, God deserves all the credit for our good works as exemplified in the following passages. "LORD, thou wilt ordain peace for us: for thou also hast wrought all our works in us," (Isaiah 26:12). "And God is able to make all grace abound toward you; that ye, always having all sufficiency in all things, may abound to every good work," (2 Corinthians 9:8). "We are his workmanship, created in Christ Jesus unto good works, which God hath before ordained that we should walk in them," (Ephesians 2:10). "It is God which works in you both to will and to do of his good pleasure," (Philippians 2:13).

Our good works are not meant to bring renown to us and certainly do not accrue to the benefit of our salvation. To the contrary, our best works are like filthy rags apart from the Savior (Isaiah 64:6). Our deeds are meant to serve God's good purposes for the salvation of mankind to **His** glory. "Let your light so shine before men, that they may see your good works, and glorify your Father which is in heaven," (Matthew 5:16). "But rejoice, inasmuch as ye are partakers of Christ's sufferings; that, when his glory shall be revealed, ye may be glad also with exceeding joy," (1 Peter 4:13).

When it comes to good works, we should be humble and thankful and give credit where credit is due. John the Baptist admitted as much when referring to Jesus, "He must increase, but I must decrease," (John 3:30). Inspired Paul expressed the same sentiment, "Let nothing be done through strife or vainglory; but in lowliness of mind let each esteem other better than themselves," (Philippians 2:3).

We should go about our daily business with great joy. "And also that every man should eat and drink, and enjoy the good of all his labor, it is the gift of God," (Ecclesiastes 3:13). "I delight to do thy will, O my God: yea, thy law is within my heart," (Psalm 40:8).

We can thank God that our faith is not dependent upon our works but rather good works flow from our God-given faith. Even our best works only reveal God's saving grace. We can be eternally thankful that the righteous work of our salvation was laid upon only one person: the perfect God-man, Jesus Christ. "All we like sheep have gone astray; we have turned everyone to his own way; and the LORD hath laid on him the iniquity of us all," (Isaiah 53:6).

The Right or Requirement to Work?

The right to earn a living and put food on the table seemed to me like a simple concept that everyone could rally around. However, we've politicized this harmless notion to the point of generating hatred and sometimes even violence. Some have argued that all workers in unionized shops should be required to join the union and pay dues while others have said they should be able to work anywhere without offering what to them amounts to tribute to a political party that doesn't represent their views or values.

For centuries, the church has dealt with the contentious subject of work too. Some Christians have vehemently asserted that our salvation is dependent upon our good works, at least in some measure, while others have steadfastly insisted that heaven is totally a free gift from God.

Originally, in the Garden, there was no such thing as work, at least not in the way we see it today. Only after the fall into sin did God require us to toil and sweat for sustenance. According to God's command, work was not just a right but more so a requirement. But it didn't take long for God to offer a solution to our predicament. As recorded in Genesis 3:15, God offered a Savior who would resolve our sin problem and conquer its consequence of death. Later He even promised to replace our sin-corrupted world with new heavens and a new earth (Isaiah 65:17).

Satan, the Father of Lies and the one who deceived Eve in the first place, couldn't stand the way that our loving God let Adam and Eve and us off the hook. From the beginning, this prideful, hateful, evil angel plotted to derail God's plan of salvation. He couldn't confront God directly so he set about his nefarious work by spreading more lies among God's children. His most popular and enticing lie was that we had to earn our way into heaven through our own good deeds. Satan knew this would be effective because it appealed to our prideful natures. To this day it has remained a bone of contention between many who call themselves Christians.

For those of us blessed enough to be steeped in Scripture, we can easily see through Satan's deception regarding works righteousness. God's word abounds in this truth but, for the sake of space and time, I'll quote one passage from Romans 10:8-9 that encapsulates God's plan of salvations perfectly. "But what saith it? The word is nigh thee, even in thy mouth, and in thy heart: that is, the word of faith, which we preach; That if thou shalt confess with thy mouth the Lord Jesus, and shalt believe in thine heart that God hath raised him from the dead, thou shalt be saved."

Ah, that simple, plain-spoken promise is so comforting. God assures us that He accomplished everything we couldn't attain for ourselves. It's a sure thing. Even the faith to believe in Jesus and confess His name is apportioned to us as a free gift from God (Ephesians 2:8-9, John 6:44). Isn't it wonderfully ironic? In a temporal sense, God requires us to work but spiritually we're set completely and leisurely free because God took up the burden for us. God made us right through Christ's work.

Sacrifice Makes Perfect

Many coaches have said, "Practice makes perfect." A wise coaching friend of mine put a new twist on this old axiom, "Practice doesn't make perfect; perfect practice makes perfect." The Pharisees taught that people could attain righteousness by perfectly adhering to the law. God said there was only one way to achieve righteousness; through a perfect sacrifice of infinite worth. As John the Baptist was privileged to announce, Jesus was the perfect Lamb of God who came to make the ultimate sacrifice for all our sins.

Some Jewish converts wavered in the aftermath of Christ's death, resurrection and ascension. They succumbed to backsliding under the heavy weight of false doctrine. Many were tempted to revert back to works righteousness. This prompted God to inspire His servant to pen an epistle to the Hebrew converts in Rome to edify and strengthen them in the one true Christian faith. Perhaps it was Paul or maybe Apollos that God used for this purpose but regardless the message was abundantly clear.

In Hebrews 6:1, God steered them away from works righteousness, "Therefore leaving the principles of the doctrine of Christ, let us go on unto perfection; not laying again the foundation of repentance from dead works, and of faith toward God." He put an exclamation point on the truth about works versus grace in Hebrews 10:4, "For it is not possible that the blood of bulls and of goats should take away sins." Then God added this seemingly contradictory statement in Hebrews 9:22, "And almost all things are by the law purged with blood; and without shedding of blood is no remission."

What did God mean? First, He said it was fruitless to offer bloody sacrifices then reversed course and declared there was no remission of sins without the shedding of blood. To top things off, God urged us toward perfection in Hebrews 6:1, an impossible task.

Of course, God didn't contradict Himself. He cleared things up perfectly in Hebrews 10:11-12, "And every priest stands daily ministering and offering oftentimes the same sacrifices, which can never take away sins. But this man (Jesus the God-man), after he had offered one sacrifice for sins forever, sat down on the right hand of God."

The blood of bulls and goats and all our deeds of the law were rendered meaningless by one sacrifice that had real power. Jesus' atoning sacrifice and the shedding of His all-availing, cleansing blood accomplished our redemption for us perfectly, once and for always.

As for our perfection, God summed up His comforting, glorious and gracious promise of salvation in Hebrews 10:14, "For by one offering he hath perfected forever them that are sanctified." When Jesus declared "It is finished," from the cross we were deemed righteous by His work and merit in God's great, gracious, cosmic exchange. Jesus suffered for us and incurred God's wrath over our sins and imputed His righteousness to us. One sacrifice of infinite worth accomplished our redemption for all eternity. We were declared perfect in the cleansing, sacrificial blood of the Lamb of God.

Pro-Choice

Are you pro-choice? I'm proud to say that I am. What, you gasp, in strident tones? No, no … I'm not talking about politics or contemporary social issues. No Christian could be pro-choice where the choice involves the killing of a baby in the mother's womb. Or for that matter, no Christian could be pro-choice when it comes to euthanizing the old, sick, infirm or terminally ill. God is the Lord of Life and we must leave those decisions to Him alone. I'm speaking of another type of choice altogether. I'm proudly pro-choice when it comes to matters of faith and salvation.

To be pro-choice in this way means to be pro-God because only God can make Christians. I hope I haven't lost any of our Baptist friends out there or members of other Christian denominations that embrace decision theology or the notion that we must cooperate in coming to faith in the Lord Jesus Christ. Some believe and teach that He does most of the doing but we have to do our part or at least give our consent. This presents a major problem since the Bible clearly teaches that we're dead in our trespasses and sins before we're brought to faith (Ephesians 2:1). And everyone can agree that a dead man can't do anything. He can't lift a finger much less decide to accept Jesus Christ.

But let's not argue from the negative since Scripture is so clear in the affirmative. Here are just a few examples. "But as many as received him, to them gave he power to become the sons of God, even to them that believe on his name: Which were born, not of blood, nor of the will of the flesh, nor of the will of man, **but of God,**" John 1:12-13. "Ye have not chosen me, but **I have chosen you**, and ordained you, that ye should go and bring forth fruit, and that your fruit should remain: that whatsoever ye shall ask of the Father in my name, he may give it you," John 15:16. "Wherefore I give you to understand, that no man speaking by the Spirit of God calls Jesus accursed: and that no man can say that Jesus is the Lord, **but by the Holy Ghost,**" 1 Corinthians 12:3.

There's much more on this subject. "But God, who is rich in mercy, for his great love wherewith he loved us, Even when we were dead in sins, **hath**

quickened us together with Christ, (by grace ye are saved;) And hath raised us up together, and made us sit together in heavenly places in Christ Jesus," Ephesians 2:4-6. "Herein is love, not that we loved God, but that **he loved us**, and sent his Son to be the propitiation for our sins," 1 John 4:10. "Being born again, not of corruptible seed, but of incorruptible, **by the word of God**, which lives and abides forever," 1 Peter 1:23. "Jesus answered, Verily, verily, I say unto thee, except a man be **born of water and of the Spirit**, he cannot enter into the kingdom of God," John 3:5. "And the LORD thy **God will circumcise thine heart**, and the heart of thy seed, to love the LORD thy God with all thine heart, and with all thy soul, that thou may live," Deuteronomy 30:6.

That should be enough to convince anyone who believes in the Bible that it's God's work; His choice and not ours. But let me close with one more for good measure. This is one of my favorites. "**Of his own will begat he us with the word of truth**, that we should be a kind of first-fruits of his creatures," James 1:18. So, the next time someone tells you they're pro-choice, loudly proclaim, "Me too!" Then explain it to them joyfully and lovingly giving all the credit where credit is due; with our great and gracious God.

Faith, Justification & Redemption

Show-Me Skeptics

Sometimes when reading Scripture, I've felt like Jesus was talking specifically to me and my fellow Missourians even though our Savior walked the earth some 1,800 years before the State of Missouri even existed. As the Show-Me State, we've been renowned for our skepticism. We've made it our motto of sorts, I'm from Missouri … you have to show me. We've basically proclaimed that I'll believe it when I see it. In truth though, we don't have a monopoly on skepticism since our Show-Me State attitude was prevalent long ago in the ancient lands of the Middle East where Jesus trod.

Jesus didn't back down when confronted by the Judean Show-Me crowd. Unlike a seasoned stand-up comic who handles a drunken heckler, Jesus didn't resort to comedy or disarmingly witty repartee. He simply used the truth and divine wisdom to overwhelm His detractors. The Lord didn't lash out in anger, bitterness or vengeance to rudely put down His critics. Instead He offered brotherly admonitions in the most loving, peaceful and patient way possible.

Jesus often used parables to get his message across to skeptical or hostile crowds. In John 10 He compared himself to a door to make the point that He represented the only way to heaven. Some did not understand so He went further and described Himself as the good shepherd who, unlike hirelings, would never desert the sheep in times of danger and leave them to the wolves. Some believed and others did not.

To that, Jesus pointed out astutely that He knew his sheep and they knew His voice and listened.

Some still complained that they could not understand and challenged Jesus to speak plainly. Jesus responded to these ancient "hecklers" as recorded in John 10:25, "Jesus answered them, I told you, and ye believed not: the works that I do in my Father's name, they bear witness of me." Christ turned their Show-Me attitude around on them and said, in effect, if you will only believe what you can see, then believe the miracles I've performed openly in front of you.

Then the Lord replied even more squarely to their call for plain talk and proclaimed, "I and my Father are one." They reacted murderously by taking up stones to kill Him. He challenged them and asked if they planned to stone Him for the good works He had performed. They replied no, that they were going to kill Him for the blasphemy of claiming to be God.

This is where Jesus delivered the stone-cold truth, the knock-out blow in John 10:36-38. "Say ye of him, whom the Father hath sanctified, and sent into the world, Thou blasphemes; because I said, I am the Son of God? If I do not the works of my Father, believe me not. But if I do, though ye believe not me, believe the works: that ye may know, and believe, that the Father is in me, and I in him." Wow, Jesus threw down the gauntlet and said if you don't believe me then judge me by my works; the things you've seen with your own eyes.

Faith Food — Steve Stranghoener

They knew that only God could have performed the miracles that Jesus had demonstrated many times over. However, some of these skeptics with their hard, deceitful and rebellious hearts refused to believe regardless of the plain facts they had seen with their own eyes. So instead of conceding and bestowing upon Christ the honor He deserved, they sought again to seize Him. Jesus provided further proof of His divine power and miraculously escaped from the midst of them.

Things are no different today since there is nothing new under the sun. Some believe by the power of God's Holy Spirit working through word and sacraments and others stubbornly resist to their own destruction. Christ through His unchanging, inspired, inerrant word is still delivering the same powerful message to all the "hecklers." If you don't believe me; then believe the ironclad proof I've set before all mankind. That's why we should always point people to the cross and empty tomb.

Jesus accomplished on the cross what no mere man could ever do. He paid the price for the sins of the entire world, redeemed us and reconciled us to God the Father. Then, in the most compelling, indisputable proof of all time, Jesus was raised from the dead; resurrected just as God had foretold in His plan of salvation from the very beginning. God has provided everything we need to believe in His plan of salvation through faith in His word of promise. But to the skeptics who still stubbornly say "show me," God has answered them the same way Jesus responded to the Old Testament "hecklers." His voice in the Bible has echoed across the centuries, *look to the cross and the resurrection; the proof positive for all time.*

God's Palette

Masterpieces are formed in the imagination but brought to life when brush meets palette. *Starry Night* offers a glimpse into the mind of Vincent van Gogh. Similarly, our world reveals much about God as noted in Romans 1:20, "For the invisible things of him from the creation of the world are clearly seen, being understood by the things that are made." However, our comprehension is limited since God used a cosmic palette when He spun His vibrant colors by the power of His word alone. To more fully understand our Almighty Father, we must turn to His revealed word of truth in the Holy bible.

Therein, color often seemed to depend on the eye of the beholder. Jacob expressed his love for Joseph by favoring him with a special coat. It contained many colors but his brothers only saw two. At first green with envy, they later saw red in plotting his demise. God painted over their dark clouds to produce rays of sunshine when, as Joseph declared in Genesis 20:50, "Ye thought evil against me; but God meant it unto good."

God sometimes appeared color blind and purposefully so. We were all miserable sinners (Romans 3:23), desperately wicked (Jeremiah 17:9) and dead in our trespasses (Ephesians 2:1) but He chose not to see the blackness of our stony hearts. Instead, God used a scarlet flood to wash our sins away as noted in Revelation 1:5-6, "And from Jesus Christ, who is the faithful witness, and the first begotten of the dead, and the prince of the kings of the earth. Unto him that loved us, and washed us from our sins in his own blood, and hath made us kings and priests unto God and his Father; to him be glory and dominion for ever and ever."

Only God could use color to this miraculous effect. Through the all-availing, sacrificial atonement of Jesus Christ, He covered our black sins in red until they vanished before His eyes leaving us as white as snow. Through Jesus, God fulfilled the promise offered through His Prophet in Isaiah 1:18, "Though your sins be as scarlet, they shall be as white as snow; though they be red like crimson, they shall be as wool." We; colored in thankfulness toward our gracious Lord and Savior, should praise our Heavenly Father and Creator for He transformed us who were destined for eternity's scrap heap into masterpieces suitable for heaven.

Spoiler Alert!

Hollywood is in the business of creating buzz. They are masters of promoting upcoming movie releases by bombarding us with trailers for thirty minutes while we're trapped in a theater waiting for the feature film to begin. Can you blame them? Smart marketing requires the producers to toy with our emotions until an avalanche of anticipation consumes our attention. Isn't it absurd how we're desperately driven toward the exciting conclusions but don't want the plot to unfold prematurely? Ironically, we're sometimes issued special warnings called spoiler alerts that disguise the outcomes we're so frantically seeking.

I can understand this apparent contradiction because my wife is a fan of true crime dramas like *48 Hours* and *Dateline* and reality shows such as *Dancing with the Stars* and the *Bachelor*. Would she and the other throngs of fans stay glued to the TV if they announced the bachelor's betrothed during the first episode or which dancing duo would take home the mirror ball trophy? What if *Dateline* opened each show by revealing who committed the murder or the jury's verdict? As for the latter, I feel they might as well since invariably the spouse did it. My cynicism aside, I agree that, when it comes to show biz, our human nature demands such secrecy.

But isn't it all the more amazing how God turned this marketing axiom on its head? God didn't keep us guessing in order to command our rapt attention. To the contrary, He revealed the final conclusion during the opening act. He unveiled His plan of salvation to our first parents, Adam and Eve, almost immediately after their fall into sin with the gospel promise recorded in Genesis 3:15. Thereafter, He repeated the promise of our Savior over and over to every generation. He didn't stop there but went so far as to reveal what would happen up to the final curtain call and beyond unto eternity.

Some people have taught that this was only done for the benefit of New Testament believers in order to maintain our focus after Christ's birth, death and resurrection. However, God gave the same insights to everyone including His Old Testament people long before the promise of the Messiah was fulfilled. The Book of Daniel chronicled the end times in much the same way as Revelation. God even offered some commentary regarding the visions in Daniel 7 that could later be traced to the rise and breakup of the Roman Empire.

The consistency of OT and NT eschatology is evident throughout. Comparing Revelation to Isaiah offers one of the clearest examples. We can read, "And I saw a new heaven and a new earth: for the first heaven and the first earth were passed away; and there was no more sea," (Revelation 21:1) in the New along with the Old, "For, behold, I create new heavens and a new earth: and the former shall not be remembered, nor come into mind," (Isaiah 65:17).

So, sometimes spoiler alerts aren't necessary or recommended. I watch *A Charlie Brown Christmas* every year even though I know the ending by heart. In a much higher way, I love to read the final conclusion to God's plan of salvation over and over again with great joy and anticipation for the Day of the Lord. God's story for mankind's redemption is that good; it's one of a kind.

Born to be Wild

Some have claimed that *Steppenwolf* was the original heavy metal band. Their seminal 1968 rock anthem, *Born to Be Wild*, launched a new music genre when their lyrics coined the phrase "I like smoke and lightning, heavy metal thunder." Oddly, their lead singer, Joachim Fritz Krauledat, hailed from tiny Tilsit, Germany. If you haven't heard of him, that's because he moved to Canada and changed his name to John Kay to more properly channel the bad boy image he exuded behind his trademark dark glasses. *Steppenwolf* became forever associated with the motorcycle crowd when *Born to Be Wild* headlined the soundtrack from the 1969 cult classic film, *Easy Rider*.

The song's third verse read, "Like a true nature's child, we were born, born to be wild. We can climb so high, I never want to die." The second sentence was easy to understand. It referred to the drug culture that proliferated in the late 1960s and the euphoric feelings produced by psychedelic hallucinogens that could also create a sense of immortality.

From a theological standpoint, it was easy to bash this lie of Satan since the Bible clearly teaches that we're all sinners and the wages of sin is death. Anyone clued into God's truth knew that it would be a horrible curse to live forever in sin. That's why God mercifully barred Adam and Eve from the Garden of Eden and the Tree of Life after the fall. Temporal death proved to be a blessing in that regard.

Thankfully, God offered Adam and Eve and all mankind spiritual rebirth from above and new, eternal life in Jesus Christ.

The first sentence of the song's third verse was harder to dismiss. As the Psalmist King David noted in 51:5, we've been sinful by nature since our conception. Thus, it seemed true that we were born to be wild, that is, in rebellion against God and His commands. Scripture aside, not a one of us could have argued otherwise based on personal experience. Nevertheless, surely *Steppenwolf* didn't have this doctrinal truth in mind back in 1968 when they released this monster hit.

I think they missed the truth that, although we were conceived in sin and born to be rebels and enemies of God by nature, that wasn't the end of the story. For most of us, a dramatic, miraculous change took place shortly after our birth into this world. For some it may have occurred later even unto old age but nevertheless was no less miraculous. In baptism, through God's Holy Spirit working through His word, He came to us from above and gave us second birth and a new nature. We were new creatures from that point on; children of God, adopted into His forever family.

We've continued to struggle with our old, sinful natures and fallen into temptation and folly in thought, word and deed on a daily basis but thankfully God in Christ has reconciled us and forgiven all. He paid the price for all of our sins; past, present and future, on

Golgotha's cross in the person of Jesus Christ and shattered the enmity between us. Sanctified by the Holy Spirit and fortified by God's Holy Word and sacraments connected to that word, we've been blessed to live anew for and through Christ and delight in His commands.

We were truly born to be wild but have been emancipated from our slavery to sin. Christ has conquered sin, death and the power of Satan and has exchanged His righteousness for our sinfulness. He accomplished this for us undeserving sinners out of pure, unconditional love. Hopefully, John Kay and his bandmates have discovered this glorious truth somewhere along the way. Wouldn't it be nice if they produced a sequel and called it *Reborn to Be God's Child*?

The Great Exchange

We love it when businesses stand behind their products. When they offer a money-back guarantee if we're not completely satisfied, it gives us buyers a sense of confidence and security. Sometimes their assurances ring hollow when we read the fine print or find out that there's a lengthy, complicated process we must navigate in order to return a product that doesn't meet our expectations.

On the other hand, some people take advantage of earnest businesses that bend over backwards to ensure customer satisfaction. Have you ever seen someone voraciously gobble down half of their meal at a restaurant before demanding restitution? However, when done properly, it can create a lot of good will when a business allows us to exchange goods for legitimate reasons.

There's just something about reciprocity that strikes a soothing chord within us. Maybe it's a golden rule thing; a basic sense of fairness that God imputes to us through His word. We see this concept expressed in our art and culture. We love it when the *Prince and the Pauper* exchange places to walk in each other's shoes.

There are endless variations of this timeless tale aimed at helping people understand their differences: black and white, rich and poor, male and female, young and old. This popular plot takes on a higher, nobler meaning when a hero trades places to save a helpless victim from some impending doom. Of course, we expect a happy ending where the knight in shining armor somehow extricates himself from the peril and overcomes the bad guys.

Isn't it ironic that the best exchange any of us have ever experienced completely violated the key principles noted above? It lacked reciprocity and fairness and the hero was unjustly mocked, beaten and tortured before suffering terrible punishment and a horrible death. Most incredibly, the hero was perfectly innocent while the intended victims He saved were wicked criminals who richly deserved the punishment the hero took upon Himself in their stead. Here's how God summed up this great exchange in 2 Corinthians

5:21, "For he hath made him to be sin for us, who knew no sin; that we might be made the righteousness of God in him."

Mankind broke every command of God over and over again while knowing that the penalty was death and eternal damnation in hell. We wickedly embraced sin and turned our backs on God. Despite knowing the consequences full well, we openly rebelled against God who had no choice but to punish our sins.

What did God do in response? He stepped into the breach in the person of Jesus Christ and took His just wrath upon Himself in order to spare us. But He did more than show mercy and instead showered us with His grace too. We deserved everything that God suffered but, incredibly, God gave us Christ's perfect righteousness in exchange for our utter sinfulness. He imputed our sins to our perfectly innocent Savior and nailed them to the cross.

The next time someone tells you about a fantastic exchange they made with a local retailer, remind them of the infinitely better, great exchange they received from our loving, gracious God, "Who his own self bare our sins in his own body on the tree, that we, being dead to sins, should live unto righteousness: by whose stripes ye were healed," (1 Peter 2:24). Eternal thanks to our merciful, gracious, loving God who saw fit to pay that terrible price in order to clothe us in Christ's righteousness and reconcile us to Him.

Silver Lining

The old saying that every cloud has a silver lining is meant to convey the notion that we should look for the good in everything, even in the midst of dire circumstances. Clouds may bring thunderstorms that cancel our grand parade but the rains still give life to the plants that feed us. Lemons are too sour to eat but lemonade is delicious and refreshing. God has expressed this same sentiment in a much higher way in Romans 8:28, "And we know that all things work together for good to them that love God, to them who are the called according to his purpose." God wants us to know that He has the power to turn around the worst tragedies and disasters in this life, even death, to suit His good purposes for us unto our eternal salvation.

The darkest cloud that ever descended upon this earth, literally and figuratively, happened during the crucifixion of our Lord and Savior. Jesus suffered God's full wrath over our sins in our place as He hung on the cross. Darkness literally engulfed the earth for three hours as Jesus suffered what we could not bear on Calvary's bloody cross. However, this most ominous of clouds contained a precious and glorious silver lining beyond what our feeble imaginations could grasp. We were reconciled to God and washed clean in our Savior's blood and declared righteous in spite of our sins.

One of the most thrilling declarations of this awe-inspiring good news came some 700 years before the birth of Jesus Christ. God offered this most precious promise through His inspired prophet (please see Isaiah 44). He revealed Himself in no uncertain terms as the only true God; the Creator of man, the universe and everything in it. The Lord left no question that He had chosen Israel as His people to serve as His witnesses not because of anything good in them but in spite of their sinfulness.

God admonished them for their backsliding and faithlessness and openly derided those who worshipped false gods and graven images. He boldly and plainly proclaimed the truth that He was not only their God and Creator but also their Redeemer. While His people, Israel and us; spiritual Israel, were wholly undeserving, He displayed His amazing grace by offering the promise of forgiveness and salvation out of true, undeserved, unconditional love.

God expressed His incredibly good news to mankind in Isaiah 44:22 with this imagery, "I have blotted out, as a thick cloud, thy transgressions, and, as a cloud, thy sins: return unto me; for I have redeemed thee." Wow, this was better than any silver lining! The cloud itself served as a blotter. Like a cosmic sponge, this cloud, by the power of God, soaked up every sin of ours and put them back on God the Redeemer.

Now when God looks at us, thanks to Jesus, Our Redeemer, He doesn't see our filthy, disgusting, putrid, wretched sinfulness. Apart from Christ, we are but a horrid stench that would turn God away from us forever. But this atoning cloud, has removed every spot, stain, blemish and offensive odor so that we are fully reconciled to God. Sing unto the Lord, sing unto the Lord joyfully!

The Great Emancipator

President Abraham Lincoln, a faithful Christian who often referred to the Scriptures in his public capacity, governed during perhaps the most tumultuous time in our nation's history. With the very union of these United States in jeopardy, he presided over a bloody, four-year American Civil War that claimed the lives of more than 600,000 Americans. Known as the Great Emancipator, Lincoln issued his famous Emancipation Proclamation on January 1, 1863 marking the beginning of the end of legalized slavery in our country.

Our Civil War produced more American casualties than any other conflict in our history including WWII. Under Lincoln's leadership, we paid an incredibly heavy price in blood and treasure to preserve the Union and remove the blight of slavery from our land.

Still remnants of the stain remained and the after-effects of slavery have troubled us even unto the present. Some legitimate issues have lingered but many have only reflected bitterness and hatred that have no place in our society. From the false hands up, don't shoot narrative that arose out of Ferguson to Black Lives Matter's war on law enforcement, we've been beset by modern-day Troublers of Israel who have only sought anarchy and destruction.

Unfortunately, we've often overlooked the one sure remedy that could heal the fractious wounds that have torn apart the fabric of our nation. We should have turned once again to the Great Emancipator; not President Lincoln but the Living Savior who has continued to bring freedom to lost souls everywhere. Jesus Christ emancipated the entire world from the spiritual slavery that originated with Adam and Eve's fall into sin and was passed on to each of us.

Scoffers, deceivers and some Confederates falsely tried to claim that the Bible endorsed slavery. To the contrary, the Bible accurately chronicled how slavery plagued nations throughout history including God's chosen people, the Hebrews, who suffered at the hands of the ancient Egyptians. While God did not denounce slavery from a political standpoint, neither did He endorse it. "Render therefore unto Caesar the things which are Caesar's," (Matthew 22:21).

However, our American form of slavery was blatantly anti-Christian because it defined some people as chattel or property whereas Christ created everyone as equals and died for all (Romans 5:18). As evidenced by Paul's letter to slave owner Philemon, God was more concerned with spiritual matters than temporal ones. Paul didn't admonish his friend Philemon for his then legal practice of slavery but rather encouraged him to consider the spiritual needs of one of his slaves, Onesimus, who aided Paul in prison.

Thankfully, God's top priority was us and our salvation. He knew that temporal matters paled in comparison to our eternal well-being since this world and everything in it will cease to matter come Judgment Day. Like America's Great Emancipator, God in the person of Jesus Christ freed us from slavery but in a much higher way. He personally paid a price that infinitely exceeded the blood and treasure lost on Civil War battlefields and gave us perfect, everlasting freedom. Let us live in this freedom as Christ instructed us, "If you continue in my word, then are you my disciples indeed and you will know the truth and the truth shall make you free," (John 8:31-32).

Have You No Shame?

We would all like to see ourselves as good, shameless people. But have you ever put this notion to the test with this simple question? Would any of us like to get up in front of family, friends, co-workers and fellow church members while hooked up to a lie detector and confess every one of our sinful thoughts, words and deeds? I don't think we'd find any takers even if we limited it to the last twenty-four hours. That's because we'd have to admit our shame and experience some very uncomfortable feelings.

Here's how the dictionary defines shame. "Shame is a painful emotion caused by a strong sense of guilt, embarrassment, unworthiness, or disgrace ... one that brings dishonor, disgrace, or condemnation. Shame can be a particularly problematic emotion because it is associated with a desire to hide, disappear, or even die." Does that last part make you think of what Adam and Eve did after the fall when they tried to hide from God and cover their nakedness?

Here's a scary thought. The hypothetical lie detector test we mused about above is going to come painfully true for many people. Paul tells us in Romans 14:12, "So then every one of us shall give account of himself to God." Jesus warns more specifically in Matthew 12:36, "But I say unto you, that every idle word that men shall speak, they shall give account thereof in the Day of Judgment."

But wait you say, that says we will **all** give an account. Not to worry my friends; we won't have to confess our sins before God as judge. That's because Jesus will be our advocate. We will be covered in His perfect righteousness and free from all condemnation.

The terrifying prospect of standing before the Great Judge, Jesus Christ, alone and unprotected will only be reserved for those who have rejected God's grace and the free gift of salvation found only in the all-availing, atoning sacrifice of Jesus. Those poor souls will have no one to blame but themselves. They will have willingly and defiantly invited God's wrath, "Whose end is destruction, whose God is their belly, and whose glory is in their shame, who mind earthly things," (Philippians 3:19).

For us and all believers, it will be a much different story; a glorious and joyful one. Christ proclaimed, "Behold, I come as a thief. Blessed is he that watches, and keeps his garments, lest he walk naked, and they see his shame," (Revelation 16:15). The garment of which He figuratively spoke is spotless and gleaming white; the robe of Christ's righteousness with which He covers us.

Listen to this incredible promise of God in Romans 10:11, "For the scripture saith, whosoever believeth on him shall not be ashamed." We **will not be ashamed** when Judgment Day comes. That's why even today, in spite of all our transgressions, we can boldly answer the question and say, we have no shame, in Jesus Christ our Lord.

Knock, Knock … Who's There?

Revelation 3:20 is one of the most well-known and beloved passages of Scripture, often accompanied by familiar images of Christ knocking at the door. Jesus says, "Behold, I stand at the door, and knock: if any man hear my voice, and open the door, I will come in to him, and will sup with him, and he with me."

Unfortunately, this passage is also quite often misunderstood. Some turn it into a proverbial knock-knock joke by adding a disconcerting punchline. That is, it is perverted into a subtle form of works righteousness known as decision theology.

Such folks say, Christ is our Lord and Savior who has redeemed us but we have to do our part. We have to decide to accept Christ. In effect, they toss objective justification overboard and make subjective justification captain of the ship. This flies in the face of the doctrine of election which is meant to be a comfort and not a foreboding, doubt-instilling source of terror. It also contradicts the clear teachings of Jesus who says in John 15:16, "Ye have not chosen me, but I have chosen you." Scripture teaches that we are brought to faith by the will of God and not man's will (John 1:13).

This doesn't stop people from using Revelation 3:20 erroneously. Private interpretation is easy when you take a single passage out of context. But, of course, with such an important doctrine, God leaves nothing to question. Jesus goes into quite a commentary on the subject of this figurative door in John 10. I encourage you to read the entire chapter for yourself but, in this short space, here's the gist of it.

First, Jesus speaks of the doorway in a parable. It's clear that who opens the door is not important. What Jesus stresses is that His sheep, that's us, must come in through the proper doorway. He explains in figurative language that other doorways are offered by imposters, false teachers, shepherds who are just hirelings who desert the sheep when the wolves appear.

But here's the rub. How do we make our way through the right doorway? Here's what Jesus says in

Faith Food — Steve Stranghoener

John 10:3, "To him the porter opens; and the sheep hear his voice: and he calls his own sheep by name, and leads them out." Then He adds in John 10:4-5, "And when he puts forth his own sheep, he goes before them, and the sheep follow him: for they know his voice. And a stranger will they not follow, but will flee from him: for they know not the voice of strangers."

Do you notice the dynamic here and who is acting and who is the object of that action? No, it's not us, the sheep, who lead the way. We follow our Shepherd's voice. He doesn't wait passively for us to decide but calls us. We respond out of God-given faith. We don't get lured away by the false teachers but rather listen to the Good Shepherd. That's because we hear His voice; the word of God that imparts and keeps us in the Christian faith.

We can't choose to follow Christ's voice, the Incarnate Word, by our own volition. Only the Holy Spirit working through the word can accomplish this feat. The only decision we can make as sheep is to disregard our Shepherd's voice and follow the hirelings, the false teachers. Such a decision would be on us completely. It would be completely contrary to the word and will of the Lord. So, in Revelation 3:20 when Jesus knocks at the door He is calling us. It is His voice, the voice of our Good Shepherd that motivates us and nothing that is within us apart from God-given faith.

To leave absolutely no doubt, Christ sums up as follows in John 10:9, "I am the door: by me if any man enter in, he shall be saved, and shall go in and out, and find pasture." Yes, who comes through the door is not the critical factor in this equation. It's the door. And Jesus makes it clear that not only is He the door but the only doorway to salvation and eternal life in heaven. In John 10:11 He leaves no question about who He is and the way to heaven, "I am the good shepherd: the good shepherd giveth his life for the sheep." Thank God for His inerrant, inspired word; the full counsel of God.

Signposts to Salvation

One year I mapped out what should have been an easy vacation trip to Gatlinburg, Tennessee. My directions said to take 64 East to 57 South to 24 East toward Paducah, KY. All I needed to do was pay attention to the signposts. Unfortunately, my concentration roamed right at the critical juncture where I should have veered to the left from Interstate 57 to 24. About forty miles later, I was startled to see a sign that read, "Welcome to Missouri." I had inadvertently stayed on 57 South. Worse yet, there was no connecting road to take us due east to Interstate 24 so I had to backtrack the entire eighty miles which added more than an hour to our drive.

Paying attention to signposts is even more critical when it comes to matters of faith. The world is filled with religions flashing signposts that supposedly lead to salvation or some variation thereof. The destinations go by different names like Nirvana or paradise and have conflicting descriptions. Some say they lead to God, others nothingness and still others a place filled with earthly pleasures like seventy-two virgins. You may even get your own planet where you can rule as your own god.

There's one thing they all have in common. Every one of these man-made religions points you to an exit through a wide gate leading to a very broad but crooked path I call the Works Righteousness Highway. These false religions say we must do something or contribute in some way to our own salvation. They make it sound like smooth sailing but their pathways all turn out to be very rough, bumpy roads. Some routes are longer than others. While some folks, usually 144,000, get to take the express lane, most have to travel through purgatory or a thousand-year detour after the rapture. Some claim that Jesus will be your tour guide but, if you look closely, you'd never recognize these imposters as the Christ of the Bible.

Don't be fooled. Thankfully, if you follow the only truly reliable road map, the Holy Bible, you will never be lost. That's because there is only one path that leads to salvation. It's very narrow with a straight gate. Jesus put it this way in John 14:6, "I am the way, the truth, and the life: no man cometh unto the Father, but by me." This truth is reiterated in Acts 4:12, "Neither is there salvation in any other: for there is none other name under heaven given among men, whereby we must be saved."

The proof is in the cross, empty tomb and resurrection. Now, here's something extremely important in recognizing the real deal versus all the false prophets and false Christs. Jesus not only leads the way to salvation, He literally **is** our salvation. Listen to the words of God's prophet in Isaiah 12:2. "Behold, God **is** my salvation; I will trust, and not be afraid: for the LORD JEHOVAH is my strength and my song; he also **is become my salvation**." How can this be?

Others claim that God provides a means for our salvation. He can guide and direct things from on high but does so through His prophets and servants in a rather detached manner. He can provide signposts and directions but we've got to take it from there. He supplies the road map but we've got to drive the bus. But that is all a lie my friends. God is much more personally and intimately involved in our salvation. He planned it out meticulously before the foundation of the world.

Here, in a brief capsule, is how God accomplished this amazing, miraculous feat for us, "For he hath made him (Jesus) to be sin for us, who knew no sin; that we might be made the righteousness of God in him," (2 Corinthians 5:21). "And the Word (God in the person of Jesus) was made flesh, and dwelt among us," (John 1:14).

This is almost incomprehensible. In fact, we can only comprehend this truth by the power of the Holy Spirit working through the word. It's unbelievable and inconceivable but irrefutable and wholly reliable. Thank God for not only personally accomplishing our salvation but for actually becoming our salvation in Jesus Christ.

Faith Food — Steve Stranghoener

Law & Gospel

Buried Treasure

The Bible is truly amazing. Its depth is bottomless. Scripture renders the greatest human intellect utterly helpless. No one can discern even a morsel of its truth without the aid of the Holy Spirit.

This fact dawned on me again recently when I came across Hebrews 8:11, "And they shall not teach every man his neighbor, and every man his brother, saying, Know the Lord: for all shall know me, from the least to the greatest." I stared for the longest time and concentrated with all my might but only drew a blank. What did this mean? Certainly, it didn't proclaim that evangelizing would cease. Was it referring to Judgment Day when every knee shall bow?

The most erudite person in the universe came to my aid and guided me by His word to follow His principles. I was reminded to let Scripture interpret Scripture within the context of the full counsel of God. I read the entire chapter and studied footnotes pointing to parallel passages. Then I enlisted the aid of scholars who had mined this treasure before. For example, *Dr. Kretzmann's Commentary* helped to guide me through other pertinent sections of the Bible. Still I only came away with a rudimentary understanding but, even at that, it blew my mind to see the vastness of God's treasure buried within such a brief passage of Scripture.

Faith Food Steve Stranghoener

Since Hebrews was written as the perfect commentary on the Old Testament, it shouldn't have surprised me that I had to plumb the Old Covenant to grasp the meaning of this short, New Testament passage. As I read more, I learned that God had inspired the writer of Hebrews to expound upon how Christ's ministry surpassed that of the Levitical priesthood to the point of rendering it obsolete.

The latter had been assigned to follow the law given through God's intermediary, Moses, to carry out the forms, rituals and sacrifices aimed at reminding the Old Testament believers of God's promise to them under the Old Covenant. However, the people of Israel were not able to hold up their end of the bargain. God knew that no one could be saved through the deeds of the law and thus He provided for a new, superseding covenant built on His promise of a perfect Savior; the promise He first made to Adam and Eve.

The writer of Hebrews was trying to enlighten many Jews who, at the time, still practiced their faith in accordance with old, outdated, ineffectual means. The Levitical priests were the only people assigned by God under the Old Testament to enter the Holy of Holies and make sacrifices on behalf of the people. But that Covenant was replaced by Christ who didn't have to enter, offer the sacrifice and leave, over and over again. The writer pointed out how Christ served as our eternal intermediary with full authority, dwelling in heaven at the right hand of the Father. Christ's sacrifice became all-availing in atoning for the sins of the entire world for all time. Jesus' sacrifice reconciled sinful mankind to God, once and for always. As God proclaimed in 1 Peter 2:9, we all became members of the royal priesthood with direct access to God through the Second Person of the Trinity, Jesus Christ.

Having this background, I was able to see Hebrews 8:11 in a clearer light. Under the Old Covenant, the people of Israel depended upon the Levitical priests to instruct them in the ways and laws of God. Christ rendered the Old Covenant moot by serving as our constant intercessor before the Father. Paul addressed this wonderful notion in Galatians 3:24-25, "Wherefore the law was our schoolmaster to bring us unto Christ, that we might be justified by faith. But after that faith is come, we are no longer under a schoolmaster."

Thanks to Jesus' atoning work, we've all been freed from condemnation under the law by the power of the gospel. Earthly mediators are no longer needed for us to understand God's plan of salvation. Under the New Covenant in Jesus Christ, God has sowed this knowledge in our hearts and sustained it through His life-giving word.

Whoever hears the gospel and believes is saved by the power of the Holy Spirit. We still are blessed to serve the Lord by evangelizing to spread the gospel but the Temple curtain has been rent and we are privileged, great and small, Jew and Gentile, to approach God without fear, covered in the blood and righteousness of Jesus Christ. "For Christ is the end of the law for righteousness to everyone that believeth," (Romans 10:4); out with the old and in with the new, hallelujah!

The Law & Gospel in a Nutshell

In the wacky 1997 movie *Austin Powers: International Man of Mystery* that spoofed James Bond, Austin's fellow spy and love interest Vanessa Kinsington proclaimed, "Always wanting to have fun, Austin, that's you in a nutshell." The irreverent British sleuth with the comically bad teeth mimed being trapped inside a gargantuan nutshell and retorted, "No, this is me in a nutshell."

Vanessa's phraseology fit that simple situation since the term in a nutshell means to express something in a few words or to sum up. However, I wondered if it could be applied to a discussion of law and gospel; one of the broadest and deepest concepts within Christian doctrine that's threaded, in some form or fashion, throughout every book of the Bible. A serious review of C. F. W. Walther's classic text, *The Proper Distinction Between Law and Gospel*, would dissuade most folks from trying to sum up this most precious doctrine in a simple one liner.

Many great theologians have spent a lifetime studying law and gospel but still its awe-inspiring and powerful meaning can be grasped by anyone. God has put it in a nutshell, so to speak, in this short passage from Romans 6:23, "For the wages of sin is death; but the gift of God is eternal life through Jesus Christ our Lord." God employed equal brevity and clarity in Mark 16:16, "He that believeth and is baptized shall be saved; but he that believeth not shall be damned." You'd have to be willfully ignorant not to comprehend this plain and simple truth: we're all sinners, consequently we're all going die but, thanks to our Savior, Jesus Christ, we will live again eternally. The law convicts and drives us to repentance but the gospel showers us with grace, love, forgiveness, faith and eternal life with God in heaven.

God's message is so wonderfully pure, plain and simple it can be captured in a single passage of Scripture. But then why bother with the entire Holy Bible? God wants us to grow in faith unto life everlasting. Everything in the Bible is provided for our edification and sustenance now and eternally. Thus, we have a treasure trove where we can dig ever deeper to mine the mind of God. We couldn't exhaust the bounty of God's blessings in Holy Scripture even if we had a thousand lifetimes. Yet, the life-giving gospel can be summed up in one little passage.

The Apostles who had the benefit of learning from the Master Himself during three years of intense instruction didn't tell proselytes to go and study the Scriptures before they could receive the gospel. They didn't subject listeners to prerequisite hours, weeks, months or years of in-depth lectures. They just got right to the point. For example, Paul with Silas responded thusly to the Roman prison guard's query as recorded in Acts 16:30-21, "And brought them out, and said, Sirs, what must I do to be saved? And they said, Believe on the Lord Jesus Christ, and thou shalt be saved, and thy house." We can do the same because that's the gospel in a nutshell.

Sanctification

Goldilocks and the Three Beers

Goldilocks was quite the stickler. Even if they could forgive her home invasion, the three bears must have been exasperated by her exacting standards. She messed with all of their porridge, chairs and beds until she found just the right one to suit her persnickety tastes.

Sometimes I used to feel the same way about our brewers when I worked at Anheuser-Busch. Quality control was more than just science to them. They elevated it to such a high art form that it was difficult for our suppliers to keep them happy. Once they produced the perfect beer, they still had to focus on getting the delicious, golden liquid safely to market. Even then, they fussed incessantly about serving techniques at the point of sale. Once I took a brew master's class where they made a single Budweiser taste like three different beers simply by pouring it at different angles into a tall, Pilsner glass.

Thankfully, you don't have to be a brew master to understand the basics of making beer. Most beer aficionados know the simple formula of water, barley malt, yeast and perhaps an adjunct grain like corn or rice. However, digging a little deeper can yield the sobering truth, pun intended, that there's a lot more to it.

For example, what is the difference between barley and malt? Barley is used to provide the sugar compounds that live yeast cells turn into alcohol and

CO_2 during fermentation. Plain barley would never do the trick. Before it's added to the wort, it has to be conditioned until, as Goldilocks might say, it's just right. Maltsters prepare huge beds of the common grain in malt houses where it is moistened and then mechanically turned over many times until germination begins. Then, at just the precise moment, it is roasted with warm air until the germination process is halted and the malt achieves the right color for the desired brew. If it germinates too little or for too long or is over or under cooked it will be ruined.

This painstaking process reminds me of God's loving care toward us as recorded in Isaiah 28:24-29. "Doth the plowman plow all day to sow? Doth he open and break the clods of his ground? When he hath made plain the face thereof, doth he not cast abroad the fitches, and scatter the cumin, and cast in the principal wheat and the appointed barley and the rye in their place? For his God doth instruct him to discretion, and doth teach him. For the fitches are not threshed with a threshing instrument, neither is a cart wheel turned about upon the cumin; but the fitches are beaten out with a staff, and the cumin with a rod. Bread corn is bruised; because he will not ever be threshing it, nor break it with the wheel of his cart, nor bruise it with his horsemen."

In preparing us for the glories of His salvation, God is constantly grooming and disciplining us for that great end. Like the master brewer who dotes over his precious product from beginning to end, God watches over us all the way as the author and finisher of our faith. Whenever necessary, He dispenses His discipline in just the right amount; not too little and not too much and never out of anger or frustration but solely from His love. He does so for our own good, our eternal good as so comfortingly revealed in Hebrews 12:11, "Now no chastening for the present seems to be joyous, but grievous: nevertheless afterward it yields the peaceable fruit of righteousness unto them which are exercised thereby." Now that deserves a hearty toast ... prost ... and thank you Lord!

Courage from Above

My pastor has been blessed with meekness and humbleness. In most circumstances, he has avoided confrontation like the plague. He has often admitted his lingering aversion to bullies like a particularly dreadful high school nemesis who harassed him mercilessly and spiteful parishioners who tried to run him out of a previous congregation for his adherence to God's word. Some who do not know him well have misinterpreted his kindness and gentle ways as timidity or even cowardice. In truth though, despite his mild manners, he has been a champion of the faith, equipped with a deep well of courage.

It can be rather easy to witness for Christ in the midst of fellow Christians but what about when we're alone facing a skeptical or potentially hostile crowd? For pastors, funeral services present a challenge under the best of circumstances because of the raw emotions that accompany the loss of a loved one. Plus, the guests come from all walks of life with a wide range of beliefs. Too many pastors are all too willing to compromise or go easy on the crucial truths about temporal death and eternal life in order to, as they might rationalize, spare the feelings of the bereaved. This is a terrible mistake since there is no more critical time to provide a faithful witness.

As I sat in a funeral parlor chapel recently with every pew filled, I couldn't help but wonder about the mourners, none of whom I knew other than the immediate family of the deceased. I assumed many were unbelievers who were there only to pay their respects. Others, I speculated, were probably practicing Christians but still I wondered how many had heard the full truth about God's plan of salvation from their pulpits?

Unfortunately, in today's world, many churches have avoided the pure gospel by substituting the prosperity gospel, social gospel, social justice or works righteousness. In such places, the fundamental truth of Scripture concerning matters of heaven, hell, death, sin and the exclusivity of salvation are considered offensive. Facing such prospects within a funeral gathering could be daunting to say the least.

Yet, my supposedly timid pastor addressed such strangers with the boldness of Peter and John in laying our sinful natures bare under the full weight of the law in order to open hearts to the sweet gospel of our Savior's atoning sacrifice. He didn't mince words but offered the hard but glorious truth that there is only one way to heaven; through God-gifted faith in Jesus Christ alone. I marveled at the power of the message and my pastor's flawless, unshakeable delivery. Surely blood-bought, immortal souls were blessed that day.

Where did my Clark Kent of a pastor receive such Superman-like strength? The answer is summed up properly in Ephesians 3:11, 12, 16, 17, 19 & 20. "According to the eternal purpose which he purposed in Christ Jesus our Lord: In whom we have boldness and access with confidence by the faith of him. That he would grant you, according to the riches of his glory, to be strengthened with might by his Spirit in the inner man; That Christ may dwell in your hearts by faith; that ye, being rooted and grounded in love, And to know the love of Christ, which passes knowledge, that ye might be filled with all the fullness of God. Now unto him that is able to do exceeding abundantly above all that we ask or think, according to the power that worketh in us." Such courage, the strength of a lion, came from above (Psalms 27:14).

Tongue-Tied

When we hear the term tongue-tied, it usually means that someone is at a loss for words. For me, this is getting to be a rare experience. It seems like everyone has something to say these days. Just ask them. I'm no exception. I can be verbose, especially if you get me fired up about something.

Faith Food — Steve Stranghoener

Everyone has an opinion and the topic doesn't really matter. When it comes to verbal blather, our society definitely has opted for quantity over quality. Talking heads have run amok on TV, radio and, in particular, social media. With talk so cheap, the truth has been in short supply. We should all emulate Christ more often since no one was more economical with their speech. The Lord said so much in so few words!

Wouldn't it be nice if we could literally tie our tongues down sometimes? They've gotten us into an awful lot of trouble, haven't they? Perhaps James 3:5-8 said it best, "Even so the tongue is a little member, and boasts great things. Behold, how great a matter a little fire kindles! And the tongue is a fire, a world of iniquity: so is the tongue among our members, that it defiles the whole body, and sets on fire the course of nature; and it is set on fire of hell. For every kind of beasts, and of birds, and of serpents, and of things in the sea, is tamed, and hath been tamed of mankind: But the tongue can no man tame; it is an unruly evil, full of deadly poison."

There's only one power strong enough to restrain these little serpents in our mouths and the deadly venom they can spew. It's only possible with the help of God. With God all things are possible, even keeping our unruly tongues in our mouths. The power of the Holy Spirit to sanctify us and our rebellious members is truly effectual. That alone doesn't do justice though. The Holy Spirit not only constrains us from evil speaking but can inspire us to accomplish marvelous, miraculous things in spreading the gospel of Jesus Christ.

Listen to David's confession in Psalm 45:1, "My heart is indicting a good matter: I speak of the things which I have made touching the king: my tongue is the pen of a ready writer." Perhaps the language is a bit difficult for some to discern but the great Psalmist is saying that God has inspired the very words that proceeded from his mouth. If you have any doubt, then let's turn to 2 Samuel 23:2 where David declares, "The Spirit of the LORD spoke by me, and his word was in my tongue." It doesn't get any clearer than that. Read further in that chapter and you will see the proof positive as David delivers a messianic prophesy pertaining to Christ the King; the coming Savior.

Yes, thanks to the power of the Holy Spirit, God's word is inspired and inspiring. "Knowing this first, that no prophecy of the scripture is of any private interpretation. For the prophecy came not in old time by the will of man: but holy men of God spake as they were moved by the Holy Ghost," (2 Peter 1:20-21).

"All scripture is given by inspiration of God, and is profitable for doctrine, for reproof, for correction, for instruction in righteousness," (2 Timothy 3:16). "Then said Jesus to those Jews which believed on him, If ye continue in my word, then are ye my disciples indeed; And ye shall know the truth, and the truth shall make you free," (John 8:31-32). So, we don't have to tie our tongues down. We can actually put them to good use. When we share the good news of Jesus Christ and His salvation, when we spread the word of God, we can truly be inspiring by the power of the Holy Spirit working through the word.

Faith Food — Steve Stranghoener

Humility

Full-Service or Self-Service?

An antique collector friend of mine recently acquired an old Texaco pump that reminded me of my childhood and going to a filling station with my dad to get gas. Back then an attendant rushed out to the car and not only filled up the tank but washed the windshield and checked the oil. By the time I started driving, there was a choice when you pulled into the gas station. There was full-service or self-service. If you opted for self-service, you paid less per gallon for your gasoline.

Nowadays, we're more likely to see a stegosaurus stroll by than come across a full-service gas station. Today we not only fill up the tank and wash our own windshield but we might also run into the adjacent quickie mart to pour our own drink and grab a donut or hot dog. If we don't need anything but gas we can even pay at the pump instead of checking out at the cash register. I kind of miss the old days of full-service but must admit things are a lot quicker now. It's too bad we don't get a discount for all of the tasks we do ourselves.

Doesn't it seem like we've become more of a self-service society in spiritual matters too? Younger folks in our country have become known famously or infamously as the me generation. According to them, instead of checking our oil, we're supposed to constantly check our self-esteem. Loving our neighbors has been replaced with self-love and looking out for number one. Charity begins at home has been superseded by "big brother's" safety net. President Kennedy's axiom has been turned on its head by demands that the government provide everything from "free" healthcare to "free" college tuition for all.

Thankfully, we still have a perfect example of selflessness to follow in Jesus Christ. God could have easily and justifiably washed His hands of the whole mess when we rebelled and fell into sin. Instead He came to earth and took on human flesh but Jesus Christ didn't act like one of us. The Lord showed true meekness and humility in spite of His omnipotent power.

When Peter unwittingly tried to derail God's plan of salvation in the Garden of Gethsemane by taking up his sword, Jesus said, "Thinkest thou that I cannot now pray to my Father, and he shall presently give me more than twelve legions of angels?" (Matthew 26:53). Christ possessed the power to quash the Romans and the Jewish leaders without lifting a finger but instead humbled Himself and suffered our punishment to redeem us out of pure, undeserved, unconditional love. Jesus set the example and taught us well, "The disciple is not above his master, nor the servant above his lord," (Matthew 10:24). He said, "If I then, your Lord and Master, have washed your feet; ye also ought to wash one another's feet," (John 13-14). Praise the Lord for He is good and His mercy endures forever!

Faith Food   Steve Stranghoener

The Gospel for Dummies

Have you ever read one of those *For Dummies* books? They've become a staple of the self-help craze and many have found them to be quite useful for simplifying some rather complicated subjects. I did a quick Google search and found a whole host of topics where I was basically clueless such as *Music Theory for Dummies*, *Organic Chemistry for Dummies* and *Spanish for Dummies*. The list seemed endless.

In some areas, I felt I had attained proficiencies beyond their target markets in subjects such as business, fiction writing and basic math. This got me to thinking and I wondered how people would react to a prank where someone offered one of these books to an expert. For example, would Bill Gates get a laugh out of receiving *Microsoft 2016 for Dummies*? How about giving *Negotiations for Dummies* to Donald Trump? Hopefully, they'd exhibit a good sense of humor but, pranks aside, I think most subject matter experts would be offended at any suggestion that they might learn something from a *For Dummies* book within their bailiwick. As a lifelong Christian who has studied the Bible diligently, would you be offended if someone handed you a book called The Gospel for Dummies?

I think most of us would probably feel slighted but should we really? The Apostles received three years of personal instruction from the greatest teacher this world has ever seen; the Master, Jesus Christ. Yet, Christ had to chide them for their unbelief after His death and resurrection as recorded in Mark 16:14, "Afterward he appeared unto the eleven as they sat at meat, and upbraided them with their unbelief and hardness of heart, because they believed not them which had seen him after he was risen." Even Peter and Paul were "dummies" when it came to the gospel, just like you and me.

By nature, we were all deaf, dumb and blind when it came to the gospel because we were dead in our trespasses and sins (Ephesians 2:1). Left to our own devices, we could never have comprehended the good news of salvation in Jesus Christ without the aid of the Holy Ghost. Paul explained this so well in 1 Corinthians 12:1-3, "Now concerning spiritual gifts, brethren, I would not have you ignorant. Ye know that ye were Gentiles, carried away unto these dumb idols, even as ye were led. Wherefore I give you to understand, that no man speaking by the Spirit of God calls Jesus accursed: and that no man can say that Jesus is the Lord, but by the Holy Ghost."

Jesus credited the Holy Ghost in Luke 4:18, "The Spirit of the Lord is upon me, because he hath anointed me to preach the gospel to the poor." He only spoke the truth when He quoted the aforementioned prophesy of Isaiah 61:1-2 but greatly angered the Jewish teachers in the synagogue when He revealed His divinity to them in verse 21, "This day is this scripture fulfilled in your ears."

We shouldn't be offended by the truth that we're helpless dummies without God's Holy Spirit to guide us. Instead, we should thank the Lord endlessly that He has made us more erudite than our teachers. When required to testify, even before hostile crowds, the Lord has promised to send His Holy Spirit to put the words of His wisdom in our mouths (Mark 13:9-11); the precious gospel of Jesus Christ.

Humble Pie

Have you come across the term humble pie lately? Upon hearing it, folks of my generation have sometimes recalled the 1960s British rock group of the same name who were famous for songs like *Thirty Days in the Hole* and *I Don't Need No Doctor*. Younger people have drawn a blank since this idiom has largely fallen out of popular use. Some others may have rightly conjured up thoughts of humiliation since to eat humble pie meant to be forced to admit to wrongdoing in a very public way. Humble pie originally was the name for a dish prepared using the edible organs of a deer or hog. Hmmmm, which would be worse, eating the literal or figurative humble pie?

Could this notion of eating humble pie be applied to Jesus' humility? Was Christ forced to submit to public humiliation, torture and death by crucifixion at the hands of his enemies? Actually, He wasn't since Jesus willfully carried out God's plan of salvation. Christ demonstrated His willingness in the Garden of Gethsemane, "He went away again the second time, and prayed, saying, O my Father, if this cup may not pass away from me, except I drink it, thy will be done," (Matthew 26:42). He knew what was coming but did not try to avoid the pain and humiliation but willingly submitted to every terrible thing out of love toward us.

But, at that point, was it too late? Did Christ then lack the power to turn back the cosmic clock and stop His murderous attackers? Jesus dispelled any such notion when Peter took up the sword in an unwitting and foolish attempt to derail God's plan of salvation. Christ admonished him and offered this stark assurance as recorded in Matthew 26:53, "Thinkest thou that I cannot now pray to my Father, and he shall presently give me more than twelve legions of angels?"

By using this graphic example, Christ reminded Peter that He had immense, omnipotent power even then. A legion in Roman times represented anywhere from 3,600 to 6,000 soldiers. Jesus could have called down 72,000 holy angels to wage war against His captors and the forces aligned against Him.

Just one angel would have done the trick. God demonstrated this dramatically when the Assyrians were encamped against Israel to destroy them like they had done to so many other nations before. God answered fearful King Hezekiah's ardent prayer by sending one solitary angel to fight the battle. As recorded in Isaiah 37:36, that one angel single-handedly slew 185,000 soldiers in one night and sent the Assyrian king packing. Of course, Jesus Christ had the power to lay waste to all of His enemies. But He humbled himself unto death even death on a cross to save us from sin and reconcile us to God.

Rest assured that God hasn't put humble pie on our menus. Instead, by His perfect example, He has called us to humility of the kind that blossoms out of love for Christ and manifests itself in faithful service to God and our fellow man.

Jesus set the example when He, the God of the entire universe, humbly washed the filthy feet of His disciples. He explained thusly in Matthew 10:24, "The disciple is not above his master, nor the servant above his lord." He added in John 13:4, "If I then, your Lord and Master, have washed your feet; ye also ought to wash one another's feet." Thank God that He has given us the honor and privilege to humbly, meekly and reverently serve the Lord!

I Am the Greatest!

Professional boxer Cassius Clay who took the name Muhammad Ali after he converted to Islam was a master of self-promotion. He was quite a showman who was renowned for his bombast and antics in and out of the ring. In 1963 at the age of just twenty-one he became the then youngest man ever to wrest the heavyweight title from a reigning champ. Leading up to the fight, he dubbed his predecessor, Sonny Liston, a big ugly bear that he would donate to the zoo after beating him. He taunted the ferocious, imposing champ and said he would "float like a butterfly and sting like a bee," and added, "Your hands can't hit what your eyes can't see."

Ali became a cultural icon when he refused to serve in the armed forces after being drafted and said, "I got nothing against them Vietcong." He was banned from boxing and convicted for refusing induction but was vindicated four years later in 1971 when the Supreme Court overturned his conviction unanimously.

His incredible success in the ring prompted Ali to famously proclaim himself the greatest of all time. His immense fame was burnished further by the witty repartee he often shared with his erudite sidekick, ABC commentator Howard Cosell. Whatever people felt toward him, there was no doubt that Ali was entertaining and his reputation was only enhanced by his outlandish behavior.

Many other celebrities followed in Ali's footsteps since they saw how shameless self-promotion paid off. Madonna, Lady Gaga and Kim Kardashian were just a few examples. The latter became famous for, well, being famous.

In some respects, Ali was more of a character than a man of character, especially early on. But the philosophical pugilist and brash social commentator became an iconic figure revered as the greatest sportsman of the 20th century according to Sports Illustrated and others. I too admired Ali's hard work and impeccable skills in the "sweet science" and his ascent to the pinnacle of boxing. While I disagreed with some of his positions, I couldn't deny that he had the courage of his convictions. He unfortunately led many away from the one true Christian faith.

This isn't meant to demean Muhammad Ali or other celebrities who have gained stardom with adoring fans and the fawning media through shameless self-promotion. They deserve their due for their hard work and God-given abilities. However, it is important to contrast temporal and spiritual aspirations and duties. The former may bring worldly accolades while the latter can result in persecution and scorn but only following God's calling can bring lasting glory.

We may, as equipped and guided by God, attain a measure of success in this world. But whether we do or not, whether we are considered high or low, we have a completely different measure of greatness as assigned by our Lord and Savior, Jesus Christ. Here like in so many things, God's view is completely contrary to the world's opinion.

These three Scripture passages convey the message much better than any commentary I could offer. "Whosoever therefore shall break one of these least commandments, and shall teach men so, he shall be called the least in the kingdom of heaven: but whosoever shall do and teach them, the same shall be called great in the kingdom of heaven," (Matthew 5:19). "But so shall it not be among you: but whosoever will be great among you, shall be your minister," (Mark 10:43). "For though I be free from all men, yet have I made myself servant unto all, that I might gain the more," (I Corinthians 9:19).

God's way certainly flies in the face of worldly, conventional wisdom. Christ put it best, "And whosoever shall exalt himself shall be abased; and he that shall humble himself shall be exalted," (Matthew 23:12). Christ didn't just talk the talk, He walked the walk. From washing His Apostles' feet to trudging to the bloody cross, His whole life was an example of selfless service, unconditional love and infinite sacrifice. If we want to draw attention to ourselves, let us do as Paul did, declaring the truth that we are chief among sinners. As for proclaiming who is greatest, let us point to the one who is truly deserving: Jesus Christ, Almighty God.

Young at Heart

Recently, Old Blue Eyes popped up on my iPod singing *Young at Heart*. Sinatra's silky-smooth voice crooned distinctively while he extolled the virtues of a youthful attitude, something more valuable than all the money in the world. As odd as this may sound, the iconic leader of the famed Rat Pack made me think of a lesson offered by our Lord and Savior to His disciples in Matthew 18:1-3. "At the same time came the disciples unto Jesus, saying, who is the greatest in the kingdom of heaven? And Jesus called a little child unto him, and set him in the midst of them, and said, Verily I say unto you, except ye be converted, and become as little children, ye shall not enter into the kingdom of heaven."

Jesus wanted them to have the humble attitude David displayed in Psalm 131:1, "Lord, my heart is not haughty, nor mine eyes lofty: neither do I exercise myself in great matters or in things too high for me." Beyond humility, Jesus' wise words contained something even more profound. What were these things that were too high for David and what did Jesus mean by becoming as little children? Christ's message had a spiritual quotient because He spoke of the mystery of faith.

Jesus taught the truth that newborn babes entered into the kingdom of heaven through baptism whereby they received faith as a free gift of God by the power of His Holy Spirit working through His word. Jesus wanted His disciples to remember that no one could get to heaven on their own, young or old. No one could lay claim to any merit. The Lord wanted them to turn from seeking personal glory and remain humbly thankful for the gift of faith like helpless, newborn babies. The inspired Apostle put it this way in 1 Peter 2:1-3, "Wherefore laying aside all malice, and all guile, and hypocrisies, and envies, and all evil speaking, as newborn babes, desire the sincere milk of the word, that ye may grow thereby: if so be ye have tasted that the Lord is gracious."

Babies at the baptismal font don't ponder the glories of heaven. The gift of faith is a concept much too high for them. This is true for adults too apart from the enlightenment of the Holy Spirit. We can't earn it or apprehend it. In order to be saved, we must receive faith as helpless little babies because we have no more power than them in such matters. Faith comes by hearing the word of God (Romans 10:17). The power isn't in the water, our comprehension or anything residing within us. Prior to our conversion we are spiritually dead in our trespasses and sins. God deserves all the glory.

Does this mean that God wants us to remain like little children in matters of faith? No, He wants us to be weaned from milk and grow through the meat of His sustenance. We're instructed thusly in 1 Corinthians 14:20, "Brethren, be not children in understanding: howbeit in malice be ye children, but in understanding be men." When it comes to evil God wants us to be childlike and innocent but in matters of faith He wants us to grow and mature as adults. Thankfully, God provides His faith-sustaining word (John 8:31-32) to help us remain grafted into the True Vine. That's how God equips us to grow in truth and faith; by the miraculous power of His holy word.

Faith Food   Steve Stranghoener

The Nature of God

Rolling in the Dough

Slang comes and goes. That's because times change and familiar idioms become unintelligible or take on different meanings. Cold is supposed to indicate low temperatures but at one time being frosted meant you were angry. Being cool means, everything is good ... or awesome according to the Fonz. Today if we're chilling it means we're kicked back and relaxing.

Back in the day, we used to say we were rolling in the dough if our pockets were full of money. I worked in a baking company as a teenager. On payday I liked to joke that I was rolling in the dough. Sometimes I'd quip that business, like our bread, was on the rise. For a while, most hip people, not just bakers, used the term bread euphemistically as a substitute for money. In the 1950s and 1960s, beatniks and hippies would say, "Hey man, can you spare me some bread?" as they panhandled for spare change.

Bread has more than one meaning in the Bible too. Sometimes the Bible uses bread as a term for universal currency or wealth of sorts. We still pray as the Lord taught us, give us this day our daily bread. It means more than just a loaf of whole wheat or rye. In this context it means everything we need for daily sustenance.

There is a distinction though in that bread normally has a positive connotation in the Bible whereas money comes with some cautions. God warns in 1 Timothy 6:10, "For the love of money is the root of all evil." Please notice that it doesn't say that money or wealth is bad or that we must take a vow of poverty to be Christians. It's a caution against making money our god or giving it too high of a priority unto itself.

Still, there is a clear tie between the use of bread and money in some places. God instructs us to remember that there is much more to life than mere money. Jesus said as much in Matthew 4:4 when responding to Satan's temptations, "But he answered and said, It is written, Man shall not live by bread alone, but by every word that proceeds out of the mouth of God." Said another way, bread or earthly wealth can sustain our bodies to a degree but more importantly we also need to be continually fed spiritually through God's word.

God doesn't decry earthly wealth per se but encourages us to use it to serve His good purposes. For example, Christ instructs us thusly in Matthew 10:8, "Heal the sick, cleanse the lepers, raise the dead, cast out devils: freely ye have received, freely give." He only asks us to share in the good things that He has already provided to us freely.

Unlike slang, God's message has a spiritual meaning that has never changed and has always stood in stark contrast to worldly wisdom. Bread or wealth can be used to accomplish great things. But there is always the caution not to get hung up on money. Sometimes the best things for us are God's chastisements which are done out of love. At times, it's better for God to withhold than to grant wealth to us.

God knew that it would ultimately be a blessing for His people to suffer through 400 years of exile and bondage in Egypt but then He delivered them. Similarly, He knew it was best for them to wander in the wilderness for forty years before crossing into the Promised Land. It caused the Israelites to draw near and lean on God rather than themselves. At that critical time, God warned them not to get caught up in the wealth He was about to shower on them in the land of milk and honey.

God still warns of potential dangers while teaching us that earthly riches can be used to accomplish great things if we remember the ultimate source of our wealth. God's words in Deuteronomy 8:18 are as valid today as ever, "But thou shalt remember the LORD thy God: for it is he that giveth thee power to get wealth, that he may establish his covenant which he swore unto thy fathers, as it is this day." When we're feeling high and mighty and full of ourselves, may God remind us that He is the source of our good fortune. When we're rolling in the dough, as we used to say, we should be happy to share God's blessings with others. As a baker might jest, it's the yeast that we can do.

Rotten Apples

We know we're not supposed to be judgmental in condemning sinners as though we are above the fray ourselves. We're all rotten apples apart from the pardoning grace of God and Jesus' blood-bought righteousness. In John 8:7, Jesus tells the angry mob with the hidden agenda, "He that is without sin among you, let him first cast a stone at her."

But many people misconstrue what Christ said in Matthew 7:1, "Judge not, that ye be not judged." Rather than taking this as a treatise on forgiveness, some use it as a cudgel against those who defend God's law and biblical doctrine. If we call a sin a sin or take any stand for truth and morality on the basis of God's word, then we're being judgmental ... bad, very bad!

We need to draw a proper distinction here. God cautions against condemning others for their sins, the small mote in their eye, while overlooking the huge beam in our own (Matthew 7:5). At the same time, He strongly condemns sin, particularly false doctrine (Galatians 1:8-9) and false teachers (Matthew 7:15). In regard to judging others, God offers this caution in 1 Samuel 16:7, "But the LORD said unto Samuel, Look not on his countenance, or on the height of his stature; because I have refused him: for the LORD seeth not as man seeth; for man looketh on the outward appearance, but the LORD looketh on the heart."

Faith Food — Steve Stranghoener

This is all pretty confusing isn't it? How are we supposed to judge without being judgmental? Even though we can't read people's hearts like He does, God gives us the answer in Matthew 7:17, "Even so every good tree brings forth good fruit; but a corrupt tree brings forth evil fruit." You wouldn't pick a rotten, mushy, worm-infested apple off the ground and eat it rather than a ruby red, crisp, delicious one hanging on a tree, would you? We need to be careful in rushing to judgment but we can learn a lot by looking at observable behavior or the fruit of someone's labor. Sometimes it's as simple as listening to what they say and watching what they do, "The labor of the righteous tends to life: the fruit of the wicked to sin," (Proverbs 10:16).

This can be challenging because people try to hide black hearts and evil motives. Abortion is a great example of how people try to polish a rotten apple to pass it off as edible. They wax eloquent about choice but all in the name of abortion. It's a culture of death; at its core it's pure wickedness. This holds true for many hot-button issues. Same sex marriage, cohabitation, climate change, euthanasia and the so-called separation of church and state come to mind. What do they all have in common? They are all contrary to God's clear word of truth in the Bible. They put the wisdom of man above God and lead us away from repentance, forgiveness, salvation and eternal life.

The battle lines are drawn in what is a cultural war. There is a clear choice: We can put our trust in God or men. The latter makes life easier for the time being but what about the long run? Here's a little help in making what should be a no brainer. "Because the foolishness of God is wiser than men; and the weakness of God is stronger than men," (1 Corinthians 1:25). "Nay but, O man, who art thou that replies against God? Shall the thing formed say to him that formed it, why hast thou made me thus?" (Romans 9:20). "It is better to trust in the Lord than to put confidence in princes," (Psalm 118:9).

This should be an easy decision if we look to God and His inspired, inerrant word for guidance. And we should take the long view of eternity in following God's path. "And fear not them which kill the body, but are not able to kill the soul: but rather fear him (God) which is able to destroy both soul and body in hell," (Matthew 10:28).

Relativity

Have you ever sat down with a two-year-old child to explain the theory of relativity? Forget that most of us don't have the faintest grasp of basic physics. Even for someone with the understanding of Albert Einstein this would be absurd. Everyone knows that a toddler's mind is incapable of understanding something so complex. But then why is it we so often have the audacity to presume to be able to comprehend the mind of God?

Scripture clearly teaches that God in the person of Jesus Christ died on the cross to atone for the sins of all people. In one infinitely mighty, divine act, Jesus justified everyone, opening the gates to heaven for all mankind. Scripture also indisputably reveals that some people will go to heaven while others will spend eternity in hell apart from God (Mark 16:16). How can this be, we ask? If God wants all people saved and sacrificed Himself in the person of Jesus to accomplish His will, how come some still wind up in hell?

The Bible offers a conundrum that we will never untangle this side of heaven: The people bound for heaven do so only by God's grace and power, apart from their own deeds, but those destined for hell have no one to blame but themselves. Since this unquestionable truth escapes our puny reason, we offer fruitless explanations aimed at appeasing our bruised egos.

All of our foolish attempts fall short and in one way or another contradict the clear teachings of Scripture. For example, double predestination; the false notion that God predestined some to heaven and others to hell, may soothe our burning curiosity for a time but eventually falls flat unless we abandon God's inerrant word that it contradicts. In frustration, this can lead some to the soul-destroying conclusion that God must be unjust. This is nothing new. Such dangerous pondering has jeopardized the faith of men since the beginning.

Paul addressed this issue in Romans 9:14-21. He tackled the attack on God's righteousness head on in a way that the Jews certainly understood. He turned to Old Testament Scripture and referred to Moses' contentious encounter with Pharaoh. Therein, God proclaimed His divine right to have compassion and mercy on whom He so chose and to likewise harden the hearts of those He saw fit, all to His glory and in keeping with His gracious will toward us. Of course, God knew that Pharaoh would never accept His gracious gift of salvation. But His foreknowledge didn't mean He predestined Pharaoh to hell. God's grace toward all, even those like Pharaoh who would reject Him, reminded me of the parable of the lord of the vineyard (Matthew 21:33-46) who kept his promise to the workers he hired first while shedding his grace on those hired later in the day.

Paul offered scathing criticism to the naysayers. That's because he understood that they weren't humbly seeking answers but challenged the truth of God with human reason out of pride and arrogance. He took the example we opened with to another, infinitely higher level. If asking a toddler to grasp the theory of relativity was absurd, how much more so was thinking that an inanimate object could contend with a living soul. By pointing out the nonsensicalness of a clay pot upbraiding the potter, Paul showed how ludicrous it was for us creatures to challenge our Creator regarding the oracles of God that He had not revealed to us.

In keeping with Paul's wise, inspired advice, let us take heed. We should focus our attention on the many promises God has shared with us for our edification and comfort and leave the mysteries of God to Him alone for now.

Proof Positive

Do you want proof of the magnificence, beauty and perfection of God's creation? Then look at women. What, you say? Women can certainly be beautiful but they're far from perfect. Yeah, yeah, I hear you but I don't mean in our fallen state but as God intended. And even after the fall, women serve a perfect purpose in God's plan in accordance with His will.

God didn't make Eve as He did Adam from the dust of the ground. He took part of Adam. Today this might be called cloning but God did something much greater. He took these same elements of flesh and bone, Adam's DNA, and reconstructed it in a new and marvelous way to compliment Adam perfectly. It was definitely a job well done.

We're of the same flesh and blood but designed differently; not just in shape and form but emotionally and temperamentally. We're each equipped to handle God-given roles in a way that makes marriages and families better and stronger.

This truth of God's wisdom came to me in an odd way. Believe it or not, we had a girl on the football team a few years back at Lutheran North where I coached. When I was younger, I would have thrown a fit about this unwanted incursion into one of the last bastions of masculinity. But times changed and, frankly, we didn't have any boys on the team who could kick worth a hoot.

Her name was Karsten and she's wasn't a girly girl in that she was tough and competitive but she was unquestionably different from our other players. She worried about the helmet messing up her hair and the frumpy look her figure took on when she donned the hip, thigh and knee pads. Her temperament wasn't the same as the boys either. Constructive criticism could bring tears instead of results. We had to tread gingerly with her emotions.

Some may have thought that this was more trouble than it was worth but she helped make us better in some unseen ways. When she was around, we took more care to dispense with salty language. The guys were less likely to bicker and let tempers flare when things went badly. The boys also complained less about conditioning drills around Karsten. She was proof positive that women were not only different but in a good way. She complimented the males and helped to make us better.

If only we could see things in the context of God's creation and His plan. Unfortunately, too often women are judged on superficial things like looks alone. When making out a wish list for prospective wives, men tend to have only one box to check. Is she a hottie? Women have so much more to offer.

Instead of only going skin deep, we should plumb the depths below the surface. God has advised us to look for hidden virtue. Here's how He put it in Proverbs 31:10, "Who can find a virtuous woman? For her price is far above rubies." He then went on to list a whole bunch of qualities that have nothing to do with external beauty. Finally, God summed it up this way in Proverbs 31:30-31, "Favor is deceitful, and beauty is vain: but a woman that fears the LORD, she shall be praised. Give her of the fruit of her hands; and let her own works praise her in the gates."

When it comes to men, women, marriage and family, like with all things, what God ordains is always good. Praise the Lord for His wonderful works!

Endless Summer

I'm a fan of surfing. This is absurd considering my home rests in Missouri. Following my passion is at best a once-a-year pursuit during our vacations at the beach. Even then, it seems like a fruitless endeavor since mastering the art of wave riding takes considerable time and practice. Never mind that our annual excursions entail exponentially more wipeouts than successful glides across glassy curls. Still my enthusiasm persists because; as the Beach Boys put it, *Catch a Wave and You're Sittin' on Top of the World*. It only takes one to make your whole vacation.

For the other fifty-one weeks out of the year, I'm left to live the dream vicariously through music and movies. Listening to Stevie Ray Vaughn and Dick Dale and the Del-Tones crank up *Pipeline* in *Back to the Beach* always gets me in the mood. Jan and Dean's *Ride the Wild Surf* gets me going too. I'm a sucker for anything in this genre: *Beach Party, Beach Blanket Bingo, Surfer Joe, Surfin' USA* and *Point Break* to name a few. Perhaps I'm most partial to *North Shore* since it offers the ludicrous proposition that a kid from mainland Arizona who learned to surf in a wave pool could compete with the best of the best on the north shore of Oahu.

Catching a wave provides an incredible rush. Still, there's something else that sets surfing apart. It embodies a lifestyle that is hard to put into words. The movie *Endless Summer* may have captured this spirit best. Two buddies follow the summer season perpetually during a trip around the globe while sampling some of the most fabulous foam this world has to offer. The message seems to be that the lifestyle transcends all geography and cultures.

This is where I have to catch myself to avoid a spiritual wipeout. Unfortunately, hard core surfing culture entails an existential element that can put it at odds with Christianity. It hearkens back to Socrates and later philosophers like Kierkegaard, Nietzsche and Jean-Paul Sartre. A central tenet adopted by many surfers is the pursuit of the good life. Another core principle is freedom. On the surface, these beliefs seem admirable. However, existentialism teaches that these ideals can only be achieved apart from a deity.

Thus, taken to the extreme, the lifestyle is focused solely on self apart from God.

Thankfully, there is no need to stop waxing down our surfboards. We can enjoy the sport and even some elements of the culture if we keep things in the proper perspective. Instead of bringing us closer to "Mother Nature," frolicking in the foam and sliding down a wall of rolling water should turn our eyes to God, our Creator.

Romans 1:20 reveals that the wonders of the natural world provide indisputable evidence of God's creative majesty, "For the invisible things of him from the creation of the world are clearly seen, being understood by the things that are made, even his eternal power and Godhead; so that they are without excuse." The thunderous roar of the tides breaking upon the beach should remind us of the omnipotent power of God, the one who commands the winds and the waves (Psalm 107:25).

The roiling of the seas should caution us against putting our faith in the things of this world (Ephesians 6:12): powers of darkness, principalities, princes and especially the false teachings of men that change like the wind (Ephesians 4:14). Finally, we should seek the everlasting joy and peace of an endless summer in heaven with our gracious God through the salvation of Jesus Christ, our Lord and Savior.

Faith Food   Steve Stranghoener

Mountain Man

The image of the reclusive, stoic, self-sufficient mountain man has remained securely embedded in American Folklore. In 2015, *The Revenant* proved to be a huge box office blockbuster. It told the saga of a mountain man who survived a horrific brush with death courtesy of the fangs and claws of a massive, marauding bear. The gruesome grizzly was just one of many seemingly insurmountable obstacles the hero had to overcome to escape the Grim Reaper. The hostile elements were bad enough but the greatest peril he faced came from a beast of another sort: the human kind. The term revenant referred to someone who came back from the dead. There was a bit of hyperbole in the title but not much, judging from the harrowing experience portrayed on the big screen.

The Revenant reminded me of *Jeremiah Johnson*, another iconic mountain man who was brought to life in film a generation ago by Robert Redford. What made these characters so appealing that they've drawn movie goers for many decades? Perhaps it was their independence more than anything else. Such rugged individualism has vanished in our modern nanny state. Nevertheless, our admiration for devil-may-care rebels who bucked the system has remained and even been extended to the comedic realm as evidenced by Jed Clampett, Ma & Pa Kettle and others.

In a far more serious vein, one mountain man has stood far above all the rest. He wasn't a product of Hollywood. This mountain man was a real nonconformist but, unlike James Dean and so many others, this rebel didn't lack for a cause. His calling was the noblest and most daunting ever undertaken by a man. No other man could have accomplished what He did. That's because it took a perfect God-man, Jesus Christ.

Jesus was quite different than silver screen heroes like Redford and DiCaprio but still fit the bill as a mountain man. Christ often sought the solitude of the mountains to pray to His Father in heaven. Some of the most memorable moments in His amazing life were set among the earthly spires. He chose the Mount of Transfiguration to reveal His divine glory to Peter, James and John. He allowed Himself to be taken up on a high mountaintop by Satan during His temptation in the wilderness. The Devil offered Him every earthly incentive possible to bow down to him but Jesus rebuffed him and thwarted Satan with the Sword of the Spirit, His holy word. Even in the end, Our Lord and Savior chose a mountain of sorts, the high hill shaped like a skull, Golgotha, from whence to claim the final victory for us.

Appropriately, Jesus chose the Mount of Olives for His ascension back into heaven in front of His disciples. He was a mountain man to the very end of His earthly ministry and accomplished so much more than all the others, real or imagined. Come to think of it, wouldn't Hollywood have been closer to the mark in recounting Jesus' life and atoning sacrifice in *The Revenant*? The revenant Jesus Christ truly rose from the dead and provided irrefutable evidence that God had fulfilled His plan of salvation for mankind in Him.

Clover and Ice

I wonder if it drives pastors crazy when people explain the Holy Trinity using simple, earthly objects like clover and ice. Maybe it makes sense on one level because everyone can relate to a typical, three-leaved clover. It has three separate leaves but is only one plant. Water might come closer since there is only one substance but it takes on three distinct forms; liquid, ice or vapor, depending upon the temperature but remains H2O in each case. Still these object lessons fall woefully, infinitely short of the truth. That's because no puny human mind can comprehend the true nature of God: Father, Son and Holy Spirit. Each person within the Holy Trinity is unique but they are not three Gods but one, perfect in harmony and co-equal in majesty.

Trying to understand this concept has caused my head to ache in the past. I've turned to my pastor for an explanation since he had the advantage of arduous seminary training. But he admitted he was in the same boat when it came to comprehending the Trinity. Still he offered this good advice. "Steve" he said, "sometimes you've just got to take God at His word in Holy Scripture and leave the secret things of God to God for now, like it says in Deuteronomy 29:29." He added, "The important thing is to believe the clear truth of God's inspired and inerrant word even if we don't fully comprehend it."

This was good advice indeed because I've encountered many people that didn't believe in the Holy Trinity because they couldn't rationalize the concept. This didn't just happen with atheists, agnostics and members of false religions like the Jehovah's Witnesses and Mormons. There were plenty of self-professed Christians that got this wrong too. Some rightly said that the word Trinity didn't appear in the Bible and falsely concluded that thus it must have been a man-made concept.

This was either ignorance or sophistry because the concept has been clearly presented in the Bible without mention of the word Trinity. Jesus referred to the Father and Holy Spirit or Comforter on numerous occasions. All three persons appeared simultaneously at Jesus' baptism: Jesus in person, the Holy Spirit descending in the form of a dove and the Father audibly with the words "This is my beloved Son, in whom I am well pleased." Jesus said "I and my Father are one," as recorded in John 10:30. Quoting from Isaiah 61:1, Jesus said "The Spirit of the Lord is upon me," in Luke 4:18.

Although incomprehensible according to human reason, Scripture actually recorded a conversation within the Holy Trinity in Isaiah 6:8 where they discussed God's plan of salvation, "Also I heard the voice of the Lord, saying, who shall I (Father) send, and who will go for us (Triune God)? Then said I,

Here am I; send me (Jesus)." All three persons were present and participated in the creation of the earth and universe. "In the beginning God created the heaven and the earth," (Genesis 1:1). In Colossians 2:16 we're told that Jesus created all things. Genesis 1:2 also credited the Holy Spirit with participation in the creation, "The Spirit of God moved upon the face of the waters."

As I read these passages my headache went away because the truth of God's word; no matter how incomprehensible, was abundantly clear. The Bible presented an open and shut case regarding the nature of one God in three persons: Father, Son and Holy Spirit. The one true and Triune God, all three Persons, were there when our world was created and when God devised His plan of salvation for us before the foundation of the world. The Triune God has never changed. He was, is and always will be one God in three Persons. My study of the nature of God left me with one more mind-blowing truth. When we see God face-to-face, Jesus will still have a glorified, human body. Imagine that!

The Great Unifier

I'm sorry to say but must admit that I've come to loathe the word diversity. That's because it no longer refers to a free and open society where different ideas and beliefs are welcomed to be put to the test of honest and respectful public discourse. In today's America, diversity has become an atrocious misnomer meant to confer nobility to identity politics aimed at pitting one group against another on the basis of skin color, ethnicity, gender, age, faith, education and socio-economic standing. The hypocrisy of the people who intolerantly preach tolerance is disgusting in its audacity.

According to the politically correct diversity crowd, the most grievous offence anyone can commit is to proclaim the gospel of Jesus Christ. Hiding behind a mythological tenet called separation of church and state, they have arrogantly banned any mention of Jesus and the one true and Triune God from our schools, halls of government and public square. Anyone who proclaims the simple truth of God's word that abortion is murder, homosexuality is a sin and marriage is exclusively the union of one man and woman is vilified as homophobic, hateful, racist, mentally ill or all of the above. If you really want to throw the diversity police into a hissy fit, just mention the immutable, all-important biblical doctrine that all steeples do not point up and Jesus is the only way to heaven.

The saddest part of the disingenuous crusade to outlaw the gospel of Christ is that so many blood-bought, immortal souls have been put in jeopardy by their outrageous lies. If they really believed in diversity, they would hail Jesus as their true champion. He is the one and only equal opportunity Savior. Thankfully, He didn't come to just redeem His own kind; the Jews. The inspired Apostle Paul, a former Jew among Jews declared in Romans 1:16,

"For I am not ashamed of the gospel of Christ: for it is the power of God unto salvation to **everyone** that believeth; to the Jew first, and also to the **Greek**." The word Greek here meant Gentiles or non-Jews. God put this truth into action by enlisting Paul as the greatest evangelist to the Gentiles that the world has ever known.

When Jesus went to the cross, He suffered an eternity of God's wrath against sin, somehow within three of our earthly hours, for everyone who has ever or will ever live regardless of their skin color, gender, nationality or other outward characteristics. Paul confirmed this glorious, inspired truth in Romans 5:18, "Therefore as by the offence of one (Adam) judgment came upon all men to condemnation; even so by the righteousness of one (Jesus) the free gift came upon all men unto justification of life."

Jesus fully paid the immeasurable price for all of our sins so we could be spared from hell. This included Simon of Cyrene, possibly a black man from Libya, who had the honor of bearing the Lord's cross for Him to Calvary. He suffered for the Ethiopian eunuch, most likely a black man, who heard about Jesus from Philip. The redeemed included the Roman slave named Onesimus who was mentioned in Philemon. Christ died for all women too including Eve, His mother Mary and Mary Magdalene who was privileged to be one of the first witnesses of Christ's resurrection at the empty tomb.

Some 3,000 people from many nations including many Jews received faith in Jesus and salvation by the power of the Holy Spirit on the day of Pentecost. Jesus even died for the Pharisees, the Jewish leaders who had Him killed. One of them named Nicodemus received faith in Christ and went to His tomb to anoint the Lord's body.

Thankfully for all of us, Jesus didn't practice today's form of intolerant, bigoted diversity. No, Jesus Christ showed through divine affirmative action that He was and is the great unifier of all mankind. Unlike ours, His house will never be divided (Matthew 12:25).

Faith Food   Steve Stranghoener

Eternal Life and End Times

Our Inheritance

Are you meek? Unfortunately, that's sometimes not the operative word in describing me. On occasion, it might be more apropos to say prideful, spiteful, cranky, impatient, arrogant, hypocritical, deceitful, short-tempered, greedy or even hateful. Even the best of us have our bad days or moments, don't we? Does that mean we've lost our inheritance? You know the one I'm talking about; the promise that Jesus offered during His Sermon on the Mount. As recorded in Matthew 5:5 He said, "Blessed are the meek: for they shall inherit the earth."

It seems impossible to remain meek given the way we're always struggling with our Old Adam; that sinful man of pride. Thankfully, we're not taken out of the will by our Heavenly Father when we give into our old, sinful natures. God is patient and longsuffering with us and always willing to forgive repentant sinners for the sake of the bitter sufferings and death of our beloved Lord and Savior, Jesus Christ.

God offers the key to remaining meek and humble in spite of ourselves. We must remember the truth of God's word that we're helpless sinners in need of the Savior. God reminds us that we are powerless to save ourselves, "And you hath he quickened, who were dead in trespasses and sins," (Ephesians 2:1). God reveals the harsh reality that only He has the power to save us through His gospel word, "For I am not ashamed of the gospel of Christ: for it is the power of

Faith Food Steve Stranghoener

God unto salvation to everyone that believeth; to the Jew first, and also to the Greek," (Romans 1:16). God gently reminds us that only His grace and not our deeds count toward our salvation, "For by grace are ye saved through faith; and that not of yourselves: it is the gift of God: Not of works, lest any man should boast," (Ephesians 2:8-9).

These simple but powerful truths are the source of our humility and meekness. By staying in the word, we can humbly remember that we can't earn our way into heaven. We're totally dependent upon the gracious work of God in bringing us to and keeping us in the faith; believing wholly in the only one who can offer us new, eternal life: our Lord and Savior, Jesus Christ.

With that settled, I have another question. What kind of earth will we, the meek in Christ, inherit? After defeating all of our enemies, Satan and his minions, is God going to turn over the keys to this earthly kingdom to us? Look around and tell me what you think. There are a lot of beautiful things in this world but look closely. There's a lot of dust that has been swept under the rug by sinful mankind.

Underneath the shiny façade, that fresh coat of paint, this is a rotting, termite-infested cesspool of a world. Inheriting this place would be a bum deal. Thankfully, we know for certain that there's something infinitely better in store for us. First, Jesus tells us that His kingdom is not of this world (John 18:36). Furthermore, this earth and the entire sin-corrupted universe are doomed to destruction. Everything is going to be burned up with fervent heat (2 Peter 3:10 &12).

Our Godly inheritance puts this world to shame. God promises to create new heavens and a new earth in 2 Peter 3:13; "Nevertheless we, according to his promise, look for new heavens and a new earth, wherein dwelleth righteousness." What will it look like? We can't say for sure but it will be grand, beyond anything we can imagine.

Although figurative, Revelation 21 puts things in perspective in describing a beautiful, bejeweled city with streets paved of gold. The best part though is revealed in 2 Peter 3:13 quoted above. When it says therein will dwell righteousness that means there will be no sin in this new world. Our home and us in our new, glorified bodies will be made fully righteous and without sin.

It will be a perfect and holy world. The Old Adam, our sinful natures will be gone for good. The very best part is that we will dwell with Righteousness, God Himself, just as Adam and Eve did in the Garden before the fall. Until then my friends, let's stay meek and humble by looking to God and His gospel promises for deliverance. Take out God's last will and testament often to avoid any doubts about our inheritance by reading the Bible often.

Quality of Life

How's your quality of life? Did you know that there are indexes available to help us assess our personal well-being in terms of four domains: ecology, economics, politics and culture? The United Nations uses what they call the Human Development Index (HDI) and they even publish something they call the World Happiness Report. Corralling composite happiness on a graph sounds overly ambitious to me; like trying to gather slippery beads of mercury.

What's the point of this anyway? Even if life is pretty good; health is okay, creditors are at bay and there are even a few bucks tucked away in the bank, does that mean that our quality of life should receive a passing grade? Some days are better than others and we're subject to mood swings that may have nothing to do with anything the UN may consider important. We're up and down, happy and sad, glad and mad. Emotions don't lend themselves well to empirical measurement and they can shift like the wind. We may not even understand why we're down in the dumps sometimes. We just are.

The more I think about it, I don't believe the UN or any government entity or think tank really cares about my personal well-being, unless it might help them wring more tax dollars out of me. So then, why is there all this fuss about quality of life and whether individuals or societies are happy or sad?

There appears to be a hidden agenda aimed at granting more power to the state. Since they consider us as their wards, the state must determine the value of our lives so they can justify dubious, even sinister means to their utopian ends. If a baby in the womb is deemed to have a health problem or a bleak future that could cost the state in terms of welfare and other assistance, then by all means we should abort the child for the greater good. If someone is old and feeble and no longer able to contribute to society, in their temporal terms, and enjoy the good life as they see it, then it's time to demonstrate our compassion and humanity by speeding up their eventual demise. It will save them a lot of pain and anguish and reduce the economic burden on the rest of us. In this context, promoting quality of life is simply a tool to aid in the promotion of abortion and euthanasia.

Sadly, the quality of life crowd is forgetting about the Lord and Giver of Life. They don't want to accept that we have a Creator God who owns us and has the final say over whether we live or die. Here's the plain truth from Genesis 2:7, "And the Lord God formed man of the dust of the ground, and breathed into his nostrils the breath of life; and man became a living soul." Thankfully, God cannot be thwarted by misguided humans who seek to play god in matters of life and death.

There is much more to life than this earthly existence and temporal death, "Then Simon Peter answered him, Lord, to whom shall we go? Thou hast the words of eternal life," (John 6:68). Here is how God measures and values human life versus the quality of life crowd. Jesus proclaims in Luke 15:10, "Likewise, I say unto you, there is joy in the presence of the angels of God over one sinner that repents." We are the pinnacle of God's creation and He values us above all else.

God created us in His own image and then, when we rebelled in sin, He didn't pull the proverbial plug on us. He came to earth in the person of Jesus Christ and redeemed us lost and fallen sinners. We were completely worthless but, thankfully, not in the eyes of our loving God. He paid that terrible price to atone for our sins and rescued each of us based on our individual rather than collective worth. He loved each of us infinitely and proved it on the cross. Heaven's holy angels have erupted in incredible joy every time a single, solitary sinner has repented and been brought to faith in Jesus Christ.

Noah, Lot and John

How did I come up with this odd grouping? There was a great expanse of time and distance between them even though Lot, like Abraham, was a contemporary of Noah's son Shem. Still, Noah and Lot were light years apart considering that the entire world as Noah had known it prior to the Flood was washed away and completely foreign to Lot apart from what others recounted to him. As for the Apostle John, he was about as far removed, chronologically speaking, from Noah and Lot as John was to us.

Here's how I connected them despite these apparent barriers of time and space. In Noah's time things had gone from bad to worse since the Fall of Adam and Eve. God described it thusly in Genesis 6:5-8. "And God saw that the wickedness of man was great in the earth, and that every imagination of the thoughts of his heart was only evil continually. And it repented the LORD that he had made man on the earth, and it grieved him at his heart. And the LORD said, I will destroy man whom I have created from the face of the earth; both man, and beast, and the creeping thing, and the fowls of the air; for it repenteth me that I have made them. But Noah found grace in the eyes of the LORD." Our gracious God chose Noah and his family to be spared from the Flood's destruction so they could be the bearers of the promised Messiah's line.

On a somewhat smaller but still supernatural scale, Lot was also spared from destruction when Sodom and Gomorrah were destroyed with fire and brimstone that God rained down from the sky. The city of Sodom where Lot lived was very similar to Noah's world prior to the Flood. It was rife with wickedness and sexual perversion, prominently including homosexuality. Naysayers have claimed that homosexuality wasn't specifically mentioned in Genesis 19 but that was pure sophistry. Although the word didn't appear, the act was clearly described and was at the center of the story.

Faith Food — Steve Stranghoener

A group of men accosted Lot seeking to know (rape) his two male guests who were in actuality angels posing as men. God's grace was showered upon Lot and his family just like Noah's before. And they provided a great and faithful, if unsuccessful, witness to their neighbors just as Noah had done for up to 120 years. Lot's wife was the only exception. She salted away (pun intended) God's grace and mercy.

Why have I included John in this trio? He didn't experience a great flood, fire from heaven or other cosmic disaster. Also, God didn't spare him from the persecution under Roman Emperor Domitian. That's what led to his exile to the Greek Island of Patmos off the coast of modern-day Turkey not far from the shore near the ancient city of Ephesus. If I wanted to stretch the comparison, I could have said that John was spared the martyrdom that, according to tradition, claimed the lives of all the other Apostles except for Judas. But that wouldn't serve any cogent purpose.

However, wasn't John much like Noah and Lot in being a messenger by God's grace? Noah warned of the Flood and Lot led God's chosen band away from the fire and brimstone. John too was a harbinger of God's destruction on the grandest scale of all. John the Revelator, by God's grace, was spared to live on Patmos and received the visions of the prophecy of things to come; the end times and final judgment.

Like Noah and Lot, John led a family, a band of believers to safety. God, through John, included you, me and all New Testament believers in this family. He forewarned us of the coming judgment and final destruction of this sinful world and universe.

Did God forget about all those Old Testament believers? Wait, I left someone out! God, through Daniel, delivered an earlier version of Revelation to Old Testament believers. Like the other three, God miraculously spared Daniel too; from the hungry lions. All four of these servants; Noah, Lot, John and Daniel, were connected by the same thing: God's grace and mercy. The world hasn't changed since it's still steeped in wickedness including rampant homosexuality. Thankfully though, we're firmly connected to Noah, Lot, John and Daniel since God has showered His grace upon us and covered us in His righteousness. God has showed us the way to safety and salvation and we can joyously say, come Lord Jesus, come quickly.

Fountain of Youth

American culture seems preoccupied with youth. Maybe it goes back to our fascination with the mythical Fountain of Youth associated with sixteenth century explorer Juan Ponce de Leon. While we're no longer searching for the conquistador's magical waters, Americans are still foolishly trying to attain immortality through fitness programs and super foods. I know good and well that nothing can turn back the hands of time that mark our inevitable march toward death but must admit to trying to improve my quality of life while I'm here through regular exercise, vitamins, supplements and a healthy diet.

Although futile in a temporal sense, there is a worthwhile spiritual lesson we can glean from healthy living. Our fitness follies can actually point to a biblical truth that forever links our past to the eternity that lies ahead. Why is it that certain foods can have a temporarily beneficial effect on our deteriorating bodies? I think it's a matter of biology. Our DNA, though hopelessly corrupted since the fall, can be traced back to our original parents and our common Creator. God originally designed our bodies to live forever and placed us in a garden perfectly suited to support our eternal bodies.

Death was not a part of the original plan before sin entered into the world. Thus, it made perfect sense for God to equip us with super foods designed to sustain us forever. No, I haven't given in to fantasy or wishful thinking. God mentioned the tree of life in Genesis 2:9 and added in Genesis 3:22 that eating of that tree would make Adam live forever. Thus, after the fall, God restricted Adam and Eve's access to the tree of life (Genesis 3:24) to avoid having them live eternally in sin.

Consequently, we cannot ever hope to attain anything close to immortality no matter what we eat as long as we occupy these earthly bodies. But the day is coming when we will shed our sin-corrupted flesh and God will transform our bodies in the twinkling of an eye (1 Corinthians 15:52) into glorious, incorruptible new bodies like those He originally designed for our famous forebears before the fall.

We will be fully formed at the perfect stage without facing developmental limitations or the prospect of death. In our new bodies we will possess powers that would make superheroes envious. Perhaps we will be able to pass through doors like our resurrected Lord did and even transport ourselves throughout the universe without any external means of transportation.

In Revelation 21:4, God affords a glimpse of what life will be like after Christ's return, our bodies are changed and the world is replaced with the new earth and heavens; "And God shall wipe away all tears from their eyes; and there shall be no more death, neither sorrow, nor crying, neither shall there be any more pain: for the former things are passed away."

It's hard to imagine the full glory of heaven but for certain we will never have to deal with pain, suffering, illness, guilt, hatred or sin. In our natural, originally intended state with the barrier of sin completely removed, the specter of death will be nonexistent and we will dwell in the presence of God. We're not told exactly what our heavenly banquet will consist of but one thing is for sure. Our bodies will be sustained through a harvest of God's perfect design. We can forget about the farcical Fountain of Youth. We will have something far better; living water, natural illumination from Jesus Christ and perhaps we will even get to eat from that tree of life.

Perfect Imperfections

No matter how diligently we study our Bibles, our understanding remains imperfect. That's because we, as imperfect, fallen human beings, cannot fully comprehend the perfect mind of God even as it is revealed to us by Him in His perfect word of truth. Of course, the problem rests with us and not in God or His verbally inspired, inerrant word. That's why it's dangerous to take a single passage of Scripture out of context. We can get things miserably wrong by doing so.

Sometimes this can even happen when we read a passage within its broader, immediate scriptural context. Take 1 Corinthians 13:10 for example, "But when that which is perfect is come, then that which is in part shall be done away." At first glance, I took this to mean that Old Testament ceremonial law with all its rituals and sacrifices were done away with at the dawn of the New Testament era when our perfect Savior came into the world as the Babe of Bethlehem, thus fulfilling all the Old Testament prophesies pointing to the Christ.

Still, I wasn't sure of my initial interpretation, so I went back and read all of chapter 13. It was immediately familiar, especially the first seven verses. This was the love chapter that I'd heard referenced so often during wedding ceremonies. Charity or love was described in beautiful, elaborate detail. This threw me for a loop and made me reconsider my initial interpretation.

As I read further, the second half of the chapter seemed to be off on a completely different tangent; especially the second to last verse that mentioned seeing through the proverbial glass darkly. Although I had read or heard all or parts of this chapter many times, 1 Corinthians 13:10 still stumped me. Perfect had to be referring to Christ, right? I read it over again several times and finally admitted I was in over my head and turned to *Kretzmann's Commentary* and enlisted my erudite pastor for help. This shed some much-needed light.

"But when that which is perfect is come" in fact referred to Jesus but not His birth in Bethlehem but rather His eventual, triumphant return on the final day of judgment. The second half of the chapter was not out of place. What seemed incongruent at first made perfect sense as a contrast to the perfect love of God.

Charity or love never fails but our knowledge does. We know of God's plan of salvation and can grasp the truth of the gospel by the power of the Holy Spirit but, because of our human imperfections, our knowledge of the truth is limited. We see through a glass darkly. Like ancient mirrors which were polished glass that provided somewhat murky, distorted reflections, our powers of comprehension are marred by our humanity.

In this context, it makes sense that 1 Corinthians 13:11 compared our understanding here on earth versus what it will be in the heavenly realm to a child's comprehension versus an adult's. Our understanding, although limited, is sufficient for our salvation. Our faith is nourished and maintained through word and sacrament but our understanding is far from perfect. There is so much we long to know but can't yet grasp.

However, in time we will be glorified and the scales will drop from our eyes. We will be able to see Him face-to-face. Many, many wonderful truths that have escaped us will be revealed in amazing glory and clarity. For now, the mysteries of God are reserved for God alone (Deuteronomy 29:29). But when our souls reach heaven and most certainly when Christ returns and we are glorified to dwell in His new heavens and earth, we shall be enlightened beyond our wildest dreams.

We who are imperfect will be made perfect. Our imperfections that now distort God's perfect word of truth shall be removed forever. Until then, we should stay in the word and read, mark and inwardly digest it over and over, in context and with the full counsel of God. We should seek the help of those blessed with the gift of interpretation and teaching as our guides. All of us, teachers and students alike, should be guided first and foremost by the Holy Spirit working through the word until that which is perfect comes again. Come Lord Jesus, come swiftly Lord.

Here Today, Gone Tomorrow

Time is a funny thing. It's always constant with sixty minutes in an hour, twenty-four hours in a day and

Faith Food — Steve Stranghoener

365 days a year. Yet, at times it seems to slow to a crawl, like when we're waiting in line at the grocery store or anxiously awaiting turning sixteen to get our first driver's license. At other times, it appears to travel at the speed of light. Sometimes we marvel, "Where did the summer go or hasn't this year flown by?" And doesn't it seem like time accelerates as we get older? We seniors are preoccupied with this; "Youth is wasted on the young and I wish I knew then what I know now." Our culture is permeated with the fleeting nature of time; "Time waits for no man, time flies, time is of the essence and we're here today and gone tomorrow."

We can see this phenomenon clearly but can't escape it; living in the moment as they say. Sometimes we're so focused on temporal things that we lose track of what's really important: eternal matters. God sums this up nicely in James 4:13-16 and offers some sage advice, "Go to now, ye that say, Today or tomorrow we will go into such a city, and continue there a year, and buy and sell, and get gain: Whereas ye know not what shall be on the morrow. For what is your life? It is even a vapor that appears for a little time, and then vanishes away. For that ye ought to say, If the Lord will, we shall live, and do this, or that. But now ye rejoice in your boastings: all such rejoicing is evil."

God says we're too wrapped up in our daily business, planning this and that while overlooking spiritual matters that are infinitely more important.

Faith Food   Steve Stranghoener

God's not telling us to neglect our duties to our families, jobs and other callings; especially our service to Him and our fellow human beings. But He's reminding us to keep our priorities straight. He wisely cautions us that we can't see into the future and thus should not bank on our man-made plans as though they were immutable.

He tells us that this life is fleeting like a vapor. Isn't that so true? We're here today and gone tomorrow. We could be called home to heaven at any age and at any time or Christ could come back at any moment. Thus, God tells us we should look to Him and His will first and foremost rather than banking on our own plans and desires. We should carry out our duties and service responsibly but keep that old hymn in the back of our minds; *What God Ordains is Always Good.*

God warns us again not to get too wrapped up in ourselves or things of this world. Rejoicing in ourselves and our accomplishments is foolish and dangerous; a temptation of the devil. We should do our best while keeping our priorities in order and, when blessings flow, we should not beat our chests and boast but turn with heads bowed and give the glory to God where it belongs. In good times and bad, we should humbly give thanks and praise to God, the author and finisher of our faith who accomplishes all things for our good, including those things which are impossible for men; in particular, the blood-bought salvation of our immortal souls.

Old Age Isn't for Sissies

The first time I heard one of the senior members of our congregation utter this phrase, I thought it was quaint and clever and it brought a smile to my face. As I've grown older, I've sometimes uttered it myself with a tinge of humor but more so a matter-of-fact acknowledgment of the cold, harsh truth. With the passage of time, things have stopped working so well: my knees, hips, back and, perhaps worst of all, my brain.

Have you ever walked purposefully into a room and then stopped and paused to try to figure out what brought you there in the first place? I've tried to find some humor to make light of such situations. Still I couldn't hide the unpleasant, unavoidable truth. Aging has provided indisputable evidence of my sinfulness and its consequences including mortality. We've all been corrupted by sin from our very conception and God pronounced the verdict in Romans 3:23, "For all have sinned, and come short of the glory of God," and issued the sentence in Romans 6:23, "The wages of sin is death."

It's depressing but we have to acknowledge that we're on a march toward death. It may be a slow trek or for some it may come swiftly and early in this life. In either case, we should expect it and never be caught unawares because it's inevitable. There's no getting around the fact that we're conceived in original sin and infected with a terminal illness. This stark reality goes even further in that even inanimate objects, the entire creation down to its core elements, are corrupted with sin. The earth and the universe are on a death march too.

Thankfully though, God didn't leave us without hope in this horrid situation. God took care of the problem for us and gave us a new nature from above (1 Peter 1:23) to go along with our old, sinful nature. As such, He imputed the righteousness of our Savior, Jesus Christ, to us (Romans 4:23-25). Furthermore, He took all of our sins upon Himself (Romans 10:4) and incurred the Father's wrath against sin for us on the cross, completely and forever. As He declared on that bloody cross (John 19:30), "It is finished!" His work of redemption reconciled us to God (2 Corinthians 5:19) and assured us of a perfect future of everlasting peace and joy in the presence of the Lord. He also promised to replace our fallen world with His new heavens and earth (2 Peter 3:13).

Of course, this doesn't change what we're facing today: pain, suffering, persecution, old age and the lies, torments and temptation of the world, the devil and our own sinful flesh. However, we can rest assured that, while we remain on this earth, God will bless us in mind, body and especially spirit as we face our travails.

This has always been true for our loving, longsuffering God of mercy and grace. When Israel faced the consequences of their sinfulness, lack of faith and idolatry, God offered this assurance in Isaiah 46:3-4 to which we are also heirs. "Hearken unto me,

O house of Jacob, and all the remnant of the house of Israel, which are borne by me from the belly, which are carried from the womb: And even to your old age I am he; and even to hoar hairs will I carry you: I have made, and I will bear; even I will carry, and will deliver you."

No matter what happens, even when our bodies and minds fail us, God will never abandon us or withdraw His gracious promise of salvation. This is our peace and joy regardless of our conditions. We have a bright, beautiful, perfect future ahead of us. We will receive new, glorified, perfect, sinless bodies and will dwell forever in the new heavens and earth with our loving God.

Home Sweet Home

My father-in-law was the last of our parents to go and this made his parting especially bittersweet. He didn't know June 29th, 2015 would be his last day on this earth but could tell that the end was drawing closer in the months preceding his death. Although the doctors didn't formally pronounce it terminal, the strength-sapping ravages of colon cancer were unmistakable. A lifelong Lutheran Christian since the day of his baptism, Les' faith seemed to grow stronger as his body grew weaker. Death did not frighten or worry him but it did raise some meaningful questions. This afforded me the opportunity to comfort Les with the truth of God's word on many occasions.

Faith Food   Steve Stranghoener

Sometimes he asked me about his dear, departed wife Laverne. In time, his curiosity turned from her eternal rest to that of his own. Would he see Laverne? What about other relatives? I delighted in providing every assurance of their pending reunion and the fact that he would be in the company of all the saints; all the believers who had died in the faith, trusting in Christ Jesus alone for forgiveness, salvation and eternal life in heaven.

He was excited to hear about what a gathering it would be. He looked forward to chatting with not only friends, family and loved ones but so many people he had never met in this life like Martin Luther, Abraham Lincoln, the Apostle Paul, Noah, Adam and Eve. Best of all, I intoned gleefully, he would get to be with Jesus, face-to-face.

After a while, our conversations took on a familiar tone with him circling back to visions of heaven. He wasn't losing control of his faculties but, I assumed, he just wanted to hear the good news over and over again. He loved to ask me what heaven would be like. Of course, I couldn't go beyond what Scripture had revealed which oftentimes used figurative imagery that was hard to translate. But I was thankfully able to offer assurances about no more death, pain or sorrow and specifics about Christ's pending, triumphant return, earth's final day, the shedding of our corrupt flesh in exchange for resurrected, glorified, sinless bodies and our eternal abode with God in His new heavens and earth.

Faith Food — Steve Stranghoener

I never sensed doubt as the end approached but felt he just wanted reassurance. With that in mind, it was important to make sure he knew I wasn't imparting opinions or matters of interpretation. Thus, we turned to the Bible and God's promises which Les knew were a sure thing. Here's one that I think said it all, not only for Les but each and every one of us. In John 14:2-3, Jesus made this personal pledge to us, "In my Father's house are many mansions: if it were not so, I would have told you. I go to prepare a place for you. And if I go and prepare a place for you, I will come again, and receive you unto myself; that where I am, there ye may be also."

Do we need anything else? By grace through faith alone in Jesus Christ, we know most certainly that when we die Jesus will be waiting to personally welcome us into the perfect, heavenly home that He has prepared for us. Shout for joy all ye saints!

Other Books by Steve Stranghoener:

A Deplorable 2018 Election Guide

Uncle Sam's White Hat

Deadly Preference

530 Reasons Why Deplorables Won

Veeper

Ferguson Miracle

God-Whacked!

Cha-Cha Chandler: Teen Demonologist

Straight Talk about Christian Misconceptions

The Last Prophet: Doomsday Diary

The Last Prophet: Imminent End

Murder by Chance: Blood Moon Lunacy of Lew Carew

Asunder: The Tale of the Renaissance Killer

Tracts in Time

All of these titles are available under Books/Steve Stranghoener at www.amazon.com.

Made in the USA
Columbia, SC
11 November 2018